The uncanny master of make-up in a new amazing shocker

CARL LAEMMLE presents

KARLOFF

in an adaptation of

EDGAR ALLAN POE'S

The RAVEN

with Bela (DRACULA) LUGOSI

IRENE WARE
LESTER MATTHEWS
INEZ COURTNEY

MIDNIGHT MARQUEE #82

Editor
Gary J. Svehla

Graphic Design Interior
Gary J. Svehla

Front/Back Cover
Aurelia Susan Svehla

Copy Editor
Janet Atkinson
Aurelia Susan Svehla

Writers
Anthony Ambrosia
Barry Atkinson
Jim Coughlin
Christopher Gullo
Gail Orwig
Ray Orwig
Gary J. Svehla
Alan Warren
Nathalie Yafet

Artist
Welcome back Allen K.

Special Thanks!
McFarland Books; Forrest J Ackerman; *Castle of Frankenstein*; *Horrors of the Screen*; David Colton and the CHFB; Richard Klemensen; Ben Ohmart; Zach Pogemiller and Heritage Auctions; Aurelia Susan Svehla; Nathalie Yafet; Allen K, and all the writers who vehemently supported the effort.

Publisher
Midnight Marquee Press, Inc.
ISBN 978-1-64430-138-8

Gary J. Svehla and Aurelia Susan Svehla, Midnight Marquee #82, October 2023, copyright ©2023 by Gary J. Svehla, 9721 Britinay Ln, Parkville, MD 21234, phone: 410-937-3723, website: www.midnightmarquee.com, e-mail: midmargary@aol.com; available from Amazon.com and any place that sells books (for ordering copies)

**Our 60th Year Anniversary
1963-2023**

Playing at the Midnight Marquee

3   Mutterings At Midnight
    by Gary J. Svehla

5   *THE RAVEN*
    Poe, Lugosi, Karloff, and Universal Pictures
    by Nathalie Yafet

24 *THE INVISIBLE RAY*
    is Radium X: "They Die!"
    by Nathalie Yafet

36 TED BILLINGS [1882-1947]
    Another Forgotten Face
    by Jim Coughlin

50 *THE SMILING GHOST*
    Briefly Re-Examined
    by Alan Warren

54 *The Wizard of Oz*
    Potholes in the Yellow Brick Road
    by Anthony Ambrosia

61 20 MILLION MILES TO EARTH
    Harryhausen in Italy: On Location

69 *TERROR IN THE MIDNIGHT SUN* BECOMES *INVASION OF THE ANIMAL PEOPLE*
    Giant Space Monster Invades Lapland
    by Barry Atkinson

75 *CURSE OF THE FLY* AND *THE PROJECTED MAN*
    A Double Bill of Teleportation Terrors!
    by Barry Atkinson

83 HORROR OF DRACULA, THE BRIDES OF DRACULA, AND DRACULA–PRINCE OF DARKNESS
    Terence Fisher and The Vampire Mythology
    by Gary J. Svehla

110 THE SADIST
    Limping, Giggling, and a Bottle of Pop
    by Christopher Gullo

122 *Midnight Marquee* Book Reviews
    by Gary J. Svehla

132 *Midnight Marquee* Movie Reviews
    by Gary J. Svehla

140 Final Mutterings
    by Gary J. Svehla

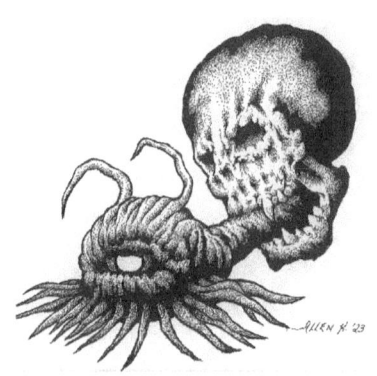

Mutterings at Midnight

This year as I hit 73, I think back to the beginning, when in 1963, I was just 13 and very wet behind the ears when it came to writing and publishing. When I think about the fanzine's maturation over the course of 60 years, the people who most helped me: my father Richard, my mother Ann, and my wife Sue. But there were others. So many others.

I am saddened by the writers who have passed away, because I cannot thank them in this 60th anniversary issue. People who wrote for the zine and the books ...

ROBERT HANCOCK
DON LEIFERT
BILL LITTMAN
DONNA LUCAS
DAVE METZLER
MARK MILLER
JOHN PARNUM
LARRY REICHMAN
TERRY ROARK
DAVID ROBINSON
DEL WINANS
TOM JOHNSON
DON SMITH
LYNN NARON
PLUS MANY BOOK AUTHORS AND FANEX GUESTS

When I think of Del Winans, I think of his dream to open a restaurant dedicated to classic horror films and how he struggled to make it happen. He never did, but I remember the times down in his cellar, in his horror film display room, several of the Baltimore boys would wheel and deal lobbies and posters and other memorabilia in hopes of improving our individual collection.

I remember Robert Hancock of Roosevelt, New York who used to come to Manhattan and, together with my father and me, would explore the latest New York sci-fi convention held in the heart of the city. He was welcome to stay over in our hotel room and crash. During the slow times he and I would explore New York city and Robert would be my guide for theaters, The Cloister Museum, favorite hole-in-the wall eateries, and we would make a weekend of it. Those were the best days.

I very well remember John Parnum, who had such a high-pitched laugh and was so serious at conventions that he often mispronounced names such as *Curse of the Undead* star Michael Pate. (Pate was pronounced to rhyme with "late," but John always called him "Pat-tay" and was so well meaning.) We teased him about it for years.

And lastly, I remember Bill Littman who use to watch movies with me when I ran the Film Program with the late Don Dohler and friend Charlie Ellis. I especially remember how Bill himself would move two sofas in front of the movie projector for us to enjoy extra comfort.

And there's even a longer list of those who still are living, a checklist too long to add here or remember. But such people know I am eternally grateful.

But the thing thast makes me saddest of all is losing contact with all those people who helped *Gore Creatures/Midnight Marquee*. Many friends from decades ago, and I do not know if they are alive or dead ... I often think of such people.

But today I want to thank the current crop of writers who contributed to issues of the recent past, the latest in a long list of staff writers and artists.

Over these 60 years we only published 82 issues, that is hardly more than little over one issue per year. But then again, our magazine was/is a labor of love, not a profit-making enterprise or

Aurelia Susan Svehla and Gary J. Svehla sandwich British actress Barbara Shelley, who was being given a Laemmle Award at FANEX 15.

business, that survived all obstacles and events over a lifetime: school, college, a secondary public school teaching career, maturing, marriage, deaths of friends and family and beloved pets, and trying to balance the obstacles that life throws at us. Let alone little things such as my recent stroke three years ago.

This is apparently the final issue, but this fact is not written in blood. I just want to give my wife Sue a break, no longer reading and re-reading text to proof-read, formatting the issue for publication, making the front and rear covers adhere to the template necessary, making all the text flow, etc.

Our analysis of classic horror is akin to literary criticism … interpreting the movie and trying to create personalized meaning out of it. Thus, films can never run out of interpretations, for films can be re-evaluated and new generations of fans will see it with fresh eyes. The richness of the original film can take on new meaning in each succeeding generation, every few years or so the movie will mean

A FANEX panel consisting of (from left to right): Gary J. Svehla, John Parnum, Del Winans, and Ed Bansak.

something different to future writers and viewers. Therefore, films can be relevant for all time. And fans shall hopefully never grow tired of writing about them.

Another format for reviewing films is to research the detailed film production of a specific movie. This is important to do, but once the production detail comes to light, what else is the critic to cover? It is done. And then there is the interview approach. But again, once the cast member or crew member is interviewed a few times, what else is there to be say? Plus, we are dealing with fading memories, distortions, and egos, which greatly distort the facts. Also, the interviewer may be guilty of selective inclusion, meaning if the interviewee answers questions contrary to what the interviewer is hoping for, those responses can be omitted from the final published interview. How the interview is edited can radically change its meaning.

Midnight Marquee has had its share of interviews and film production histories, and as stated they are very important, but our emphasis has always focused primarily on personalized film criticism and evaluation. That has allowed us to cover Universal and Hammer horror classics for 60 years without repeating ourselves.

But if this is to be the final issue, I must thank all the fans who supported us for over 6 decades. Many have been with us through the maturating of the magazine, the FANEX conventions, and filming genre spoofs. A magazine cannot survive without readers and supporters. As we fans, who wrote about Universal and Hammer, now acquiesce to the exploration of newer movies and directors and

Musical and horror star Russ Tamblyn does a handstand for Gary Svehla, media magnet Ted Bohus, and director Fred Olen Ray at FANEX.

Top: Don Leifert and Ed Bansak at FANEX; Bottom: Christopher Lee and Ingrid Pitt at FANEX behind the scenes.

stars, we wish the newer generation of horror film writers and historians all the very best. The journey continues! What a wild ride it's been and hopefully continues.

—Gary J. Svehla
May 2023

THE RAVEN
POE, LUGOSI, KARLOFF, AND UNIVERSAL PICTURES

BY NATHALIE YAFET

"I became insane with long intervals of horrible sanity." Edgar Allan Poe, January 4, 1848, in a letter to George W. Eveleth, a medical student who started corresponding with the reclusive writer in 1845, which continued up until Poe's death in 1849. Eveleth was an elusive, seldom-seen person who is characterized by the online Poe analyzer, "Blogger of the *Grotesque and Arabesque*," as "the one person who could out-weird Poe himself." *The Amazing Mr. Eveleth* (Blogger of the *Grotesque and Arabesque* September 17, 2009). That could almost describe Dr. Richard Vollin in *The Raven* (Universal 1935), one of Bela Lugosi's most memorable characters who, had he been real, might well have outweirded the "Blogger."

With the unexpected success of *The Black Cat* (Universal 1934), the first Karloff and Lugosi pairing, it made financial sense to continue the Poe theme with the same stars. (Unfairly, *The Raven* [Universal 1935] is the first and only time that Bela Lugosi was billed above the title by surname only.) While most genre film criticism has *The Black Cat* as superior to *The Raven*, each movie really merits its own evaluation. Maybe they should not be compared. (Interestingly, UMR, Ultimate Movie Rankings, a website ranking movies since 2011, combining box-office results, critical, and audience reception,

The original Universal title lobby card

and award recognition—ranks *The Raven* higher than *The Black Cat* by critical and audience reception—77% for *The Raven* vs 72% for *The Black Cat*; *The Raven* earned $39.6, whereas *The Black Cat* earned $26.9. So, the UMR for *The Raven* is 78.7 and *The Black Cat* is 69.3). *The Black Cat* (with its only legitimate Poe tie-in being a real black cat) earns the famous Karloff quip, "Poor Poe, what we did to him when he wasn't around to defend himself," but *The Raven*, largely thanks to the bravura Lugosi portrayal of Dr. Richard Vollin, is suffused and surrounded by the author's aura.

Startlingly, *The Raven* begins with heroine Jean Thatcher (lovely Irene Ware) speeding on a dangerous road in a downpour and unexpectedly encountering a detour which sends the car and driver off the cliff. Louis Friedlander (later known as Lew Landers)—recognized for directing serials at Universal: *The Vanishing Shadow* 1934, *The Red Rider* 1934, *Tailspin Tommy* 1934, *Rustlers of Red Dog* 1935, and *The Cry of the Savage* 1935—puts us right into the action delivering brisk pacing and absorbing vignettes throughout. Edgar Ulmer's brooding psychological introspection, a perfect fit for *The Black Cat*, might be out of place here. Filmsite.com, in discussing serials cites, "Attractive heroines, action heroes, and villains in melodramatic sequences ... and diabolical villains with evil devices ... narrow escapes, fistfights, close calls, and hair-raising situations." (Dr. Jerry Halden is not an "action hero" but heroic enough.) Friedlander keeps the film moving even in the few humorous moments, while giving us plenty of serial-style scenes: Bateman coming up through the floor of Jean Thatcher's room, Judge Thatcher and the pendulum, and Jean

A lobby showing Judge Thatcher (Samuel S. Hinds) introducing his daughter Jean (Irene Ware) to Dr. Vollin (Bela Lugosi) after Jean's *Spirit of Poe* dance.

Dr. Vollin's Poe Museum is sought out by many enthusiasts, including Mr. Chapman (Arthur Hoyt).

and Jerry in "the room where the walls come together." The only problem with the serial approach, at least in *The Raven*, is that we're interrupted just when things get interesting. Frustrating, but at least it replicates the cliffhanger endings at the end of each chapter. (Music used here by J. Franke Harling was the *Storm Scene* track from *Destination Unknown* [Universal 1933], a hurricane at sea drama starring Pat O'Brien as a rum runner and Ralph Bellamy as an enigmatic stowaway who vanishes after helping the survivors.)

Our next glimpse of Miss Thatcher is in the emergency room with her father, Judge Thatcher (Samuel S. Hinds), and her fiancé, Dr. Jerry Halden (Lester Matthews). For most people, Hinds will always be Peter Bailey, George Bailey's father in *It's a Wonderful Life* (RKO Radio Pictures 1946), but for golden age horror fans imperiled Judge Thatcher is his signature role. He started acting in his 50s—eventually appearing in over 200 films—including: *Murders in the Zoo* (Paramount 1933), *Deluge* (RKO Radio Pictures 1933), *Berkeley Square* (Fox Film Corporation 1933), *She* (RKO Radio Pictures 1935), and *Night Key* (Universal 1937). *Night Key* starred Boris Karloff as kindly inventor Dave Mallory, with Samuel S. Hinds as unscrupulous Stephen Ranger, who takes advantage of him; both were cast against type. Other genre-related roles were *Man Made Monster* (Universal 1941), *The Strange Case of Dr. Rx* (Universal 1942), *Son of Dracula* (Universal 1943), *Cobra Woman* (Universal 1944), *Jungle Woman* (Universal 1944), and *The Boy with Green Hair* (RKO Radio Pictures 1948). Lester Matthews (playing Paul Ames) was fresh from comforting Valerie Hobson as Lisa, the bride of the *Werewolf of London* (Universal 1935). He also appeared in *Between Two Worlds* (Warner Bros. 1944), *The Invisible Man's Revenge* (Universal 1944), and *The Son of Dr. Jekyll*

Dr. Vollin immediately falls in love/lust with Jean Thatcher.

After surgery, Dr. Vollin seems to enjoy touching Jean's neck.

Bela Lugosi's hypnotic eyes render Jean helpless.

(Columbia Pictures 1951). He rejoined former *Raven* star Boris Karloff in *British Intelligence* (Warner Bros. 1940).

With the judge and the fiancé are Dr. Cook, Jonathan Hale (who was in *Dead Man's Eyes* (Universal 1944) and numerous uncredited roles, but he was the definitive J.C. Dithers in the *Blondie* series (Columbia Pictures 1938-1943), Dr. Hemingway (Walter Miller), who appeared in *The Utah Kid* (Tiffany Pictures 1930]), and *King of the Wild* (Mascot 1931), two pre-code films with Boris Karloff and an unnamed, sympathetic under-five nurse played by Madeline Talcott, previously seen in *Night Life of the Gods* (Universal 1935), as one of the three Graces with future *Raven* leading lady Irene Ware as the goddess Diana.

The doctors give Jean's father no hope, when suddenly Jerry wonders aloud about "Dr. Vollin," echoed by Hemingway and Cook. "Vollin? Can we get Dr. Vollin? Dr. Vollin? Dr. Vollin? Get Dr. Vollin here." (Inappropriately, it recalls the Oscar nominated Three Stooges short, *Men in Black* (Columbia 1934): "Calling Dr. Howard, Dr. Fine, Dr. Howard."

As Jean Thatcher's doctors stand around her in the operating room apparently doing nothing, Bela Lugosi's Dr. Vollin is reading from *The Raven*. The one-man audience is Mr. Chapman (a delightful Arthur Hoyt, from Preston Sturges' unofficial stock company. The actor did 17 other films in 1935, besides *The Raven*. He also appeared in *The Criminal Code* [Columbia 1931] with Boris Karloff, and as Professor Summerlee in *The Lost World* [First National Pictures 1925]). Undercoring the reading is Clifford Vaughan's *Raven Theme,* one of the three special pieces he composed for the film.

"... Suddenly there came a tapping as of someone gently rapping, rapping at my chamber door ... Open then, I flung the shutter, when, with many a flirt and flutter, in stepped a stately Raven ..."

Poe's poem has "open here" not "open then." Either Bela Lugosi changed the line and director Friedlander wasn't aware, or he let it go. Perhaps screenwriter David Boehm did let it go, but it hardly matters today. Most important was the effect of the Lugosi voice, giving us a tantalizing introduction to Dr. Richard Vollin, a madly intense Poe fanatic. He tells Mr. Chapman that the raven is his "talisman," because "death" is also his "talisman," as "the one indestructible force, the one certain thing in an uncertain universe. Death!" A deliciously uneasy Mr. Chapman would rather discuss the "very hand-

Judge Thatcher begs Dr. Vollin to operate on his daughter Jean.

POSTERS that sell seats!

THE 24 SHEET STAND

THREE COLOR WINDOW CARD

TWO-COLOR JUMBO WINDOW CARD

MIDGET CARD

ONE SHEET "A"

THREE SHEET "B"

THREE SHEET "C"

SIX SHEET

ONE SHEET "D"

Copyright 1935—UNIVERSAL PICTURES CORP. Member Motion Pictures Producers and Distributors of America, Will H. Hays, Pres.   Printed in U.S.A.

Boris Karloff (in make-up) and Bela Lugosi (also in make-up) have a relaxing cigar and peruse the script together.

some price" that his museum will pay for the Vollin "Poe collection." (Perhaps first editions and letters?) The museum and the audience at this point are unaware of the contents of the basement dungeon. All of this is interrupted by a phone call from Judge Thatcher begging for the doctor's help. As Vollin's only doing "research" right now (the subject of which is never revealed), he refuses and hangs up. Getting Dr. Vollin's address from the nurse (her only line, "Hillview Heights"), Judge Thatcher goes there to ask Vollin's help in person. Cut to Dr. Vollin dismissing Mr. Chapman, claiming fatigue, and offering a future invitation to see the "torture and horror devices that Poe describes in his tales, especially, *The Pit and the Pendulum*." Mr. Chapman enthuses, "That's a thriller isn't it," which is met with a signature Lugosi sinister "deadpan." Not noticing, Mr. Chapman forges on, commenting about "a very curious hobby." Bela Lugosi's Dr. Vollin responds with a line dear to Monster Kids, "It's more than a hobby!" (Another is from *Freaks* [MGM 1932]: "One of us, one of us, one of us …")

After Mr. Chapman leaves, Judge Thatcher arrives and pleads with the doctor to save Jean, offering money and reminding him of his responsibilities as a doctor. Vollin dismisses any "obligation" because he is "a law unto" himself. "But have you no human feeling? My daughter is dying." The chilling reply, "Death hasn't the same significance for me as it has for you." It's only when Judge Thatcher, narcissistically manipulating him, says that the other doctors think Dr. Vollin is "the only one" who can save the dying girl, that he agrees to operate. At the hospital, Dr. Vollin has a visceral reaction to his patient's gorgeous face which her fiancé worriedly notices. Bela's closeup here is one of many in *The Raven* by Charles J. Stumar, a sensitive and talented Hungarian American cinematographer, whose camera almost becomes another character in the film. He previously worked on three other Universal horror films: *The Hunchback of Notre Dame* 1923, *The Mummy* 1932, and *Werewolf of London* 1935. Tragically, he died in a plane crash shortly after *The Raven* wrapped.

Immediately following a point-of-view shot of the anesthesiologist which effectively puts us all under, we see dramatic flames in the fireplace with Jean Thatcher reclining seductively on a nearby sofa, listening to and gazing dreamily over at Dr. Vollin, as he plays Bach's *Toccata and Fugue in d Minor* on the organ. (Bela looks very convincing here. One of his best Hungarian-American musician friends was Ervin Nyiregyhazi, a pianist who was often at the Lugosi home. Bela admired his passionate virtuosity which sometimes had him leaving blood on the keys. Possibly he picked up some hand movements from the man described by Arnold Schoenberg as displaying "… a power of the will, capable of soaring over all imaginable difficulties in the realization of an idea …")

Languidly, Jean swoons, "Extraordinary man! You're almost not a man. Almost …" Vollin says, "A god?" To which the captivated girl simply answers, "Yes." Not disagreeing with her assessment, he adds, "A god—with the taint of human emotions. Stumar's camera shares a Vollin's eye view of Jean as he looks down at her satin-clad figure while she looks up at him, agreeing that he is "almost— a god." Overwhelmed by her physical closeness, the besotted doctor leans over his patient and touches the surgical scar on her neck in a decidedly unprofessional manner, covering himself by asking if it still hurts. (It doesn't.) Backing away from her, his voice trembling, Vollin says, "A month ago, I didn't know you." Jean

Most of the cast of *The Raven* assemble on set to discuss the next scene.

responds warmly, "And now I owe my life to you. I wish there was something I could do." Displaying his "taint of human emotions," he replies, "There is!" Standing up, she answers with infatuated admiration, "Tell me!" Fervidly grasping her shoulders and obviously referring to himself, Vollin declares, "The restraint that we impose upon ourselves can drive us mad!" Confused and battling her own "human emotions," Jean pulls away, telling Vollin that she doesn't know what he means (although she does.) Changing the subject, Jean says she now owes him "another debt" because the doctor has made her fiancé, Jerry Halden, his assistant which means the engaged couple can "be married that much sooner!" (Jerry's last name is pronounced as both Holden and Halden throughout the film. The credits say "Halden.") Hearing his rival's name, Vollin drops his hands from her shoulders and, with unmistakable intent, says, "You owe me nothing. I did it to give him something. To take the place of what he's losing," then tries to embrace her. Jean locks eyes with him as her smile fades, yearning to return his ardor, reluctantly breaking free of the spell, and lamely excusing herself for dinner plans. Even after all this, she reminds Vollin of her dance performance the next evening. "Nothing can keep me away." Jean teases that she has "a surprise" for him, says goodbye, and presses his hand for a moment longer than necessary. With his hand outstretched in a touching gesture of longing, Vollin watches her leave, beseeching her to return.

This is a tantalizing love scene and—slyly—sound supervisor Gilbert Kurland

Judge Thatcher appeals to Vollin's ego and the doctor looks very distressed.

thought so too as musically he chose hints of Franz Liszt's ominous *Piano Sonata in b-minor*—harking back to *The Black Cat*'s Hjalmar Poelzig ogling Joan Alison—to underscore Vollin's fervently eyeing Jean, which then changes abruptly to the *Cat Love Theme* track when he bends down to her and touches her neck. Written for newlyweds Joan and Peter Alison, the *Cat Love Theme* was based on the mesmerizing *Overture-Fantasy to Romeo and Juliet* (Tchaikovsky, Pyotr Ilyich, TH42, CH39) which was modified because of concerns over copyright restrictions.

The shooting script at this point says that Vollin "pulls her toward him in an embrace," and she, "fascinated attracted—and still resisting," gives him "a quick impulsive kiss" and starts to leave. The film omits the embrace and kiss. (Lenning, Arthur G., *The Immortal Count: The Life and Films of Bela Lugosi* Lexington: The University Press of Kentucky, 2003, 227).

Despite this omission, the actors convey the same, "human emotions" without a kiss. Vollin tries to seize her as Jean looks directly into his eyes. Using these scripted but un-filmed directions from the shooting script would have resulted in less conventional horror movie character types and a conflicted, more compelling heroine.

"(Jean) ... performs her dance-interpretation of his favorite poem: "The

Dr. Vollin does not seem phased by criminal Bateman holding a gun on him.

Lester Matthews (would he play heroes today?) and Irene Ware from *The Raven* pressbook.

Raven." This mutual and rather noirish obsession could plunge two people right over the edge of madness. So, I think it's interesting that Jean tries to thank him by assuming the same dark avian aspect. It's as though she is trying to become part of him as she ecstatically flits across the stage for the eyes of all ... but really for the gaze of one. For Vollin, not for her dull, dependable fiancé ... In attempting to be a stagey revenge thriller rather than a sinister one, Gothic romance worthy of Poe ... the film as shot ... throws it all away and turns Vollin into an embarrassingly obvious loony and Jean into every other bland, squealing horror heroine. What a waste." *The Nitrate Diva* (Online blogger October 25, 2012.)

Alluring Jean and seductively handsome Dr. Vollin could have been weaving in and out of a perilous *pas de deux*, a relationship from the dark side, beguiling with forbidden what ifs! Richard Vollin, embodying danger, and Jean almost caught in his web. The shooting script had them doing just that, but it never came to be.

Bela Lugosi and Ms. Ware were no screen strangers. She played Princess Nadji to his evil Roxor in *Chandu the Magician* (Fox 1932), in which he kidnaps her as a gift for one of his accomplices, even while leeringly admiring her himself en route to his goal of world domination. (A "law unto" himself.)

Being attractive to women was not unusual for Bela Lugosi, the man, and the actor. Carroll Borland, his vampire daughter in *Mark of the Vampire* (MGM 1935), said:

"Bela had an incredibly wonderful devilishness—that devilish charm! I have never known a man who could sit still in a room, and all the women were just drawn to him like pieces of metal to a magnet. He was incredible—the sexiest man I ever knew!" (Borland, Carroll and Mank, Gregory William, *Countess Dracula, A novel by Carroll Borland with a biography of Carroll Borland* [Absecon: MagicImage Filmbooks, 1994] 23.)

When he made *Black Dragons* (Monogram Pictures Corporation 1942) Lugosi was almost 60 years old, but the magic was still there. The small talk between Bela's character, Dr. Melcher/Monsieur Colomb, and female lead Joan Barclay, as Alice Saunders, is flirtatious from the start with most of the energy coming from her. After their initial meeting, he excuses himself and leaves her with male ingenue, Clayton Moore, playing Dick Martin. Alice remarks, "Handsome devil, isn't he?" The future *Lone Ranger* says he'd "... hate to meet him in a dark alley." Alice disagrees, "Well, I don't know. Make it a moonlight night and a park bench. Might be exciting!" In another scene, she gets scared and runs right into Bela/Colomb's embrace as he says, "... It's time she might take refuge in a strong man's arms." Joan/Alice smilingly replies, "I just ran into yours. Mine might be dangerous." Alice then proceeds to sit right next to him. Ms. Barclay also worked with Bela Lugosi again in *The Corpse Vanishes* (Monogram Pictures Corporation 1942), this time as Alice Wentworth, one of the suspended animation brides.

Some years ago (while hunting for photoplay editions and old Nancy Drew books) on a rainy Sunday afternoon at the Chatham Bookseller, a used bookstore in

Bateman is welcomed at Vollin's door by the butler.

Edmund Bateman (Boris Karloff), wearing a bushy beard and hat for disguise, poses for a publicity photo.

Vollin prepares to fix Bateman's face by only having him loosen his tie and covering him with a sheet.

Madison, New Jersey, I got into a conversation about movies with a man who was subbing for the owner, and he mentioned that his mother was in a nursing home with Joan Barclay who often talked about being in two movies with Bela Lugosi (specifically *Black Dragons*), and that no one believed her. Almost 60 years after acting with him, she still fondly remembered the legendary Lugosi charm and appeal!

The surprise for Dr. Vollin? … "Special Attraction. Miss Jean Thatcher. Dance Interpretations." We see Jean on the stage from *The Phantom of the Opera* (Universal 1925) set with an actor embodying Edgar Allan Poe, who recites movingly.

> Once upon a midnight dreary,
> while I pondered, weak and weary,
> Over many a quaint and curious
> volume of forgotten lore—
> While I nodded, nearly napping,
> suddenly there came a tapping,
> As of someone gently rapping,
> rapping at my chamber door.
> "'Tis some visitor," I muttered,
> "tapping at my chamber door—
> Only this and nothing more."

> Ah, distinctly I remember it was
> in the bleak December;
> And each separate dying ember
> wrought its ghost upon the floor.
> Eagerly I wished the 'morrow;
> vainly I had sought to borrow
> From my books surcease of sorrow—sorrow for the lost Lenore—
> For the rare and radiant maiden
> who the angels name Lenore—

The Poe here is Raine Bennett, a 44-year-old actor (1891-1981, Los Angeles, CA) famous for narrating *The Pacific Frontier*, a Broadway Brevity (Vitaphone 1942) short which, according to IMDb, was a "Tour of Hawaii, Midway, and other Pacific Islands, subject to Japanese attack, aboard the Pacific Clipper." Mr. Bennett's Edgar Allan Poe is arrestingly vivid. (He says, "tried to borrow" rather than Poe's original "sought to borrow," but he correctly quotes, "... whom the angels name Lenore." Bela says, "whom the angels call Lenore." The editorial decision to remove any reference to "Nevermore," Poe's haunting refrain from, *The Raven*, is contrary to what the author wrote about his most famous poem. (Bela/Vollin and Raine Bennett/Poe never say "Nevermore." The shooting script did have Dr. Vollin ranting "Nevermore" several times near the end of the movie, but it was not used in the release print.)

"This led me at once to a single word as the best refrain. The question now arose as to the character of the word. Having made up my mind to a refrain, the division of the poem into stanzas was, of course, a corollary: the refrain forming the close to each stanza. That such a close, to have force, must be sonorous and susceptible of protracted emphasis, admitted no doubt: and these considerations inevitably led me to the long "o" as the most sonorous vowel, in connection with "r" as the most producible consonant. The sound of the refrain being thus determined, it became necessary to select a word embodying this sound, and at the same time in the fullest possible keeping with that melancholy, which I had predetermined as the tone of the poem. In such a search it would have been … impossible

Bateman awakens from his operation to observe his new look in the mirrors.

Disfigured Bateman reacts when Jean apologizes for being scared when he came to her room earlier.

to overlook the word "Nevermore." In fact, it was the very first which presented itself." (Poe, Edgar Allan, "*The Philosophy of Composition*," Philadelphia: *Graham's American Monthly Magazine of Literature and Art*, April 1846.)

Dance double for Irene Ware—Nina Golden—puts Poes' raven in sensuous motion as she jetes and pirouettes, making her filmy costume "flirt and flutter." *The Spirit of Poe* dance music is another one of the unique pieces composed for the film by Clifford Vaughan. Stumar's camera cuts away several times from the stage to show Jerry and friends, Geoffrey and Mary Burns in one box, while also displaying Judge Thatcher and a rapt Dr. Richard Vollin in another. Judge Thatcher can't help but notice Vollin's deep absorption as well as his overly vigorous applause. After 12 curtain calls, Jean and Jerry banter lightly in her dressing room, as she asks him to remove her ballet slippers, something she would never ask Dr. Vollin to do. Before Jerry can attend to her, Geoffrey and Mary enter and praise her performance, as does her father who wonders what she calls the dance, which was new to him. "I call it, *The Spirit of Poe*." Hearing that, Dr. Richard Vollin makes an entrance as Jean smilingly asks him if it was "a great surprise." Kissing her hand, he sighs, "Whom the angels call Lenore." Jean and Dr. Vollin stare at each other as he kisses her hand again. Charles Stumar provides us with a marvelous closeup of the two of them with Judge Thatcher in the background, dead center.

Russian ballet actor, dancer, and choreographer Theodore Kosloff was responsible for the *The Spirit of Poe*. He acted and danced in silent films throughout the 1920s. His last role was in *Stage Door* (RKO 1937), and you can miss his uncredited appearance as a dance instructor. Information on Nina Golden is scarce, IMDb only mentioning that she is known for *The Raven*.

Dr. Vollin appears in his office through a moving bookcase. His butler, and apparently man of all work, since we don't see any other servants around, is played by Cyril Thornton, (uncredited here and similarly unrecognized in *Tower of London* [Universal 1939], *The Invisible Man Returns* [Universal 1939], and *The Man They Could Not Hang* [Columbia 1939]. Both *Tower of London* and *The Man They Could Not Hang* starred Boris Karloff). He's surprised to see Dr. Vollin emerging from behind the bookcase, who sharply reprimands him for being in the room without being summoned. The unnamed butler announces that Judge Thatcher has come. Vollin was expecting Jean. The anxious father observed the dynamic between his daughter and the doctor after the performance, so he presses her for an explanation. Jean admits she's "in danger of becoming infatuated." Naturally, the judge expects the doctor to discourage the girl, instead Vollin's passions rapidly escalate, saying Jean has "fallen in love" with him, and the judge doesn't "approve." Alarmed, Judge Thatcher watches Vollin unable to conceal his feelings and angrily break a test tube in his hand. Seeing this, the judge now wants Jean to marry her fiancé "more than ever," and tells Dr. Vollin not to see his daughter anymore. Furious, the doctor calls the judge a "trifling fool" and vehemently states—with another fabulous Stumar closeup. "Listen, Thatcher. I'm a man who renders humanity a great service. For that my brain must be clear, my nerves steady, and my hand sure. Jean torments me. She has come into my life, into my brain." Sympathetically, the father suggests, "Forget it man, forget it." Vollin insists that the judge send his daughter to him. Horrified, Judge Thatcher calls Dr. Vollin "stark, staring mad," and quickly leaves, even while the doctor keeps insisting that Jean be sent to him. "Send her. I warn you." Vollin never asks for Jean's hand or admits to loving her. Rather, what the doctor feels is a delirious concoction of obsession, lust, and *droit de seigneur* with perhaps a smidgeon of love in the mix. "Send her to me." He is bewitched by a

Bateman is standing in front of the giant machine that controls the house.

Bateman in the process of kidnapping Judge Thatcher for Dr. Vollin to torture.

woman who has become a fever in his brain. "Send her to me."

A saloon. Boris Karloff is Edmond Bateman—murderer, bank robber, and San Quentin escapee who needs a face change and hopes Dr. Richard Vollin can do it. Composer Vaughan's *Bateman Theme* swirls around him. The fugitive is dressed in an ill-fitting jacket, wrinkled shirt, baggy pants, and over-brimmed hat.

Stumar gives us a good look at the man's face and his scruffy beard as he makes for the doctor's house, slouching and dodging. Clifford Vaughan was one of three composers credited with scoring *The Raven*, the others being Heinz Roemheld and Y. Franke Harling. Vaughan, a child prodigy pianist, and organist, had recently been hired by Universal, where his first job was orchestrating Franz Waxman's *Bride of Frankenstein* (Universal 1935). Bateman finds the house's nameplate, "Dr. Richard Vollin," and rings the bell. Cyril Thornton's butler answers, instantly trying to shut out the seedy man, who forces his way in and announces, "I want to see Dr. Vollin." "I'm Dr. Vollin," rings out from Bela on the stairs. Standing militarily straight, Adonis-like, and dapper in an immaculate suit, the contrast couldn't be greater, but Batemen nevertheless removes his hat in an attempt at being a gentleman. Imperiously, Vollin commands him into his office, without asking him to sit down. He recognizes Bateman from the paper, telling him his bad beard is "no disguise." Bateman wants Vollin to "change" his face. Annoyed with the uninvited guest, Dr. Vollin flings out, "I'm not a plastic surgeon—Bateman!" The visitor shows a gun, and the doctor revises his answer and tells him that he can change his appearance, just not in the usual way. Desperate Bateman doesn't care. Any way is "all right" with him. Vollin will do the surgery but wants something in return. Bateman uneasily asks, "Like what?" Coldly Vollin assures him, "It's in your line." Even to a wanted criminal, this is sounding worse and worse, "Like what!" Chillingly, the mad doctor tosses off, "Torture and murder." Honestly protesting, Bateman pleads, "That's not my line! My line is …" We never find out because Dr. Richard Vollin interrupts, "You shot your way out of San Quentin. Two guards are dead. In a bank in Arizona a man's face was mutilated—burned—cashier of the bank." Bateman's excuse? "Well, he tried to get me into trouble! I told him to keep his mouth shut. He gets the gag out of his mouth and starts yellin' for the police. I had the acetylene torch in my hand …" Vollin breaks in—savoring the details— "So you put the burning torch into his face! Into his eyes!" Bateman's explanation. "Well, sometimes you can't help things like that! Even after such a heinous act, Bateman gets our sympathy with, "I'll tell you somethin' Doc … Ever since I was born, everybody looks at

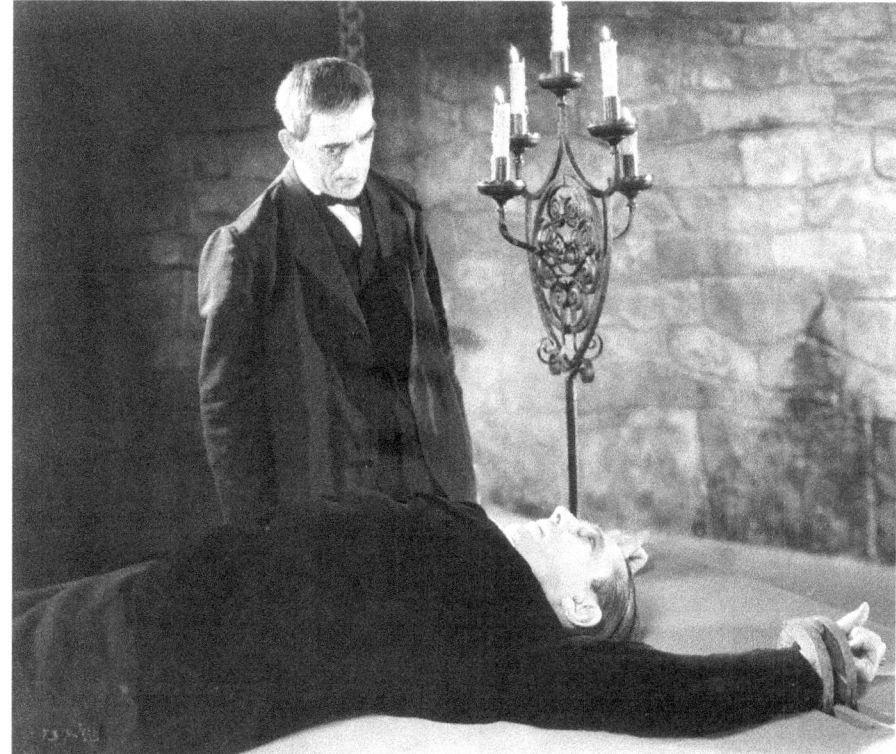

Vollin, who is demonstrating his pendulum torture device to Bateman, finds himself trapped in the device, much to Bateman's joy.

Judge Thatcher, who is startled from his sleep by Bateman, is ready to face the tortures of the swinging pendulum, devised by Vollin.

me and says, you're ugly." Makes me feel mean! Dr. Vollin is once again irritated and attempts to stop the man with, "Why are you telling me this, Bateman, I'm not interested in your life story." Lugosi's emphasis on "life" rather than "story" is perfect for a man who really doesn't care about anyone else's life, while Karloff's Bateman draws us in with his almost patented heartbreaking vulnerability, "Maybe because I look ugly, maybe if a man looks ugly, he does ugly things. (Charles Stumar's magical closeup highlights Karloff's beautiful, sad eyes.) "You are saying something profound, a man with a face so hideously ugly." "Profound," indeed. Vollin may just have found his "muscle."

Still hoping, Bateman accepts the doctor's offer to do the operation immediately but keeps his gun when Vollin tries to take it. As we hear the *Second Movement* of the *Schumann Piano Quintet in e-flat major*, Bateman follows Vollin through the bookcase door. (This music also accompanied Poelzig leading Werdegast down to the cellar in *The Black Cat*. The main musical theme of this movement is in c-minor, a funeral march.) The operating room is decidedly unhygienic. Dr. Vollin simply hangs up his jacket on a coat tree and slips into a surgical smock (which is also hanging on the same coat tree), assuring his patient that the procedure will only take 10 minutes. Perfect tight closeups of Boris and Bela, with Boris' Bateman still hunched over, hat in hand, and hanging on the words of Bela's Vollin as he says, "I who know what to do with these nerve ends can … make you look anyway I choose." All Bateman does is lie face up and loosen his collar (tie still on), while the great surgeon just covers him with a sheet. No hospital gown. No sanitizing. Further proof that Dr. Richard Vollin is truly "a law unto himself."

His patient is still sedated, so Vollin returns later to remove the bandages which bizarrely only cover half of Bateman's face. (Make-up genius Jack Pierce made one side attractive with a shave and haircut; the other ruined in ghastly paralysis, with a staring, useless eye.)

We can't help but sympathize with Bateman, as he continues to accept Vollin's hokum explanations as to why it's difficult for him to talk. Innocently happy— "I want to see myself"—he believes he will "look good." Vollin disappears. Slowly the curtains open one after the other to reveal mirrors, which shows Bateman what Vollin has done. Enraged, he shoots out every single mirror, emptying his gun. Sadistically, the doctor laughs insanely and forces Bateman to agree to "torture and murder." "My brain, your hand." Karloff's poor trusting man barely whispers a "yes," as he resignedly hangs his head. We remember Bateman's pitiful, "Make me look good." The betrayed man has no options. He could give himself up and tell police about the doctor's murderous plans, but he wouldn't be believed because the unscrupulous Vollin would probably turn him in first, anyway. All friendliness gone, the doctor returns,

Bateman drags Dr. Vollin unconscious into "the room where the walls come together," as Jean and Dr. Jerry Halden watch.

pointing a gun, and roughly throws servant's clothes at the man he maimed. Lugosi's Vollin in this scene foreshadows his brilliant Ygor, Lugosi safe behind his upper-level protective grill, as he cackles at Karloff's Bateman.

We see the weekend party invitation note, "My dear Jean … Richard Vollin." Against Judge Thatcher's wishes, Jean and Jerry, on their way to the Vollin party, are talking about Vollin being, "a little mad," and that the doctor also, "kind of likes," Jean. Also, at the Vollin bash are Geoffey (nicknamed "Pinky") Burns and wife, Mary, as well as the Colonel and Mrs. Harriet Grant. Illinois born Ian Wolfe, in his Universal debut here, was often cast as an Englishman, years older than he was and usually uncredited as when he played Colin Clive's stepfather, Henry Orlac, later that year in *Mad Love* (MGM 1935). Other genre films include *The Invisible Man's Revenge*, (Universal 1944) with Lester Matthews; *Bedlam*, (RKO 1946) starring Boris Karloff, where he was one of the unfairly incarcerated "loonies"; dignified scientist Sidney Longmand; and in *The Lost World* (20th Century Fox 1960), as Amazon basin explorer Burton White, with Claude Rains. Wife Mary was played by Inez Courtney, who was a musical theater actress, singer, and dancer and provided *The Raven* with some of its rare humorous moments. This film was her sole genre credit. More comic relief came with Colonel Grant played by prolific character actor (220 films) Spencer Charters, who appeared with Bela Lugosi in *Postal Inspector* (Universal 1936), and Charles Laughton in *The Hunchback of Notre Dame* (RKO 1936). American movie and Broadway actress, Maidel Turner, was cast as the colonel's wife, Harriet. She previously joined Irene Ware in *Night Life of the Gods*, (Universal 1935). We see them all together at the Vollin party enjoying a weird mechanical horse racing game. After various exclamations, Jerry's bet wins. Did brilliant surgeon and Poe fan, Richard Vollin, build this thing?

The *Jeu de Course* (or *Petits Cheveaux*) was invented in Wales in 1887 by Dai Ceffyl, a blacksmith … the English invaders destroyed all examples and burnt his patent application. Not to be beaten, Dai sailed to France and sold them his idea; they started manufacturing this mechanical wonder in 1890 … Players would place bets and pull the handle to make the horses rotate at random speeds. The horses cross the finishing line several times, but the winner is the horse which is closest to reaching the finish line when they stop.

Circa 1911, the author Saki wrote a short story ("The Way to the Dairy"), which was largely based on playing *Petits Cheveaux* in a French casino. (Dennis', Phil Internet blog, *Antique and Vintage Games*.

Dr. Vollin and Edmund Bateman smiling and holding each other between a take.

Mechanical Horse Racing Games. March 29, 2020.)

"… At his private house party, glancing over to the lovely Jean, who is having the back of her hair twirled by fiancé Jerry Halden, Lugosi flashes a quick, dynamic glance of hatred in seeing his love being fingered by his younger assistant. Quickly, he regains his composure and assumes a pleasing host-like smile. But that poison-dagger glance lingers long in the viewer's mind." (Svehla, Gary J., *Midnight Marquee Actors Series Bela Lugosi* [Baltimore: Midnight Marquee Press, Inc.] 97, 98.)

Vollin may be planning Jean's demise, but he is still jealous. Jean goes upstairs to fix her hair and Karloff's Bateman enters, startling the merry group with his ghastly appearance, croaking, "Man to see you." It's Judge Thatcher, none too pleased at being there. Vollin looks over to him, profusely apologizing for, "… all the stupid things I said to you the other day." The judge is not so willing to forget, only hesitantly acquiescing when Vollin mentions being "… under a terrible strain … and if you can feel in any way indebted to me, clear your debt by forgiving me for what I said." Still not convinced but remembering that this man saved his daughter's life, he allows the beaming host to present him to the others. (Karloff's Bateman is a hoot here, as he stares at the party guests and tentatively moves forward as if to join them.) Everything is interrupted by Jean's scream when she sees Karloff's Bateman (with that eye!) reflected in the mirror, who is there on Vollin's order that he tell the girl her father has come. Terrified, Jean runs downstairs, grateful that her father arrived. He takes Jean's hand as if he was leading her to the dance floor. The smoothly lying Vollin has them all sit down and claims that Bateman was in his regiment, tortured by Arabs. "The poor fella…" Continuing, he compares the fictional "Arab bandits" with his idol, Poe, as having "… A genius for devising torture…" Explaining his Poe obsession to the guests (Jean and her father are especially interested), Vollin points to the stuffed raven in his study which prompts Harriet to exclaim, "A pretty thing to have around the house." Ignoring her, Jerry and Jean again ask the doctor about the poem and its author. Vollin obliges with, "… Poe was a great genius … But he fell in love. Her name was Lenore …" Soulfully, directly to Vollin, Jean murmurs, "Longing for the lost Lenore." Vollin wistfully echoes, "Longing for the lost Lenore." "… When a man of genius is denied his great love, he goes mad … so he begins to think of torture for those who have tortured him!" Stumar's camera makes us look directly at the very uncomfortable Judge Thatcher on this last remark, and the camera moves over to Bateman clearly thinking

Bateman stands by the elevator entrance of Jean's room.

of getting back at Vollin for paralyzing his face. Dr. Vollin then backs away from his "torture" comments, but he winds up digging in deeper, claiming, "A doctor is fascinated by death—and pain. And how much pain a man can endure …" Only Jerry finds his voice and objects. (Poe's "great love" was not Lenore. His wife was his cousin Virginia, who was only 24 years old when she died from consumption [tuberculosis]). Lenore was used because the name rhymed with "Nevermore."

The sleepy colonel starts a general movement to retire for the evening. Jean agrees, mentioning the "windy cold" night and "nice warm beds." (Considering that she's costumed in a fanciful gauzy sleeveless number that reveals more than it covers, actress Irene Ware probably could relate!) Feeling badly about Bateman, she stops on her way upstairs to apologize for her fright. Karloff's hangdog Edmond Bateman seems as if he's falling in love with Jean, too. It may well have been the only time in his life that anyone was kind to him.

Gracious host (also brilliant surgeon, Poe fanatic, and deranged madman) Dr. Richard Vollin escorts his guests to their rooms. After he leaves, Judge Thatcher proves that he was never taken in by the apology and wisely tells Jean and Jerry that, "This man Vollin is stark staring mad …" adding, "Let's go home." Unwisely, the engaged couple laugh this off, with Jerry going so far as to say that Vollin's crazy talk about Poe and torture and pain was just the doctor "… being amusing." Reasonably, the judge objects, "I'm afraid there's something wrong with my sense of humor." Jean unhelpfully offers that she can't believe her former crush would do anything to harm them. "… He's not going to cut our throats." Getting serious finally, Jerry worries, "You're afraid that in the middle of the night, he might …" (*The Raven* has dozens of these unfinished sentences. Jerry's line could easily be an intertitle in a silent film with the lascivious villain bursting in on the heroine in the next scene.) The comment must remind Judge Thatcher of Dr. Vollin's commanding, "Send her to me." Amusingly, Jean wonders if her fiancé will be safe, which allows Jerry, who's costumed in a stunning polka dotted robe, to imitate William Powell in *The Thin Man* (MGM 1934). Suavely leaning against a cabinet, he snarks, "Well he

In an unused scene, Bateman grabs the Colonel, one of Vollin's party guests.

certainly isn't coming into my room." So, they switch.

Joining Vollin for a dungeon torture device tour, Bateman is now dressed as a servant. The music is the track used for Poelzig visiting all his glass encased embalmed women—the Chopin *Prelude No. 2 in a-minor*. (This prelude significantly uses tritones, the devil's interval—making the music sound more like Liszt than Chopin.) Lugosi and Karloff swap evil and good characters.

Stumar's eerily smooth tracking shot reveals an Iron Maiden which was never used in a Poe story, but we see it in Vollin's private museum of torture devices.

"The Iron Maiden was a device so fiendish it was once thought to be fictional. It's an upright sarcophagus with spikes on the inner surfaces. Double doors open on the front, allowing entrance for the victim. In one example, eight spikes protruded from one door, 13 from the other. Once the victim was inside, the doors were closed. There, the strategically placed spikes would pierce several vital organs. However, they were relatively short spikes, so the wounds wouldn't be instantly fatal. Instead, the victim would linger and bleed to death over several hours." (From the website, *HowStuffWorks: 10 Medieval Torture Devices*).

Barbara Steele's unfaithful wife, Elizabeth, gets the Iron Maiden treatment in the Vincent Price Poe movie, *The Pit and the Pendulum* (American International Pictures 1961). But a background glimpse is all we get in *The Raven*. Next comes an alarmingly dreadful looking flatbed with slats which might have been another type of Iron Maiden, but the only photos that appear online of it are from *The Raven*!

Adding to the grisly collection is a metal cage. Similar ones in various horrible constructions were widely used in the Middle-Ages. Victims could be locked up and left to die or suspended from an outside structure so that the inquiring public could literally watch them perish from exposure and starvation. ("A pretty thing to have around the house.") Vollin's cage is accessorized by manacles, and large iron balls, and chains.

Usually thought of as the go-to medieval torture device, the rack was used to stretch a prisoner's limbs and joints in an unimaginably ghastly manner, as to encourage confessions. The poor victim gained nothing from this because they were usually executed afterwards. Vollin adds that the nasty things are, "… Rare older pieces, all of them, but … ready for use." The prize dungeon ornament is a stone slab with a fiendish pendulum knife

The hero and heroine: Irene Ware and Lester Matthews

hanging above, illuminated by two large candelabras. Vollin proudly demonstrates by lying down with arms outstretched on the slab and tells Bateman that a side switch locks the manacles, which starts the blade swinging downwards. (It's still hard to believe that Vollin "built" it as he claims to have done.) Perhaps remembering, "Your monstrous ugliness breeds monstrous hate …" and unable to resist the opportunity, after Vollin lies down, Bateman pushes the switch accompanied by Liszt's *Piano Sonata in b-minor*, joyfully exclaiming, "Gotch you!" Bateman has been no innocent, but we rejoice with him in this moment of triumph. Ever cool Vollin is not so calm now and nervously laughs, telling his temporary servant to let him go. Bateman does not comply and unnervingly watches the moving pendulum knife arcing downwards on Vollin. Trying to hide his growing fear but still commanding, the manacled doctor reminds Bateman that he is the only person who can "fix" him. "You remain the hideous monster that you are." That's too much for the grotesquely disfigured man to bear, so he stops the blade. With audible relief, Vollin gets up from the slab. "It's all quite simple, isn't it Bateman?"

As the girl sleeps, Bateman tries to enter her room via a trap door in the floor but is stopped by a tree breaking the window, and Jean's scream. In her clingy satin nightgown, Jean runs to Jerry who takes her back to the same room and laughs off the broken window but helps her into a robe more notable for style interest than warmth. She tells him that she, "… saw a man coming up through the floor." That same man, Bateman, is now facing an angry Vollin sporting a cravat, smoking jacket, gun, and riding whip. He asks, "You were looking for the girl, weren't you?" Vollin's wrath is like Archdeacon Claude Frollo's when he sees Esmeralda's kindness to Quasimodo.

"Then he felt jealousy begin to awaken confusedly in him, a jealousy which he would never have expected … The captain is bad enough … but *that* creature! The thought overwhelmed him." (Hugo, Victor Marie, *The Hunchback of Notre Dame* [New York: Bantam Books, Inc. 1965] 213.)

Thinking about Jean who he fell in love with instantly, Bateman gasps out a yes. Vollin sadistically strikes him with the whip but stops to answer the colonel's knock at the door, appearing as the solicitous host. Mrs. Grant needs a sleeping powder. Vollin gives him two. "One for you." The colonel gets a cute comic closeup as he gushes, "Such a nice man, so thoughtful!" Laser focused on Lugosi's Vollin, he tells of Karloff's Bateman, "The job begins."

Bateman grabs Judge Thatcher from his guest bed, who struggles and tries to yell for help. (Liszt's *Piano Sonata in b-minor* again) Jerry hears him—taking his sweet time going down the stairs—and gets to the study in time to see Bateman roughhousing the judge through the bookcase door. Then just as in *The Black Cat*, the male ingenue is knocked out before he can offer immediate assistance. The judge, with bare feet, and in pajamas, faces a smiling Vollin in the cellar, who apologizes for his "uncivilized" servant. On Vollin's command, Bateman forces Judge Thatcher down on the slab and starts the pendulum. The orchestral version of the Brahms' *Rhapsody in b-minor for Piano*—already familiar from *The Black Cat*—cascades in the background.

> Judge Thatcher: What's that thing?
> Dr. Vollin: A knife.
> Judge Thatcher: What's it doing?
> Dr. Vollin: Descending.
> Judge Thatcher: Oh … try to be sane, Vollin!
> Dr. Vollin: I am the sanest man who ever lived! … 15 minutes … Torture waiting, waiting …
> Bateman gets a tight closeup with his functioning eye trained on the pendulum again.

Back in the study, Jerry comes to and tries to get through the wall. Down in the cellar, Vollin goes to an impressive control panel marked with telephones, room, shutters, office door, clock, elevator, and 1st floor. He slides the elevator switch, and Jean's room descends. Jean screams again, calling for Jerry. Stumar and the editor give Bela a significant closeup here where his face hints of regret and perhaps even a trace of lingering love, as he waits for Jean, standing like a prospective bridegroom at the altar. Subtle, powerful, and short-lived. As steel doors close her in, Vollin tells his obsession that he has a "pleasant surprise." In a serial movie moment, Jerry hears Jean, goes to her room, and falls, swinging precariously from the door leading to her disappeared room. Pulling himself up, he wakes Geoffrey and Mary, who follow him. Quick cut back to the action in the cellar, with Stumar giving us an aerial view of the lowering pendulum above Judge Thatcher. Jerry again is reunited with Geoffrey and Mary. We find out that the colonel and his wife are probably drugged. Jerry tries to call the police. Vollin slides the telephones and shutters switches, saying to a watching Bateman, "There is now no way of getting in. No way of getting out." Back to the judge, Vollin asks, "Do you mind if I smoke?" Final screenplay writer, David Boehm, got this suggestive line past the censors somehow, just as Edgar Ulmer in *The Black Cat* managed to keep the outrageous Poelzig solo cellar walk.

Angry because Jean continues to call for Jerry, Vollin tells Bateman to, "Tell her to stop." Jean can't help cringing when Bateman comes in. "Yes, I'm ugly. He did it!" She tells him Vollin won't help him, but she will. He is torn but closes the steel door because he wants to "look good."

With the action ramping up in Rococo style, we are suddenly in the study. The bookcase opens and Jerry, Geoffrey, and Mary go to the cellar, despite Mary's misgivings. They see Bateman standing near the still trapped Judge Thatcher, who Geoffrey can't free because the switch is locked. (Bateman has the key.) He grabs Jerry from behind and hustles him over to Jean.

Tall, dark, handsome, and insane, Dr. Vollin holds them at gunpoint and talks about their "wedding ceremony." Jean begs for her father's life, but the doctor "dismisses" that plea. "I'll soon be rid of my torture, rid of it!" With the Liszt *Piano Sonata in b-minor* orchestrally boiling in the background and pointing his gun, Vollin tells the couple that the sinister room is his "gift." "A humble place, but your love will make it beautiful." Bela's Vollin is wickedly enjoying his speech with inherent evil heart and orders, "All right, go in. Go in!" What else can they do? Lunge at

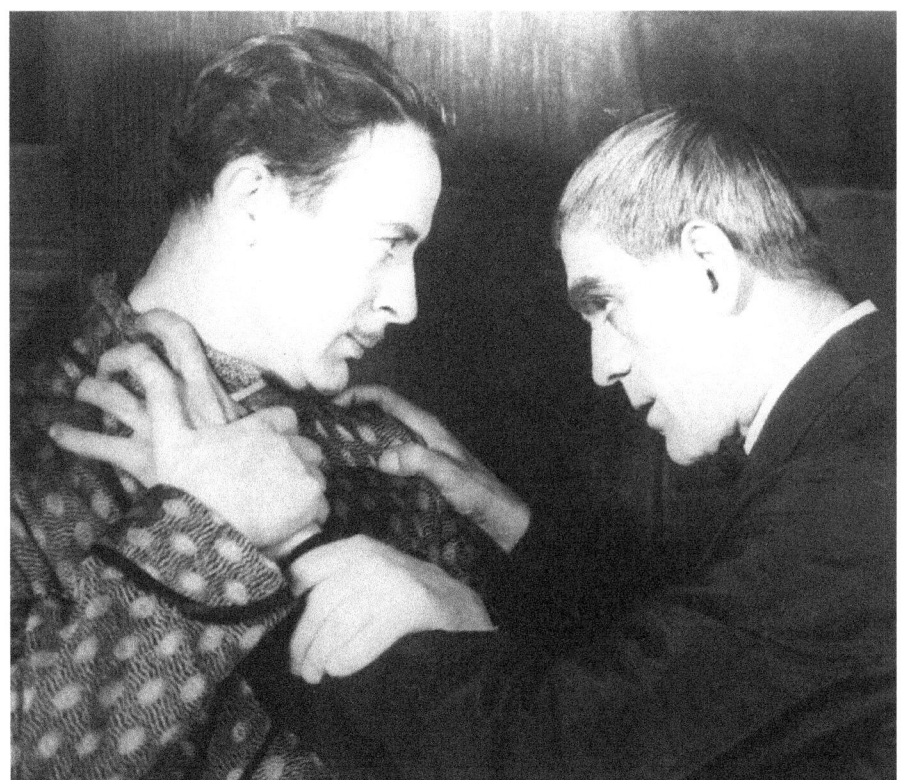

Bateman puts his hands near the neck of Dr. Jerry Halden, in a most threatening manner.

Vollin and get shot immediately, or take a chance on getting help, however hopeless. Quick switch to the judge and the pendulum, getting much nearer. Back to Vollin, looking right at Jean and Jerry with what he thinks will be his final sight of them. "You will live in this place forever and ever. It'll be the perfect marriage, the perfect love …" He shouts at a very reluctant Bateman to close the steel door, which he finally does as Lugosi/Vollin deliriously rants and laughs insanely about torture and Poe, waving his arms and declaring, "Poe, you are avenged!" (We don't find out why crushing a young couple to death and murdering a judge would avenge Poe, but it's a plummy line and Bela doesn't hold back.) Bateman demands to know what happens in the room and Vollin happily answers, "It's another one of Poe's devices. It's the room where the walls come together." The pendulum is descending on the judge; Jean and Jerry are in the death room, yet mad Vollin strokes his handiwork on Bateman's face and promises, he'll "do nobly" by him. Bateman can't stand it, "She crushed to death?" No. No!" He goes deliberately to the panel. "First, I'll let her go." Vollin warns that he won't fix him and worse, "If you touch that switch …" Bateman pulls the lever. Vollin viciously shoots him in the back. Mortally wounded, Bateman clutches himself but turns around to face the monster who mutilated him (with a clever blurry closeup paying homage to the ruined eye), leans in, knocks the gun out of his hand, and takes down Vollin. A stunned Jean and Jerry, who thought they were done for, stumble out as Bateman drags Vollin into the room, then slides the room switch on the control and dies, trapping Vollin inside. The doctor regains consciousness just in time to see the door close. "Bateman! Bateman! Bateman!"

(After watching the scene 25 times, it seems as if Boris Karloff's stunt double, Monte Montague, and likewise, Bela Lugosi's George DeNormand, are briefly in this scene as Bateman struggles to get up and drag Vollin into the room. There is a quick edit where we do see Karloff's face, but it's his double, not him climbing over Vollin, and it's not Lugosi being dragged.) Karloff's dying Bateman stumbles to the panel and falls as he pulls the lever, while Lugosi's Vollin in utter terror futilely puts his hands on the walls.

Geoffrey grabs the key from Bateman's pocket, and they all rush over to the judge who is freed just in time. Jean fusses over her father, while Stumar shows us the

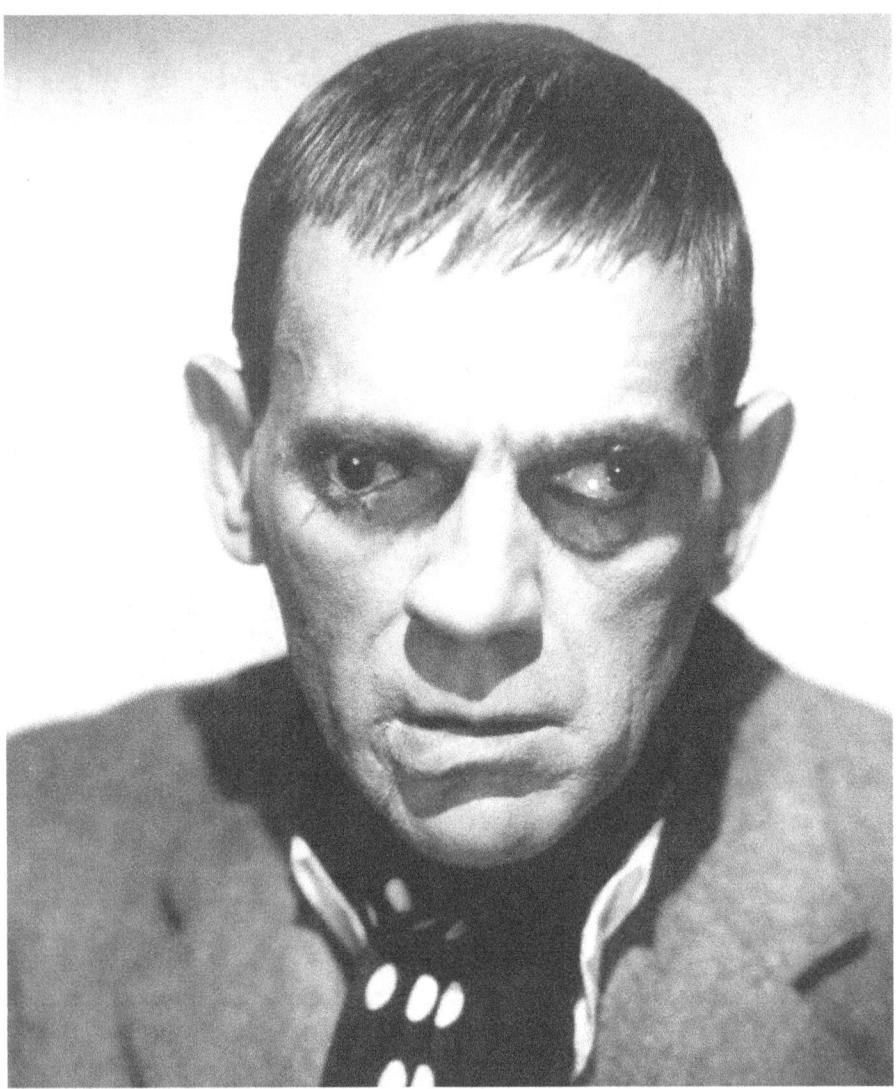

An unused mock make-up for Bateman, with each eye staring in different directions.

dead Bateman and the soon to be crushed Vollin, holding onto his head and screaming as he falls.

Shouldn't the movie end at this point? Edmond Bateman has saved at least three lives and maybe seven, giving up his own. Richard Vollin has discovered that death does indeed have the same significance for him as it does for everyone else. But no. We get Mary Burns screaming about, "The Colonel ... and his wife who are shown safe, sleeping, and snoring in their guest beds. As if that were not bad enough, the final scene shows Jean and Jerry in the car again, at least appreciating Edmond Bateman sacrificing his own life to save theirs, but the moment is immediately trivialized by Jerry saying, "He saved us from being crushed all right ..." "I think I better finish the job don't you, only a little more gently." Smiling as he hugs her and takes his eyes off the road, Jean calls him, "... the big bad raven."

Specially, how does the movie *The Raven* tie-in to Poe literature?

Poe's tale, *The Pit and the Pendulum*, does have a room of sorts "where the walls come together," but we're not immediately sure if it's reality or a fever dream. And of course, there's a pendulum.

"While I gazed directly upward at it, (for its position was immediately over my own,) fancied that I saw it in motion ... Its sweep was ... slow ... again I cast my eyes upward ... it had perceptibly descended ... and the under edge as keen as a razor ... down—relentlessly down! It vibrated-within three inches of my bosom!"

"There had been a second change in the cell—and now the change was obviously in the *form* ... The room had been square. I saw that two of its iron angles were now acute—two, consequently, obtuse. The difference quickly increased with a low rumbling or moaning sound ... I could have clasped the red walls to my bosom as a garment of eternal peace ... I shrank back—but the burning walls pressed me resistlessly onward ... I felt that I tottered upon the brink—I averted my eye ..." (Poe, Edgar Allan, *The Works of Edgar Allan Poe, Volume II: Tales* [New York and London: Harper & Brothers Publishers, 1910] 184-193.)

Whether intentional or not, the end of the story is reflected in the end of the movie: the story's unnamed narrator is saved from falling into the pit; Jean and Jerry are saved from being crushed.

According to Wikipedia: "*Deus ex machina* (is) a plot device whereby a seemingly unsolvable problem in a story is suddenly and abruptly resolved by an unexpected and unlikely occurrence." In the movie, it's Edmond Bateman.

A thirst for vengeance is a frequent theme in Poe's works, even in his literary criticism! Dr. Vollin is determined to get his revenge ("I'll soon be rid of my torture"). In, *The Cask of Amontillado*, the narrator Montresor has a pent-up fury over "the thousand injuries of Fortunato." Those injuries remain a mystery, but Montresor ostensibly lures an intoxicated Fortunato down to his family's combination crypt and wine cellar to give a connoisseur's opinion on some rare Amontillado he has supposedly obtained. Montresor appeals directly to Fortunato's vanity by trying to discourage him from going into a damp cellar because he has a cold, suggesting that another expert, Luchesi, will taste the wine. Fortunato objects to this because, "Luchesi cannot tell Amontillado from sherry." Getting Fortunato drunker and drunker, Montresor chains him to a wall in a niche and closes him up inside. Gradually, the intoxication begins to wear off and Montresor hears moans, then screams, "For the love of God, Montresor!" He coldly answers, "Yes ... for the love of God." (Poe, Edgar Allan, "*The Cask of Amontillado,*" *The Works of Edgar Allan Poe, Volume II: Tales* [New York and London: Harper & Brothers Publishers, 1910)] 221-229). Vollin hopes the deaths of Jean, Jerry, and Judge Thatcher will free him from his inner torment, instead he dies by the "delicious torture" he had planned for them. "The measure with which you measure will be measured out to you." (Matthew 7:2) Montresor supposedly gets away with murdering Fortunato, but he will never have peace.

"No answer still. I thrust a torch through the remaining aperture and let it fall within. There came forth in return only a jingling of the bells. (Fortunato is dressed as a jester with bells on his cap for the carnival festivities.) My heart grew sick—on account of the dampness of the catacombs." (Poe, Edgar Allan, "*The Cask of Amontillado,*" *The Works of Edgar Allan Poe, Volume II: Tales* [New York and London: Harper & Brothers Publishers, 1910] 229.)

Another possibly unintentional Poe tie-in appears in the torture dungeon tour scene with Dr. Vollin and Bateman, as we see the cage against a wall with manacles, and iron balls and chains. The cage (in many different forms) could be used to hoist the victim(s) into the air and left to die. Similar deaths occur in *Hop Frog*, one of Poe's most gruesome stories. The title character is a cripple, dwarf, and court jester, who vows revenge on the king and his council for insulting and shaming his fellow jester and dwarf, Trippetta. Hop Frog persuades the king and his men that it would be a real lark to scare his guests by dressing up as orangutangs. Hop Frog helps them into tight fitting supposedly protective costumes, and then, essentially tars and feathers them. Before they realize what's happening, the jester chains them together and an unseen hand pulls them up until the king and councilors are suspended from the ceiling, halfway up. Handily clambering up the chain with his torch, Hop Frog feigns inspecting them with his torch to see who the masqueraders are. Horrifyingly, he sets them all on fire instead and addresses the guests.

"I now see *distinctly,*" he said, "what manner of people these maskers are. They are a great king and his seven privy councilors—a king who does not scruple to strike a defenseless girl, and his seven councilors who abet him in the outrage. As for myself, I am simply Hop Frog, the jester—and *this is my last jest.* (Poe, Edgar Allan, *Hop Frog Complete Stories and Poems of Edgar Allan Poe* [Garden City: Doubleday & Company, Inc, 1966] 289.)

Edgar Allan Poe's works have never been filmed by major studios without significant changes. Often, only the title of the tale survives. But *The Raven* honors the author with over the top excesses, horrors, and flamboyance as it simultaneously delights us with two magnificent star performances. "It's almost a celebration of Bela and Boris." (Mank, Gregory William, *Bela Lugosi and Boris Karloff: The Expanded Story of a Haunting Collaboration,* Jefferson, North Carolina and London: McFarland & Company, Inc., 2009, 269).

The Raven could have been titled *The Spirit of Poe*. Edgar Allan Poe would not have objected.

A studio portrait shot of Bela Lugosi, used in promotion for *The Raven*.

THE RAVEN (1935)
CREDITS: Director: Louis Friedlander (Lew Landers); Associate Producer: David Diamond; Screenplay: David Boehm; Suggested by the poem *The Raven* and the short story *The Pit and the Pendulum* by Edgar Allan Poe; Director of Photography: Charles Stumar; Film Editor: Albert Akst; Editorial Supervision: Maurice Pivar; Dialogue Director: Florence Enright; Art Director: Albert S. D'Agostino; Assistant Directors: Scott Beal & Victor Noerdlinger; Sound Supervisor: Gilbert Kurland; Musical Score: Clifford Vaughan, Heinz Roemheld & Y. Franke Harling; Dance Staged by Theodore Kosloff; Make-up: Jack P. Pierce; Released July 22, 1935 by Universal Pictures, 61 minutes

CAST: Karloff ... Edmond Bateman, Bela Lugosi ... Dr. Richard Vollin, Lester Matthews ... Dr. Jerry Halden, Irene Ware ... Jean Thatcher, Samuel S. Hinds ... Judge Thatcher, Spencer Charters ... Colonel Grant, Inez Courtney ... Mary Burns, Ian Wolfe ... Geoffrey "Pinky" Burns, Maidel Turner ... Harriet Grant, Arthur Hoyt ... Mr. Chapman, Jonathan Hale ... Dr. Cook, Walter Miller ... r. Hemingway, Cyril Thornton ... Butler, Nina Golden ... Dancer, Raine Bennett ... Poe actor, Madeline Talcott ... Nurse.

MUSIC:
Storm Scene, track from the score for *Destination Unknown* (Universal 1933) (Harling, J. Franke)

Raven Theme, from the score for *The Raven* (Universal 1935 (Vaughan, Clifford)

Toccata and Fugue in d-minor (Bach, Johann Sebastian, BWV, 565)

Piano Sonata in b-minor, S178 (Liszt, Franz)

Cat Love Theme, track from the score for *The Black Cat* (Universal 1934) (Roemheld, Heinz)

Based on the *Overture-Fantasy to Romeo and Juliet* (Tchaikovsky, Pyotr llyich, TH42, CH39)

The Spirit of Poe ballet music. From the score for *The Raven* (Universal 1935) (Vaughan, Clifford)

Bateman Theme from the score for *The Raven* (Universal 1935) (Vaughan, Clifford)

Piano Quintet in E-Flat major, Opus 44. II: I modo d'una marcia: Un poco largamente-agitat (Schumann, Robert Alexander)

Prelude No. 2 in a-minor, Opus 28 (Chopin, Fryderyk Franciszek.)

Rhapsody in b-minor for Piano, Opus 79 (Brahms, Johannes)

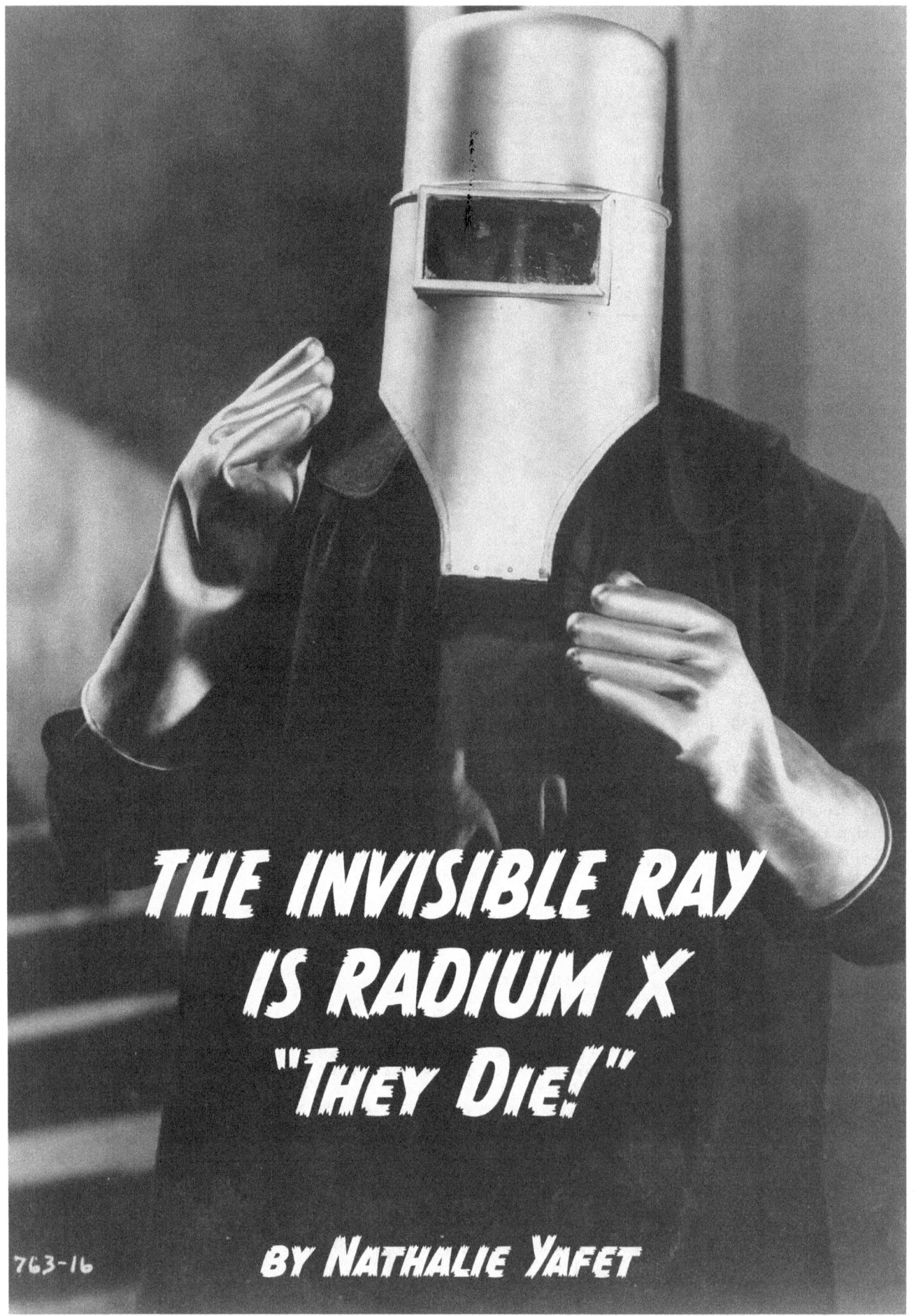

Before the movie was properly cast, here is an early trade ad for a 24-sheet.

Eight films. Karloff and Lugosi. Karloff and Bela Lugosi. Boris Karloff and Bela Lugosi. There were eight. Technically, not always together: *Gift of Gab* (Universal 1934) and *Black Friday* (Universal 1940). *Gift of Gab* is a bizarre conglomeration of various singers and actors joined together by the slimmest of plotlines. Bela Lugosi appears in an opened closet—handsome in a raffish tilted beret and holding a gun—asking Roger Pryor what time it is and gets the information he requests. Pryor and his sidekick, Chester Morris, close the door and that's it. Boris Karloff has a bit (just a bit) more to do as the Phantom—in cape and top hat—entering through a window, gets assistance finding a "little black book" from a corpse who isn't quite dead, blows smoke in Roger Pryor's face, laughs ghoulishly, and goes out through the same window. Their characters do appear together on a Holy Grail lobby card, but not in the film. The infamous *Black Friday*, inexplicably and inexcusably co-starring Boris Karloff and Stanley Ridges, with Bela Lugosi tossed off to the side, does not have them sharing one single scene. The decidedly non-horror actor Ridges (who should not have been Professor George Kingsley/Red Cannon) gets most of the star treatment with the showy dual role which should have been Karloff's. Nineteen-forties horror movie fans must have been confused. Karloff (should have been Lugosi) played Dr. Ernest Sovac, and Lugosi (could have been Stanley Ridges) was gangster Eric Marnay. The mess that was *Black Friday* makes even less sense when we remember that *Son of Frankenstein* (Universal 1939) came right before it. Boris and Bela were both billed after Rathbone but still above the title. *Son of Frankenstein* gave us a great gift of Lugosi's unique Ygor. Funny and chilling and poignant simultaneously. It is also—fortunately and unfortunately—forever married to *Young Frankenstein* (20th Century Fox 1974).

A German program book

The original pressbook herald

1 sheet from 1936

Their double association began magnificently in *The Black Cat* (Universal 1934), with Karloff as devil worshiper Hjalmar Poelzig, and Lugosi playing cat phobic psychiatrist, Dr. Vitus Werdegast, as the two top horror stars sparred stylishly in a blurry-lined battle of good versus evil. *Gift of Gab* followed anticlimactically and insultingly. Then came Bela Lugosi's one star turn among the eight—*The Raven* (Universal 1935), Bela's sexy Dr. Vollin facing off with Boris' warmhearted escaped murderer, Edmond Bateman. In the movies, at least, the Lugosi and Karloff combo ended with one of the best horror films of any decade, *The Body Snatcher* (RKO Radio Pictures 1945). Bela's underappreciated Joseph character role was admittedly smaller than Boris' Grey, but it was expressive and one of his best. Right after *Black Friday* came the entertaining but overlong, *You'll Find Out* (RKO Radio Pictures), where Karloff and Lugosi team up with Peter Lorre facing off against musical comedian, Kay Kyser. The trio is out to dispose of an heiress, take her money, and continue bamboozling her aunt. They are stopped byKyser, his band, and a dog named Prince. Although they're amusing—to a point—the movie needed less Kyser and company and more terror triumvirate.

After the censorship smoke cleared from *The Raven*, Universal decided to go sci-fi horror in 1936 with *The Invisible Ray*. "*The Invisible Ray* is the most maligned of Universal horror classics … *The Invisible Ray* has never been given its due, but when examined closely today, the film rises to become one of Universal's greatest horror movies ever, with two solid performances by Karloff and Lugosi." Svehla, Gary J., (Baltimore, Maryland: Midnight Marquee Press, Inc., 1994) 114.

It should have been classed with *The Black Cat* and *The Raven* as one of the top three with Karloff embodying obsessed sinned-against mad scientist Dr. Janos Rukh, paired with Lugosi's benevolent astrophysicist, Dr. Felix Benet. Refreshingly, it also has a cosmopolitan feel to it as we go from the Carpathian mountains to Africa to Paris, an evocative Franz Waxman score, stylish Brymer costumes, special effects guru John P. Fulton's magic, moodily engaging George Robinson's cinematography, and well-cast supporting players. Or are they? There's Frances Drake as Rukh's wife, Diana, who could easily have been one of painter Edward Burne-Jones' pre-Raphaelite models; stuffy Walter Kingsford (just right as Sir Francis Stevens), twice nominated for the Best Supporting Actress Oscar; Beulah Bondi, *The Gorgeous Hussy* (MGM 1936) and *Of Human Hearts* (MGM 1938), who fully inhabits the annoying Lady Arabella Stevens, big game-hunting bodice-ripper writer. Then there's Frank Lawton, effective in *David Copperfield* (MGM 1935) but a

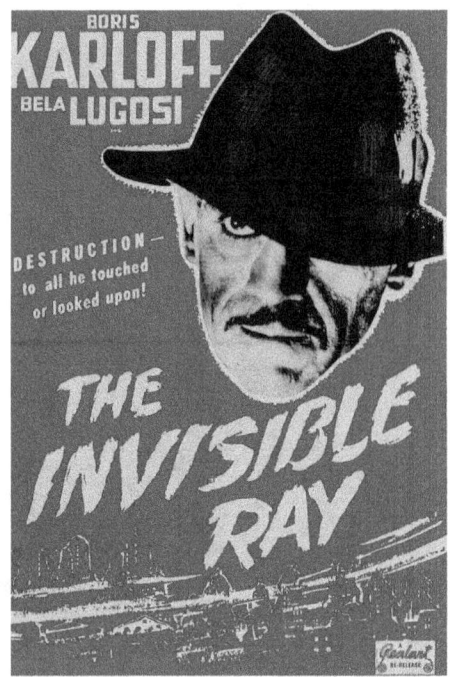

washout as male ingenue, Ronald Drake. His character has supposedly crossed the Mountains of the Moon.

The "Mountains of the Moon" is an ancient term referring to a legendary mountain range in Africa. The Ruwenzori Range is a series of six separate glaciated masses and is often celebrated as the "Mountains of the Moon." At an elevation of 5,119 meters, it is Africa's mightiest mountain system. (Google web search)

We're supposed to think that Lawton is believable playing the irresistible guy who steals the Mad Scientist's wife. Except we don't and he isn't. Frank Lawton's

The stars of the show: Boris Karloff as Janos Rukh and Bela Lugosi as Dr. Benet

This montage lobby card focuses on Frank Lawton and Frances Drake embracing.

Drake enters uninvited with the Benet group for Rukh's scientific demonstration, and already we're not buying it. Even at 5'9" his dainty physical characteristics and unimposing manner make him appear diminutive next to 5'11" Karloff and 6'1" Lugosi. It doesn't improve. The actor fails to convince even from the first as his character is meant to fall hard for Diana Rukh, instantly. Stares and averted glances do not compensate for zero chemistry. Giving him a huge hat appears comical, not manly. He even flops on what should have been a foolproof line as Lady Stevens remarks, "Would anyone ever expect to find anything like this atop the Carpathian Mountains?" Clearly, she meant the whole castle setup. Also clearly, Drake was expected to make us think he was commenting on Diana Rukh. He looks at her and flatly says, "No." No love at first sight vibes, no overwhelming attraction. Nothing. Weirdly, Diana has fizz with Bela's sedate Felix Benet and certainly some with screen husband, Janos Rukh. (Watch the sweet little exchange they have when Diana tells her husband that his guests are driving up.) So, who else would have been better as Drake? Reginald Denny, Patric Knowles, or Douglas Fairbanks, Jr., that's who.

Five-foot-11-inch Reginald Denny had already been successful as Leslie Howard's double-dealing doctor friend, Harry Griffiths, in *Of Human Bondage* (RKO Radio Pictures 1934). Howard's sad sack Philip Carey is desperately in love with Bette Davis' psycho slattern waitress, Mildred Rogers. His supposed friend, Griffiths, seduces the girl and dumps her afterwards. Immediately following *The Invisible Ray*, Mr. Denny and Frances Drake were a delightful romantic team in *The Preview Murder Mystery* (Paramount 1936), a better than average programmer. They connect charmingly in every scene they have together. It's a pairing so winningly natural that it would surely have guaranteed a better Diana and Drake combo. Reginald Denny was not associated with the horror movie genre. The closest he ever came was in several murder mysteries and most famously as Maxim de Winter's (Lawrence Olivier) agent and best friend for life, Frank Crawley in *Rebecca* (United Artists 1940). Denny had worked before with Frank Lawton in the dark James Whale-directed *One More River* (Universal 1934), in which he is Jane Wyatt's boss and eventual love. This seldom seen movie reveals that *The Invisible Ray* was not the first time that Frank Lawton was miscast as a wife-stealing hottie. His tender scenes with the Amazonian Diana Wynard are excruciating. The film is memorable for

Frances Drake and Reginald Denny in *The Preview Murder Mystery*

Valerie Hobson and Douglas Fairbanks, Jr. in *Jump for Glory* (aka *When Thief Meets Thief*)–A similar camera composition occurred in *The Werewolf of London*.

Kay Francis and Patric Knowles in *Give Me Your Heart*

Diana (Frances Drake) thinking her husband Janos dead, marries current lover Ronald Drake (Frank Lawton), as Dr. Benet and others look on.

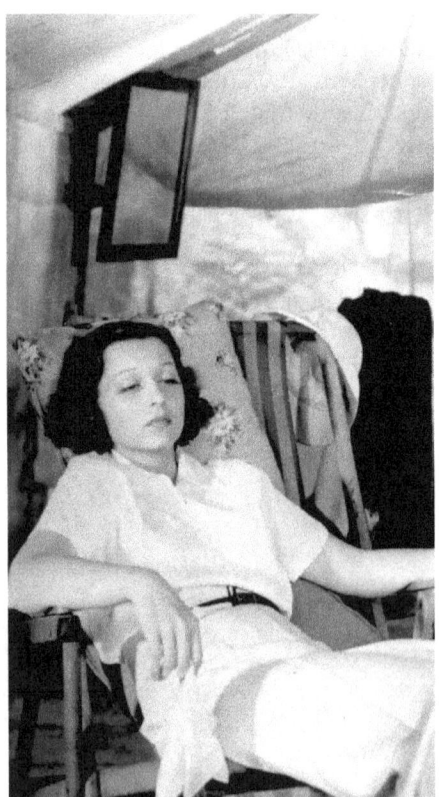

Frances Drake sweats it out in Africa, but suffers less "humidity" with lover Frank Lawton.

Whale's direction and Colin Clive's beastly class A wife-abuser husband, but not for any crackling moments between leading lady and her male ingenue. A Reginald Denny Ronald Drake would surely have been the calmest of the three alternative choices. Diana would have gravitated to him as a sanctuary from her husband's growing insanity.

At a high six-foot-two-inches, Patric Knowles was the tallest of the three. He was best known as Robin Hood's (Errol Flynn's) sincere friend, Will Scarlet, in *The Adventures of Robin Hood* (Warner Bros. 1938). He was cast against type in *Give Me Your Heart* (Warner Bros. 1936). As Robert Melford, he cheats on his crippled wife, Rosamund (Frieda Inescort), with Kay Francis' Belinda Warren, who's in love with him. Then he caddishly lets his father, Lord Farrington (Henry Stephenson), deal with the fallout from the ensuing pregnancy. Mr. Knowles' genre credits would all be in the 1940s at Universal: *The Wolf Man* (1941), *The Strange Case of Doctor Rx* (1942), *The Mystery of Marie Roget* (1942), and the beloved *Frankenstein Meets the Wolf Man* (1943), where his Dr. Frank Mannering morphs from local doctor to detective to lover to nearly full-blown mad scientist with intoxicating speed. Ronald Drake played by Patric Knowles could have been equally effective as a gentle presence or a rakish Lothario, but he also would have confidently faced off with Janos Rukh. There might have been a possible conflict with filming as *Give Me Your Heart* was also in 1936, but that film came out in September, while *The Invisible Ray* was released much earlier in January of that same year. Ironically, Patric Knowles and Reginald Denny eventually shared the same role, Harry Griffiths. As mentioned, Reginald Denny played him first (*Of Human Bondage* 1934). The movie was remade 11 years later (Warner Bros. 1946) with Paul Lukas as Philip Carey and Eleanor Parker as Mildred Rogers. Despite strong efforts, they are unable to match the original version. But it's Mr. Knowles who wins with his shockingly callous betrayal of his friend and Mildred. It was 10 years after *Give Me Your Heart* but proves that the sweet-faced actor could ably play bad boys, given the opportunity.

Six-foot-one Douglas Fairbanks, Jr. was the only one of the three possible Drake fantasy replacements who had been consistently cast in leading roles. In 1936, he was one year away from his dazzlingly charming villain, Rupert of Hentzau, in *The Prisoner of Zenda* (United Artists 1937). Prior to that, Mr. Fairbanks had unintentionally almost made a cottage industry out of playing men who take women away from their husbands, lovers, and boyfriends.

Such as in *Chances* (First National and Warner Brothers 1931) he takes his brother's beloved away from him, regretfully, after she pursues him relentlessly. He pretends to be kissing another to discourage her. She becomes engaged to the brother out of spite. Both men enlist. The girl shows up as a transport driver and soon hooks up with her original crush. Anthony Bushell is cuckolded brother and fiancé, Tom, and Rose Hobart is Molly. She was also in: *Dr. Jekyll and Mr. Hyde* (Paramount 1931), *Tower of London* (Universal 1939), *The Mad Ghoul* (Universal 1943), *The Soul of a Monster* (Columbia 1944), and *Isle of the Dead* with Boris Karloff (RKO Radio Pictures 1945). Fairbanks, Jr. plays Jack who eventually wins over the girl both

Boris Karloff in 1936 as he looked while engaging in studio publicity for his latest film from Universal, *The Invisible Ray*.

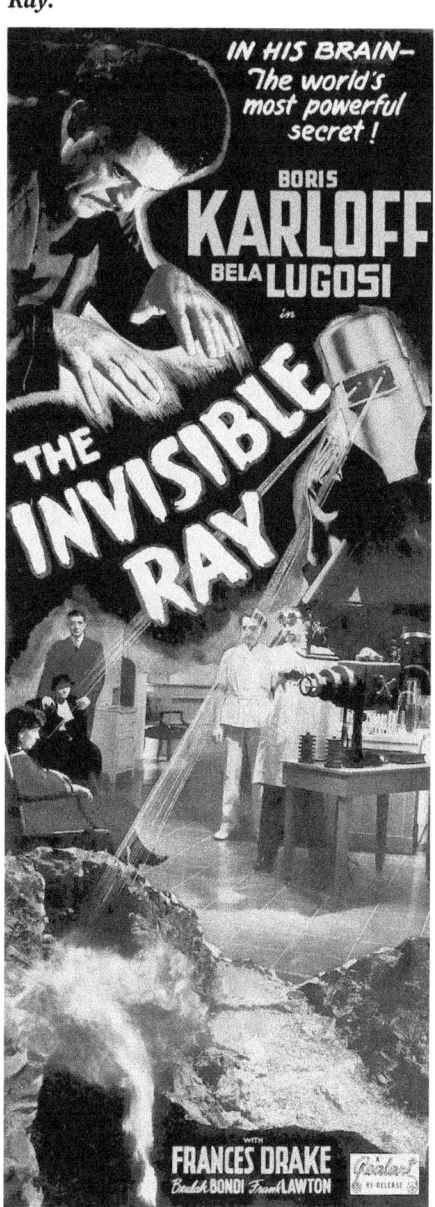

before and after his brother is killed in action.

In *I Like Your Nerve* (Warner Bros. 1931) he romances a gorgeous sweet young thing away from her much older rich fiancé, who her uncle is forcing her to marry. Loretta Young as Diana, Edmund Breon as Clive, and Henry Kolker as Areal Pacheco, the uncle. Fairbanks is Larry. Appearing as Pacheco's butler, Luigi, and clearly meant for better things is Boris Karloff. He and Fairbanks, Jr. literally pass by each other but do not really share any scenes.

The Narrow Corner (Warner Bros. 1931) is loosely based on a Somerset Maugham novel of the same name. Fleeing a murder charge, a young man is whisked away on a dead of night sailing vessel with a hard drinking but capable captain, which is arranged by his wealthy father who curtly bids him goodbye, telling him he hopes his son will stay out of trouble by getting "acetic acid on that handsome face of yours." Trouble starts soon after as the boy winds up on a remote island, where he gives in to an engaged girl's first sight obsession with him after trying to resist her. Clueless as to her faithlessness, the fiancé bonds with the young man but then tries to kill him after seeing him in a compromising situation with his affianced. Later despondent over losing her and believing that he has murdered his new best friend, he commits suicide. Patricia Ellis appears as Louise and Raymond Massey as Eric. Fairbanks is Fred. (Arthur Hohl plays boozy Captain Nichols and was a heartbreaking Montgomery in *Island of Lost Souls* [Paramount 1932], demonstrating this actor's considerable ability for creating both sympathetic and unsympathetic characters).

Captured! (Warner Bros. 1933) is when his best friend's wife falls for him, and he goes along with it. Asked if she loves him, he says, "I don't know. I think so. I hope so." Both men become World War I prisoners. The captain friend sacrifices himself by wildly machine gunning the enemy so that all his comrades can escape after he nearly allows his wife's lover to be executed by firing squad for a rape/murder that he did not commit. Leslie Howard is Captain Fred Allison. Margaret Lindsay is his adulterous wife, Monica. Ms. Lindsay was also in *British Intelligence* with Boris Karloff (Warner Bros. 1940) and *The House of the Seven Gables* (Universal 1940). Fairbanks is Lieutenant Jack Digby. Arthur Hohl pops up again colorfully as another POW, Cocky.

Success At Any Price (RKO Radio Pictures 1934), Fairbanks, Jr. plays a ruthlessly ambitious man who dumps his fiancée, marries his boss' mistress, is caught with shady business practices, and then tries to shoot himself. Colleen Moore is Sarah, Ralph Morgan is Raymond, and Genevieve Tobin, Agnes. Fairbanks is Joe.

In *The Amateur Gentleman* (United Artists 1936), Fairbanks, Jr. is a principled son

The third montage lobby card from *The Invisible Ray*

who goes undercover, posing as royalty to save his father from hanging for stealing a watch that he did not steal. In the process, he exposes the true villain and lures away his fiancée. Basil Sydney is bad guy Lord Chichester, and Elissa Landi is conflicted Lady Cleone. Fairbanks is Barnabas Barty. (Also appearing is Vincent Price's last wife, Coral Browne, as Pauline, Chichester's spark plug-conniving murderous mistress).

Jump For Glory (Criterion Films 1937) is an exquisite noir where Fairbanks is Ricky Morgan, equally accomplished violinist, thief, and cat burglar who, while attempting to rob Glory Howard (Valerie Hobson), rapes her instead. Astonishingly for a 1937 film, they fall in love after this. Unfortunately, the woman is a thief too, whose last fiancé shot himself in the head over gambling debts she helped to cause. Despite this, she becomes engaged to Colonel Fane (Alan Hale, Sr.), who is only posing as a wealthy, respectable colonel. Fane is really Jim Dial, a former disreputable colleague of Ricky's, who fingered him to slip out of his own punishment. "The Colonel" and Glory marry anyway. On the wedding night, Ricky breaks in, grapples with Fane/Dial, and appears to have killed him in self-defense, but it is new wife and widow, Glory Fane, who is arrested for murder that night. At the trial, it looks worse and worse for her, but Ricky convinces the judge to let him demonstrate how he jumped up to a window and down again, which will give Glory an alibi. Ricky reaches the balcony but falls to the ground and is badly injured. Fairbanks did all his own stunts in this film, as he did in most of them from the 1920s onwards. (Valerie Hobson was in three 1935 Universal horrors, *The Mystery of Edwin Drood*, *Bride of Frankenstein*, and *Werewolf of London*).

Fairbanks, Jr. would have been the best choice for Frank Lawton. As proof that audiences (and producers) liked him as a wife/lover/fiancée stealer, he repeated the theme with quirky variations in: *The Rage of Paris* (Universal 1938), *Safari* (Paramount 1940), *The Corsican Brothers* (United Artists 1941), *Sinbad the Sailor* (RKO Radio Pictures 1947), *That Lady in Ermine* (20th Century Fox 1948), and *The Fighting O'Flynn* (Universal Pictures 1949). Sidenote: In *The Corsican Brothers* he battles his separated-at-birth Siamese twin brother for the lady fair, in addition to saving her from marrying Akim Tamiroff's murdering Baron Colonna, while *The Fighting O'Flynn* has him winning the lovely fiancée of future television *Robin Hood*'s Richard Greene (terrific as traitor Lord Sedgemonth) with poetic speeches, twinkling Irish charm, and eye-popping physical feats.

Apparently, several Diana/Drake romantic scenes were cut from *The Invisible Ray*, ostensibly for pacing. Scissored because they fizzled? Think of Frances Drake's fetching Diana and Douglas Fairbank, Jr.'s alluring Drake with the enticing possibility of Janos Rukh catching them in an embrace, resulting in stronger motivation for Rukh's simmering obsession boiling over into madness, fueled by Radium X contamination. Remember Arabella's remark, "Would anyone ever expect to find anything like this atop the Carpathian Mountains?" Fairbanks, Jr. had a unique, discreetly seductive way of laser-focusing on a woman by almost swooning but keeping his cool while delivering the message, all in a few seconds. Frank Lawton's boring, "No," as he summarily looks at Diana is not in that class. The Mountains of the Moon buildup would have been plausible if audiences could envision the athletic Fairbanks, Jr. traversing them. Frank Lawton's dinky Drake and the Mountains of the Moon journey do not inspire similar visions.

Franz Waxman was given the job of scoring Universal's latest horror thriller, The Invisible Ray, which was Karloff and Lugosi's third film together. Waxman wrote an exciting and very moving score of about 25 minutes' duration. It is to a

Dr. Benet looks distressed by the maid, who in turn looks quite distressed.

Janos' scientific group arrives at his Carpathian castle and is welcomed by wife Diana. The group consists of Lady Arabella Stevens (Beulah Bondi), Sir Francis Stevens (Walter Kingsford), Ronald Drake, and Dr. Benet.

large extent fashioned out of four themes: an ascending heroic one, usually played on brass and associated with the scientist Janos Rukh (Karloff); Clifford Vaughan's discordant agitated music for the bandage scene in The Raven (1935) heightens the horror considerably as Bateman's (Karloff's) horribly disfigured face is unveiled by Dr. Vollin (Lugosi). That sweep is reminiscent of Strauss's Don Juan, a pentatonic theme associated with the mysterious "Radium X" which bears some resemblance to the melodic minor theme in Hajos' score for Werewolf of London; a pretty theme associated with Diana, Rukh's wife (Frances Drake), which is very similar to a theme in the first movement of Chopin's Piano Concerto no. 1; and a theme for Diana and Ronald Drake (Frank Lawton), who fall in love. Again, the score was orchestrated by Clifford Vaughan.

The music accompanying the opening sequence of The Invisible Ray, where the Rukh castle in the Carpathian Mountains is shown, is entitled "Castle in Hungary" and is a reworking of the "Storm Scene" from Harling's Destination Unknown score. (This was the same Harling cue which was previously tracked for the opening scene of The Raven.) The only difference between Harling's and Waxman's cues is that Waxman interpolated a theme of his own ("Diana's theme") in one spot. Ironically, Waxman's theme in the cue was deleted in the final dubbing so that what is heard in the film is Harling's music alone. (William H. Rosar, Music for the Monsters Universal Pictures' Horror Film Scores of the 1930's [Washington, DC: Quarterly Journal of the Library of Congress 1983] 413.

So basically, we enter to the same music which accompanied Jean Thatcher's wild ride from *The Raven* except this time there's a castle apparently serving as both Rukh's dwelling and laboratory. Mother Rukh and Diana are waiting for son and husband Janos' guests to arrive for a demonstration, which he hopes will validate his theories previously dismissed by the scientific community. Mother Rukh was Violet Kemble-Cooper, a fine British actress, who made only one other genre film, an uncredited bit as a "Woman" in *The Invisible Man* (Universal 1933). Leading lady Frances Drake had two genre credits as well. She was a ravishing Yvonne Orlac in *Mad Love* (MGM 1935). After she sees

The scientific team gathers around itself while Janos Rukh remains alone and isolated, looking through his telescope.

Janos is about to begin his demonstration as the scientific observers sit behind protective glass.

In Africa, Rukh and his native guides/protectors explore Radium X.

the car lights at the window, Diana—in a princess fantasy gown paired nicely with a vampiric cape goes to alert Janos. As was probably usual, Boris' Dr. Rukh is utterly absorbed, even after Diana calls his name twice. He responds, quite affectionately, to his wife's loving smile and leaves with her. After some preliminary group chitchatting, Rukh appears and greets the guests, not entirely cordially. Doctors Rukh and Benet frostily meet for the first time, shooting barbs. Bela's Felix says, "We have never seen eye to eye." Boris' Janos tops him with, "That's because I've always looked 200 years ahead of your theories."

The group—Dr. Felix Benet, Sir Francis Stevens, Lady Arabella Stevens (uninvited), and nephew non-scientist also uninvited Ronald Drake—all settle in behind special protective glass at the Gothic laboratory and observatory to watch the Rukh show, "Tour of the Universe," courtesy of John P. Fulton's special effects wizardry of heavenly miniatures culminating in a big boom as a meteor from the distant past lands somewhere in Africa. It's impressive enough to leave the skeptics gasping and causes Dr. Felix Benet to drop his negative body language and congratulate Rukh. There's another fleeting Diana Drake moment right after the boom, which should have been symbolic of their mutual interest, but it just looks as if he sat on the lady's dress by mistake. Benet and Stevens invite Janos to join their expedition, which he agrees to do. His mother warns, "Your experiments are your friends. Leave people alone." Sensible, and it turns out, prescient advice, which Rukh, tragically for him and others, ignores.

Once there, Boris' impatient Dr. Rukh takes off in search of Radium X and Bela's Dr. Benet continues his perpetual experiments in astrochemistry. Sir Francis Stevens spends his time complaining about the heat and physical ailments, Lady Arabella Stevens kills animals to display on her wall at home, Diana sits around bored out of her mind, and Ronald Drake apparently does pretty much nothing except look at Rukh's wife, wondering what he's supposed to do. It's bizarre that Diana and Drake and Arabella are there at all, since their contributions to the expedition are worthless. On the other hand, Arabella does get her bloodlust satisfied to a degree, although she longs for a rhino to annihilate. And—most importantly for the extramarital subplot—Diana and Drake get some alone time, which turns out to register nowhere near as hot as Africa. As mentioned before, sto-

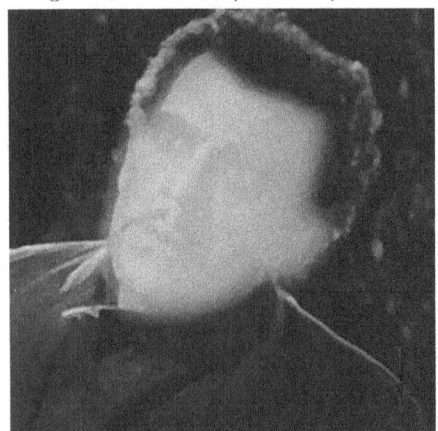

Rukh begins his deadly glow from Radium X poisoning.

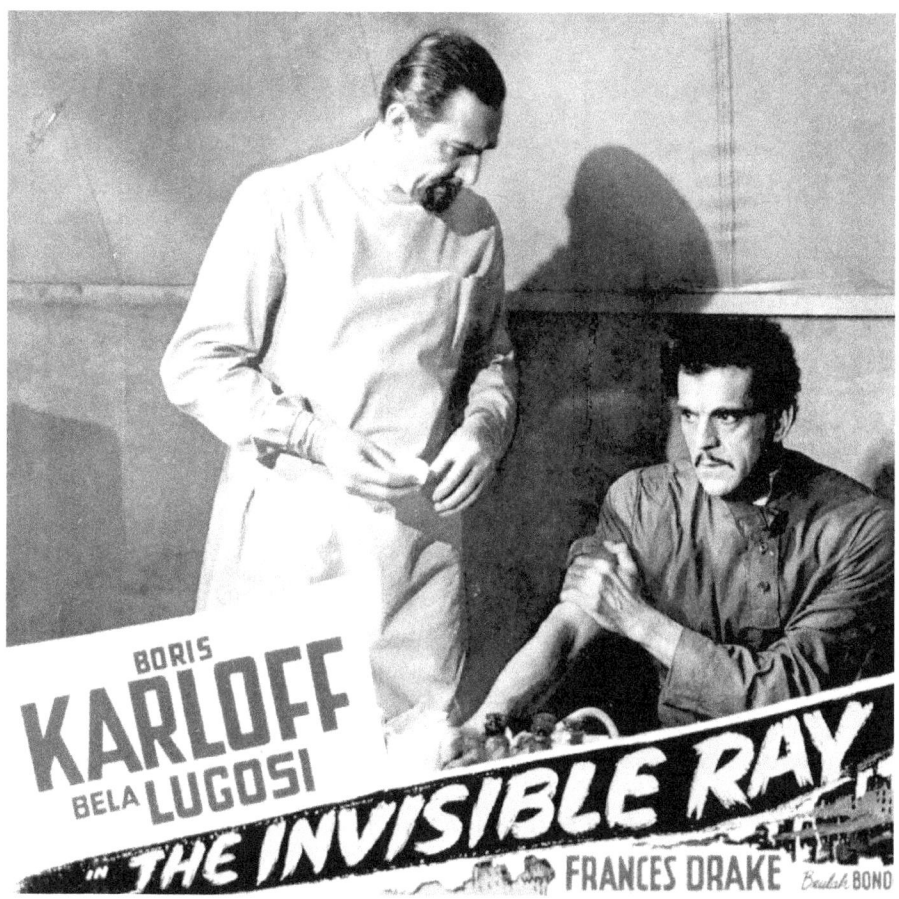

In this Realart lobby card, Dr. Benet administers the antidote to Rukh.

In shock, Dr. Benet finds The dead body of Sir Francis.

len clinches were edited out for "pacing." In retrospect, given the casting, this was wise.

Rukh, garbed in a strange metal suit and helmet with a glassed-in eye area, does find the meteorite site going down into a hellish pit as central casting natives stand nearby modeling the usual stock non-PC frightened behavior. Later alone in his tent, Janos discovers his touch is death and that he glows in the dark. The first victim is his Great Dane who should not have been along on this trip, either. Following this tragedy, Diana who had previously told Drake that her place was with Rukh, in yet another failed mini love scene, shows up to see her husband who tells her to leave immediately the next morning. She's unaware that Janos is protecting her from himself; he's yearning to see her but can't. Karloff and Ms. Drake play this very movingly. Terrified, he runs many miles to get Benet's help, arriving in a state of near collapse. The astrophysicist is sympathetic but warns that the counteractive he will compound is not a cure but a lifelong injection regimen which could eventually damage his brain, even as it allows him to live day by day.

No longer glowing from Radium X poisoning, at least until the next treatment, Janos returns to his camp. Shortly afterwards, Benet goes to him there with a dear Janos letter from Diana and the unwelcome news that Sir Francis Stevens has taken his Radium X sample back home, because it could not be trusted to one man alone. Boris' Rukh understandably

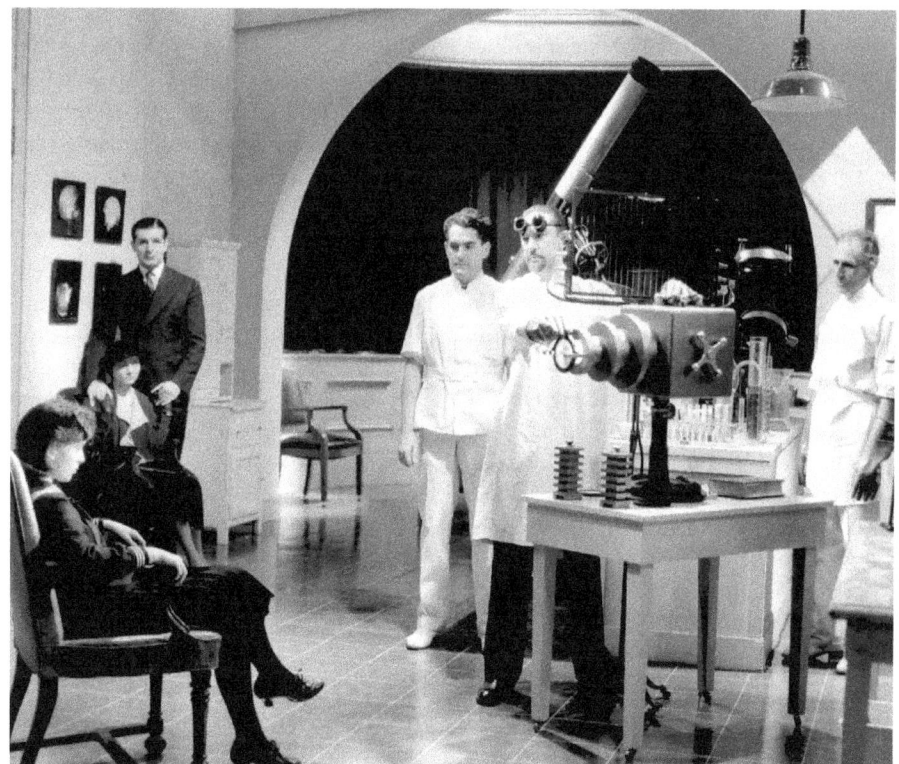

In Benet's Radium X laboratory, he cures a young lady with the mysterious ray.

Janos Rukh touches Dr. Benet, who dies instantly.

explodes all over the place, repeatedly calling the group "thieves" and accusing them of stealing "everything" from him. He shouts and threatens with his Invisible Ray gizmo, "Get out of here, Benet! Get out before I ..."

Back at the castle, Rukh does use his discovery for good. Impressively, John P. Fulton's special effects show us the healing rays from the Radium X gun directed at his mother's blind eyes. She can see again and says, "You have work to do which will take you all your life." Stubbornly and spitefully, he wants to go to Paris to avenge the theft of his discovery and shows up just as Benet has cured a blind girl. Karloff's Janos isn't soft-soaped by all the warmth and gratitude. He glowers at the girl and her parents, which is very effective. Still upset by the theft of his work and his wife, he hangs around with Benet, asking about Diana. The good doctor tells his visitor that Diana and Drake are "in love," but Diana is waiting to hear from her husband. All this begs the question, why is this eminent astrophysicist and busy Radium X miracle man wasting his time getting involved in an extracurricular romance? It's the second time he's discussed it with Janos, and while both actors do well, might it be considered unethical for Benet to be talking about it at all?

Janos Rukh does tell Felix Benet that he, "... Won't stand in their way." While Benet seems snowed by this, we're not because in the very next scene, accompanied by cheesy Parisian cafe-type music, we see Janos cruising for a likely substitute who can—literally—play dead for him. He fixes on a man peacefully eating his soup in the corner, played by Walter Miller, who was recently one of the doctors standing around Jean Thatcher in the emergency room in *The Raven* (Universal 1935). Mr. Miller and Mr. Karloff were together in *The King of the Kongo* (Mascot Pictures 1929) and *The Utah Kid* (Tiffany Pictures 1930). Seemingly dead to all emotions save his need for revenge, he sizes up the poor man, distastefully lying that he wants to help him, "I want to do you a benefit, the greatest benefit one man can do another." No surprise to us, but shockingly for Diana and Arabella, the paper reports the death of Janos Rukh, his face burned beyond recognition.

Tears from Diana are indecently and speedily replaced by wedding bells for her and Ronald Drake. The cathedral set was used in *The Hunchback of Notre Dame*, starring Lon Chaney, Sr. (Universal 1923). The whole group is there, with Dr. Felix Benet in formal attire. Also attending from the outside is very much still alive Dr. Janos Rukh, which makes this happy occasion both bigamous and illegal. Waxman's cheerful wedding recessional music ominously darkens as Rukh peeks around one of the outside pillars, watching his wife and her lover, not technically her husband. Looking up, he sees six generic male and female statues which, thanks again to Fulton magic, appear as the African expedition group of six. Now nearly fully mad, he finds a room opposite the cathedral so he can conveniently and unobtrusively melt the statues with his ray gun after he offs the person it represents for him. "Sir Francis Stevens, thief," is first. Dr. Benet, who seems to be thick as thieves with Sir Francis and Lady Stevens and either lives with them or next door, is downstairs when Sir Francis is murdered. Dr. Benet photographs the corpse's eyes with an ultraviolet camera which naturally is handy! A tiny little image of a menacing Rukh appears on the plate which Benet breaks right after he looks at it. In the morning, the papers gleefully announce the second Radium X death and rapidly scream out yet another one, "Lady Stevens, matchmaker," so labeled by Rukh. Two statues are now molten messes, drawing large crowds each time, including Janos Rukh's landlady.

All of this highlights the second problem with *The Invisible Ray*. We don't see these murders in real time or the statues melting. We get information on the deaths of the unfortunate soup man, Sir Francis Stevens, and Lady Stevens, as well as the latest on the destroyed statues duly reported in the papers every day. "Also, all this would have been far more memorable if we *saw* it" ... Mank, Gregory William, *Bela Lugosi and Boris Karloff: The Expanded Story of a Haunting Collaboration* (Jefferson, North Carolina and London: McFarland & Company. Inc. Publishers 2009) 294. "... but it would have been *nicer* if a bit more of Rukh's mayhem could have been recorded on Universal's film!" Weaver, Tom, Brunas, Michael, and Brunas, John, Second Edition Universal Horrors: The Studio's Classic Films, 1931-1946 (Jefferson, North Carolina and London: McFarland & Company, Inc. Publishers 2007) 157. Just suppose that Universal had greenlighted more in the budget for their special effects. Fulton was more than capable of doing astonishing things with small budgets, but it made no sense to lowball this one, effectively their first science fiction horror film. And surely there could have been a way to show the murders even creatively, Lewton-style in shadows, and still appease the censors. We should have seen Rukh killing the soup man, not heard about it. We should have been able to watch Rukh exacting his vengeance on Sir Francis and Lady Stevens. Instead, it's all watered down and compounds the problem the film has already with the ridiculous casting of Frank Lawton as Ronald Drake.

Ms. Drake and Mr. Lawton have another love scene after Arabella's demise, where he declaims pompously that they "belong together." All the juice here is coming from Frances Drake. Frank Lawton overdoes it with the drama, enjoying the sound of his own voice.

Benet and Drake talk with the police, proposing that a scientific conference be held to bait Rukh with easy accessibility to his last three targets. Benet tells them that if Rukh gets inside, despite needing a name card for entry, the house can be darkened at midnight and Janos will glow. The French police chief wonders what would happen if Rukh touched someone. Bela's Benet, with one arched eyebrow and grim tones replies, "They die."

Rukh is on the loose in heavy rain, injection delayed, so he can easily eliminate Benet, Drake, and Diana. He runs into Professor Meiklejohn (fabulous Frank Reicher, *King Kong* [RKO Radio Pictures 1933], *Night Monster* [Universal 1942] *House of Frankenstein* [Universal 1944] and many others). Oddly, "Meiklejohn" becomes "Mendelssohn" in the end credits. Crazy Janos is still clever, claiming to be "Jones of the University of Wales." Since he needs a card to get into Benet's event, he leads the trusting man into an alley and apparently poisons him with "Napoleon Brandy." The professor drops heavily to the ground, groaning. Remorseless, Rukh filches his card. Once there, he stays outside. As all the invitees have checked in, Drake whines that maybe Rukh "won't come." Bela's Benet brilliantly responds, with deadpan black humor, "He will be here. Probably's here now." Armed with a gun, he heads for his laboratory but never gets out the door because Rukh backs him up inside, which begins one of the best Bela and Boris death scenes.

> It began to affect my brain almost immediately. I could feel it coming and crawling for cells.
>
> Aren't there ever moments when you think as you used to think, when you are human?
>
> Not often now, not often.
>
> And because of that, we must die.
>
> No, because you're thieves. Five thieves. All thieves. It will be easiest just to shake hands. It will all be over in a second.

Without his antidote which is destroyed by his mother (Violet Kemble-Cooper), Janos erupts in flames and becomes a human fireball.

Benet reaches for his gun, Rukh touches him (rather gently). Benet dies. Both actors are superb in this grim death duet. The pace escalates as Drake laughs idiotically about things being over, "one way or the other." The police and Drake then find Benet's body, with Rukh's glowing mark on him. The mad scientist is already upstairs and finds Diana calling out for "Ronnie," which seems to really put him over the edge, but he cannot bring himself to kill his wife, especially lovely in a stunning backless black nightgown. Thinking of "Ronnie," he says, "But he must die!" Downstairs, Mother Rukh and her silver headed cane have arrived. She finds her dear mad son, Janos upstairs grasping at his counteractive and pleading for time so he can finish off Ronald Drake. With her cane, she sends his medicine crashing to the floor, "My son, you have broken the first law of science." Perhaps in a last moment of sanity, Rukh tells her she's right. "It's better this way. Goodbye Mother." John P. Fulton has smoke coming out of Rukh as he runs down the hall, crashing through a window, and fireballing into the rainy street below. Mother Rukh intones, "Janos Rukh is dead. But part of him will go on eternally, working for humanity." It should end here. Fulton's special effects are magnificent and anything else is anticlimactic. But? *The Invisible Ray* ends with another unconvincing Diana and Drake embrace. Why?

The Invisible Ray had so much going for it. Karloff and Lugosi are both perfectly in tune with their characters. Karloff's been accused of overacting and Lugosi of underacting. But doesn't it make sense? Bela is a scientist to the core. Sensible, thorough, and logical. Why does he need to rant? Boris is playing not only a man driven mad by Radium X contamination, but one that is reclusive, hair-trigger tempered from the start. They are not the problems. Director Lambert Hillyer does a fine job as does cinematographer George Robinson. The issues are Frank Lawton and putting restraints on the special effects budget. These two factors alone keep *The Invisible Ray* from being one of the best. It's a rotten shame.

CREDITS: Producer: Fred S. Meyer; Director: Lambert Hillyer; Cinematographer: George Robinson; Screenplay: John Colton; Music: Franz Waxman; Special Effects: John P. Fulton; Costumes: Brymer; Make-up: Otto Lederer; Technical Advisor: Ted Behr.

CAST: Boris Karloff (Dr. Janos Rukh); Bela Lugosi (Dr. Felix Benet); Frances Drake (Diana Rukh); Frank Lawton (Ronald Drake); Violet Kemble-Cooper (Mother Rukh); Walter Kingsford (Sir Francis Stevens); Beulah Bondi (Lady Arabella Stevens); Frank Reicher (Professor Meiklejohn); Derelict: Walter Miller

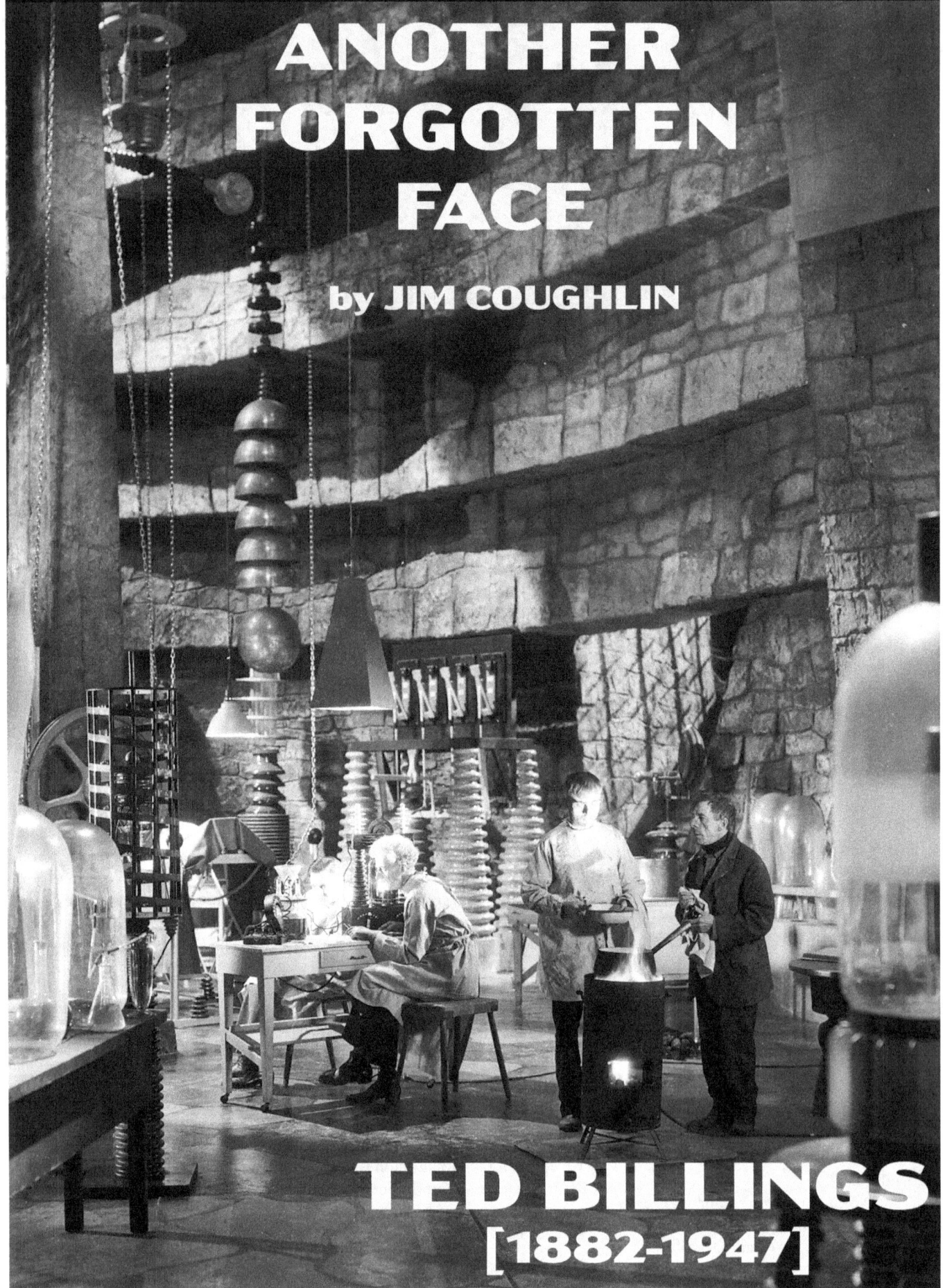

ANOTHER FORGOTTEN FACE

by JIM COUGHLIN

TED BILLINGS
[1882-1947]

Photo by the John Kobal Foundation/Getty Images: *Bride of Frankenstein* with Ted Billings, right

Performers in the acting craft, particularly in film, can be construed as part of a caste system system. At the top are the lead performers or stars. Next in line are the supporting players or character actors, who have substantial parts and billing. Then there are the bit players who have clearly defined small roles, either with or without dialogue, and are usually unbilled. At the bottom of the system are the extras who are considered "background talent," generally without any lines, and never receiving billing. Although some stories may be apocryphal (as there has been minimal record keeping as to appearances by extras), there have been individuals like Sarah Schwartz, who allegedly appeared in over 2,000 films for Universal (after having performed an act of heroism at that studio, when she was a young girl, with the reward she received being first dibs on extra bits in all their subsequent films). There will never be a full and accurate record of appearances for film extras.

Ted Billings was a minor actor, alternating between bits and extra work, whose claim to fame was having appeared in significant Universal horror films such as *Frankenstein*, *Murders in the Rue Morgue*, *The Invisible Man*, and particularly *Bride of Frankenstein*. Back in 2007, he had fewer than 50 credits listed in IMDb. Thanks to attentive film buffs, Billings now has 161 known (as of late 2022) appearances, but even that seriously underestimates his body of work. Billings only received on-screen credit two known times (*The Babes in the Woods* and *Bride of Frankenstein*) and had an actual character name fewer than 10 times. More often, Billings just served as background window dressing. If he spoke a line, as in *Road Gang*, *Hangover Square*, or *Two Years Before the Mast*, it was a rare occurrence. Just as in the "Where's Waldo" series of children's books by British illustrator Martin Handford, it takes a perceptive eye to spot Ted Billings in the panorama of the screen when he does a five second walk by in a film like *Stagecoach*.

Ted was born Edwin Theodore Billington in London, England, on April 8, 1882 (although other sources report "April 7" and "1880," including Ted himself at different times). Young Edwin was baptized on May 6, 1882, at the Eton Mission in Hackney, London, as a member of the Church of England. He was the youngest of seven children born to Henry John Billington (1846- ?) and the former Mary Ann Poynton (1848-1891), who were married on December 22, 1867. His father Henry worked as a stationer warehouseman, while his mother Mary Ann labored as a book folder. Their four older sons were: Henry (1870-1965), Arthur (1873-1936), Ernest (1877-1946), and William (1880-1934). The couple also had two daughters, Minnie (1875-1967) and Emily (1878-1982). Prior to Ted's birth noted by the English Census of 1881, the Billington family lived at 58 Jodrell Road in Hackney Parish, Middlesex, near Victoria Park in the East End of London. The Billington children attended the Baker Street School in London during their developmental years.

By 1891 (according to the English Census), son Henry (21) was living with the Abrey family (he would marry their daughter Kate) as a lodger, while daughter Minnie (only 15) was living with the Player family as a servant. Apparently both parents died during the 1890s (mother in 1891), as the 1901 Census had Henry (now 31) as the head of the Billington household, living with his wife Kate, son Leonard, and siblings Arthur, Minnie, and Emily. Presumably, Ted had already immigrated to Canada prior to this time.

By self-report (*Buffalo Courier-Express Pictorial*, 10/20/46, p. 13), Billings, standing between 5'1–5'2 and weighing roughly 110 pounds, plied his trade as a jockey in England in the mid-1890s. His relative success at this endeavor is unknown. In any case, Ted decided to venture to Canada around the turn of the century. It is undetermined if he continued to competitively ride after making this journey.

Billings apparently crossed from Canada into the United States on at least two different occasions. He traveled via the Great Northern Railway from Nelson, British Columbia, Canada, to Marcus, Stevens County, Washington, entering the U.S. on November 27, 1903. Billings later journeyed from Lethbridge, Alberta, Canada, to Sand Point, Bonner County, Idaho, also by train, arriving in December 1904. He provided his name as Edwin Billington at that time. It is uncertain as to when he started utilizing Ted Billings as a professional name.

Working his way to California in 1905, Billings found employment in the

The Babes in the Woods (Fox, 1917): Ted Billings as the Witch, one of his two credited screen roles

fledgling motion picture industry. He valued himself as a "jack of all trades," but specialized in locating props and costumes to meet the needs of whatever was being filmed on a lot any given day. Billings was listed as a property man with the Selig Polyscope Company in 1915, at which time he resided at 212 Grand Avenue, in Los Angeles, California. He also maintained a small office at 304 South Broadway, Room 446, Los Angeles, from the mid-teens through the early 1920s. In addition to Selig, Billings labored for virtually all the early film companies in Hollywood, with much of his service provided for Fox Film Corporation.

While at Fox, Billings appeared before the cameras in two of the Fox Kiddie Pictures, playing Sullivan in the second entry of that series, *Aladdin and the Wonderful Lamp* (1917). Another of Billings' earliest known film roles (and one for which he received on-screen credit as "Teddy Billings") was that of the Witch in the Fox production, *The Babes in the Woods* (1917), the third in the same series in which child performers enacted most of the adult roles. Using the "Hansel and Gretel" fairy tale as a story within the film, the Witch, who has been promised wealth by the Bad Prince (Violet Radcliffe), sends a raven to guide the children (Francis Carpenter and Virginia Lee Corbin) to her gingerbread house. A title card, after Billings' Witch

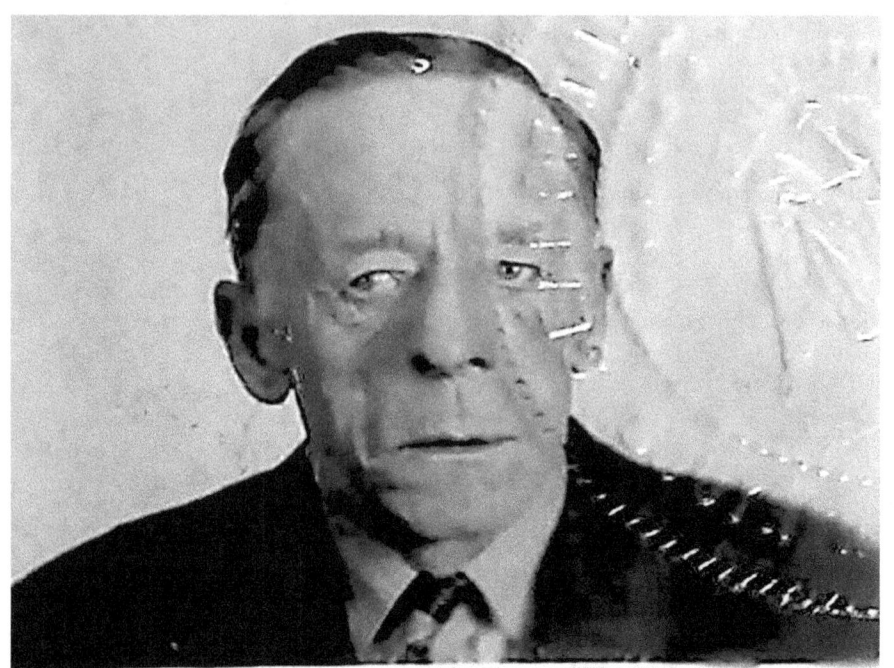

A 1943 Naturalization application photo of Billings, signed with his real name: Edwin Billington.

is introduced, states, "Nibble, nibble, little mouse. Who's nibbling at my little house?" She fattens Hansel to eat him but is tricked into climbing into the oven by Gretel, who is aided by the Good Fairy (Carmen de Rue). It is interesting that the directors (Chester M. and Sidney A. Franklin), in the tradition of British pantomime, had the Witch played by a male and the prince played by a female. It may be that Billings' atypical facial features and small stature led to this casting.

Throughout the early silent era, Billings kept busy in many jobs behind the scenes of countless films. He earned the reputation as an individual who could secure virtually any prop, large or small, in rapid time when required. In addition to a variety of objects, Ted amassed an extensive collection of caps and hats that he would eventually utilize to help him be noticed, even in minor bits. Billings even tried his hand at songwriting, penning the words and music to "Don't Turn Your Back on Uncle Sam, Boys," copyrighted April 3, 1918.

Ted's World War I registration card, completed on September 12, 1918, listed his sister Emily in London as his closest relative (Emily Billington Phipps would live to be 104, passing away in 1982).

On his naturalization "Declaration of Intention" application filed on October 3, 1918, Billings provided his full name as "Edwin Theodore Billington" and described himself as having a fair complexion, brown hair, blue eyes, and a broken nose. Interestingly, Billings would not receive his actual Certificate of Naturalization until September 14, 1945.

On February 19, 1920, Billings was married in Santa Ana, California, to the former Margaret E. (Maggie) Hennessey (1878-1939), a widow. Margaret had five children from her first marriage with Benjamin B. Ludwick (1877-1913). The Ludwicks had lived in numerous locations, including Kentucky, Missouri, and Colorado, before ending up in California shortly before Benjamin's death on May 9, 1913.

Maggie and Benjamin Ludwick's oldest child was Anna May Ludwick (1898-1992). Anna was briefly married to Joseph Conk, but the marriage did not last, as by 1920 she was living with the newly constituted Billings family. Eventually (1944) she married for a second time to Eugene Buntell.

Catherine June Ludwick (1900-1997) was the second child. She married Freeman Michael Dunn in 1918 and bore him a son (Freeman Michael, Jr.), but Catherine's marriage was also short-lived. She later was married (1940) to Edward Krog.

Benjamin (Bennie) Ludwick, Jr. (1903-1923) tragically passed away at the young age of 19 on May 9, 1923. As a child he had appeared in a few silent films including *The Birth of a Nation* (1915) and *Live and Let Live* (1921), in the latter playing Jim and billed as Bennie Billings.

The other two Ludwick children, sons Richard and Elmo, both of whom

Stepsons Elmo and Richard Billings to the right and left of large youth in center, from *Three Cheers,* 1923, a "Juvenile Comedy" short.

made minor marks of their own in the film industry, also used their stepfather's last name of Billings.

Richard Eugene Ludwick Billings (1908-1965) was among the seminal members of "Hal Roach's Rascals" (later to be known as "Our Gang"). He appeared in *Fire Fighters* (1922), the second short of the long-lived series, as well as three subsequent entries, including *The Champeen* (1923), which still exists and has been shown on TCM, and *The Big Show* (1923) as Muggsy. Richard played Herbert Atwater, Jr. in *Gentle Julia* (1923), with Bessie Love, but soon after gave up performing before the cameras. He remained involved in the industry, however, working primarily in the editing department of 20th Century Fox on films like *Jesse James* (1939) and *Stanley and Livingstone* (1939), before enlisting in the military (9/22/42) during World War II. In later years, Richard worked in television, editing an episode of *Hong Kong* (3/15/61), for example.

Freckle-faced Elmo Gerald Ludwick Billings (1912-1964) also worked for Hal Roach, partaking in seven "Rascals" shorts, including three with Richard. He had a lengthier acting career than his brother, though, working in at least 22 films, including his playing Kit Mason opposite Tom Mix in *Tumbling River* (1927). Elmo even appeared with Lon Chaney in *The Monster* (1925). Like Richard, he then transitioned to the production aspect of motion pictures, mainly as a laboratory technician and later editor (e.g., *Silver City*—1951, *Terry and the Pirates*—TV—1952). Elmo was married to Hazelle and had two sons, Richard, and Russell. He died following a stroke at Cedars of Lebanon Hospital in Los Angeles on June 24, 1964, at the age of 51.

The 1920 U.S. Federal Census recorded the Billings family as living at 18 Swall Street, Sherman Oaks, California. Ted's occupation was listed as property man for Fox Studios.

Now with a family to support, Billings expanded his involvement in the motion picture industry by working as an extra or bit player, in addition to his efforts as a prop man.

Billings had a substantial role as the villain Derrick's nephew, who hopes to marry Meenie (Daisy Robinson), the daughter of the re-appeared Rip (Thomas Jefferson) in *Rip Van Winkle* (1922), a film

All the Brothers Were Valiant (Metro, 1923): Billings third from left, with Lon Chaney (center, raising cap), William V. Mong (in chef's hat) and Billie Dove, Malcolm McGregor, Robert McKim, and Bob Kortman, among other cast and crew

which fortunately still exists. The nephew, attired in fancy clothes and white wig of the rich, wrongly claims Meenie's childhood sweetheart Heindrick (Hal Craig) has been lost at sea, only to be proven wrong. In addition to playing a villainous role, Ted also served as head prop man on the film.

Metro's *The Prisoner of Zenda* (1922), with Lewis Stone in the dual lead role, included Billings as a train passenger eating a banana who proceeds to toss the peel out onto the platform. With his knowledge of props, Ted often brought small pieces of business into notice in a film. He then was glimpsed as a peasant in *Robin Hood* (1922), starring Douglas Fairbanks, Sr.

In the summer of 1922, Billings received four notices in the pages of *Camera* magazine, all pertaining to his work behind the scenes. In *Camera* (6/24/22, p. 8), it is noted that "Ted Billings has landed himself a nifty job when he agreed to rustle props and dress the sets for Jack O'Brien Co." John B. (Jack) O'Brien, was an actor and director during the silent era, focusing mainly on Westerns. It is uncertain what projects of O'Brien that Billings worked on in this period, as Jack has no known directing credits for 1922. On August 19, 1922, Billings placed an ad in *Camera* (p. 16), stating he was an "A-1 Prop Man" who was currently in actor's parlance, "at liberty." A week later (8/26/22, p. 15), the following item ran in *Camera:*

Ted Billings, who was a prop man when Los Angeles was a flag station and is still making good at it, is seeking an honest position that he can prop 'em up some more as of yore.

He eventually secured work at Universal, as stated in *Camera* (9/9/22, p. 14):

Chas. Clary, Melbourne McDowell, Helen Ferguson, Al McQuarrie, and others are working under the direction of Ed Sedgewick (sic) at Universal. Ted Billings is propman, while Harry Webb is assistant director.

The production referenced was *The Flaming Hand* (1922). Although Billings had served as prop man for literally hundreds of silent films from the early days of motion pictures in Hollywood, this and *Rip Van Winkle* are his only confirmed credits as prop man.

Billings' next known acting role came in Metro's adaptation of Ben Ames Wil-

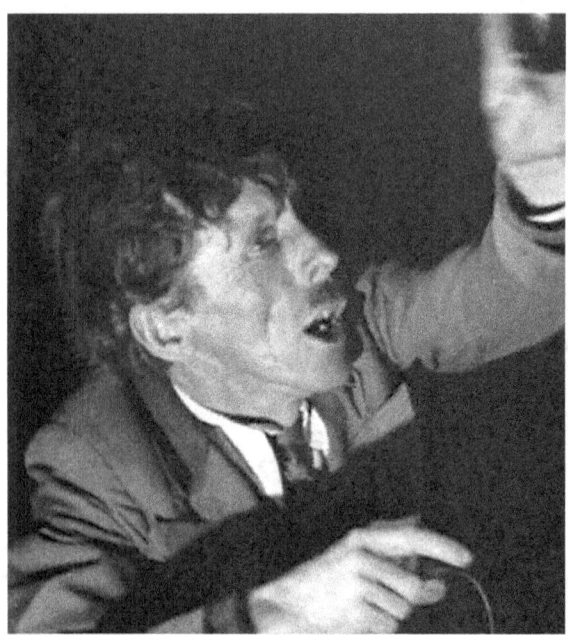

Frankenstein (Universal, 1931): A screen grab of Billings as a villager at the windmill

liams' novel, *All the Brothers Were Valiant* (1923). Ted portrayed a crew member of the whaling ship "Nathan Ross," amidst a fine cast including Lon Chaney, Malcolm McGregor, Billie Dove, Robert McKim, and William V. Mong.

Although Billings undoubtedly did extra work in addition to his responsibilities as property man throughout the 1920s, he has no more known film credits until the advent of the sound era in 1929. In *On with the Show!* (1929), a musical filmed in an early color process, Billings was seen as a stagehand wearing one of his innumerable caps during many of the backstage moments. The film, concerning a theatrical production of *The Phantom Sweetheart*, featured Joe E. Brown, Sally O'Neill, Betty Compson, Arthur Lake, and Ethel Waters, who provides a solid rendition of "Am I Blue?"

The *Daily Record* (June 3, 1929), out of Ellensburg, Washington, was one regional newspaper that ran the following publicity item by Robin Coons, under the headline "Celebrity":

> In Hollywood, if a man isn't a celebrity, he usually is related to one. Ted Billings, diminutive prop man at Warners, seems to carry a whole warehouse of small props in his bulging pockets, claims Josh Billings, the noted American humorist, as his great grandfather.

Michael Hoey, in his book *Sherlock Holmes & the Fabulous Faces: The Universal Pictures Repertory Company*, debunks this story (p. 141) in that Ted's real last name was "Billington" and that "Josh Billings" was a *nom de plume* for 19th Century writer Henry Wheeler Shaw. Such was the Hollywood publicity game.

In the opening sequence of *Disraeli* (1929), starring George Arliss, Billings is among the crowd assembled in Hyde Park (in 1874) listening to a speaker (George Atkinson) inquiring as to what Disraeli has done for England. Intoxicated and attired in glasses, a bowler, and tie, Billings, hands in his pockets, yells out, "Nothing!" Ted later would appear as a hungry peasant in another Arliss period piece, *Voltaire* (1933).

Billings was a panhandler in *The Fall Guy* (1930), with Jack Mulhall and Mae Clarke. In *Moby Dick* (1930), with John Barrymore as an effective Ahab, Ted, sporting a thin mustache, was a sailor on deck as the captain addresses his crew. Ahab tells his men, "If you don't like it, swim home," as the camera cuts to Billings to catch his reaction. He later is viewed aboard the "Shanghai Lady," watching the men in the whaleboat harpooning Moby Dick.

Billings was one of the villagers chasing the Monster (Boris Karloff) up the hill toward the windmill after Little Maria (Marilyn Harris) is found dead in *Frankenstein* (1931). As the men divide into groups, Ted is seen with the burgomaster (Lionel Belmore) and Maria's father, Hans (Michael Mark). At the windmill, he is among those yelling up at the tormented Monster before the edifice burns to the ground.

James Whale liked to utilize familiar faces in his films, from stars to supporting performers to bit players. Following *Frankenstein*, Billings would be seen in six more movies directed by Whale: *The Impatient Maiden* (1932), *The Kiss Before the Mirror* (1933), *The Invisible Man* (1933), *Bride of Frankenstein* (1935), *Remember Last Night?* (1935), and *The Man in the Iron Mask* (1939).

The seedy pre-code melodrama *Safe in Hell* (1931) featured colorful supporting efforts by genre veterans Gustav von Seyffertitz, Charles Middleton, Ivan F. Simpson, and Noble Johnson. Near the conclusion, star Dorothy Mackaill, in a wonderful performance, is put on trial for murder, with the impromptu court being presided over by judge Lionel Belmore. In addition to Billings, with a goatee and

Murders in the Rue Morgue (Universal, 1932): Billings (far left in cap) observes the fortune teller, along with Edna Marion, Bert Roach, Sidney Fox, and Leon Waycoff (Ames).

The Invisible Man (Universal, 1933): Billings (2nd from left in foreground) among the villagers, including D'Arcy Corrigan in back, watching the constable (E.E. Clive) deal with the mysterious visitor (Claude Rains).

mustache as the juror sitting closest to Mackaill, the rag tag jury also included Rondo Hatton in an early film bit.

The opening scenes of *Murders in the Rue Morgue* (1932), directed by Robert Florey, had Billings among the onlookers gawking at all the sideshow exhibits, glancing between two elderly gentlemen to see the Native Americans. Ted is seen behind leads Leon Waycoff (Ames) and Sidney Fox, before they are enticed to view Professor Mirakle (Bela Lugosi) and his ape, Erik.

James Whale presented Billings with the interesting role in *The Important Maiden* (1932) as a lunatic in an asylum who thinks he is Napoleon. Ted had a character name Len the railbird in *Devil's Lottery* (1932). Billings did many Westerns at this point in his career, playing a townsman in the 12-chapter serial *Heroes of the West* (1932), a rider with Rigby (Tom Mix) in *The Rider of Death Valley* (1932), and Ed, the livery stable worker, in *The Texas Bad Man* (1932), also with Tom Mix. *Sherlock Holmes* (1932), with Clive Brook as the famous sleuth, had Ted up to no good as a carnival thug. Billings was seated in the third row of the gallery adjacent to the windows of the courtroom during the trial of Sarah Padden, in *Women Won't Tell* (1932). He still managed some bits of business to garner attention, shifting his left hand over his ear and then wringing both hands while exiting the courtroom.

Ted was seen as the man laughing in the movie house in *Cynara* (1932), with Ronald Colman.

Frank Lloyd's award-winning *Cavalcade* (1933), featuring a slew of British expatriates in Hollywood, had Billings as a paperboy, bringing news of the second Boer War as he sells a newspaper to Una O'Connor. Ted acknowledges, "Thank you, Ma'am, thank you lady!" as he continues to hawk papers … "All about the war!"

Billings played a member of a chain gang (that included Walter Long and Fred Kohler, Jr.) in *Laughter in Hell* (1933) and was a prison inmate in *Pick-Up* (1933), starring Sylvia Sidney. For James Whale and Universal, Billings had a bit as a courtroom spectator in *The Kiss Before the Mirror* (1933). He also was seen as a Cockney soldier, in *The Eagle and the Hawk* (1933), with Fredric March and Cary Grant as WWI fliers.

Billings can barely be glimpsed as a villager in *The Vampire Bat* (1933). As Herman (Dwight Frye) enters the Kleinschloss Morgue, following the murder of Martha (Rita Carlyle), Ted, hat in hand, is the diminutive villager at the top of the stairs.

In the respected *Hollywood Filmograph* (12/24/32, p. 1) review of *Hallelujah I'm a Bum* (1933), starring Al Jolson, it was noted:

> Ted Billings did a very fine job as "The Fiddler." His work stood out very far above the many bits in the picture and is worthy of special attention and commendation.

Set in Central Park in the early portion of the Great Depression, Billings was one of an army of tramps following the charismatic Bumper (Al Jolson). Wearing

Bride of Frankenstein [Universal, 1935]: Henry Frankenstein (Colin Clive) gives directives to Ludwig (Ted Billings) and Karl (Dwight Frye).

Bride of Frankenstein (Universal, 1935): As Karl (Dwight Frye) struggles with the Monster, Ludwig (Billings) looks up in shock.

a straw hat and a blazer, while sporting whiskers and a mustache of sorts, Billings sings a line and plays his fiddle to Rodgers and Hart's "Bumper Found a Grand." As Bumper sings an ensuing number, "What Do You Want with Money," there are several cuts to Billings (whom Bumper refers to as "Rich," the fiddler). Billings probably has as much or more screen time in *Hallelujah I'm a Bum* than in any of his film roles.

In the opening sequence of *The Invisible Man* (1933), at the "Lion's Head Inn" in the village of Iping, Billings is among a group of men playing darts. When it comes Ted's turn to throw, he adroitly hurls the dart left-handed for a bullseye. After Hall (Forrester Harvey) is hurled down the stairs by the mysterious new arrival, Jack Griffin (Claude Rains), Billings is among those hovering over the injured man. Ted later follows Constable Jaffers (E.E. Clive) up the stairs to Griffin's sitting room, but he looks aghast when Jack unravels the bandages around his head to reveal his invisible state.

The bits for Billings remained brief and barely noticeable. Ted was a drinker in a pub in *The Mystery of Mr. X* (1934), a man in the park in *City Park* (1934), a townsman at the dance in *Smoking Guns* (1934), a man in the nightmare sequence in *Whom the Gods Destroy* (1934), a passerby at the murder scene in *Limehouse Blues* (1934), a waiter in *The Red Rider* (1934), and a sailor in a Chinese café on the Barbary Coast, in *Wharf Angel* (1934), with Victor McLaglen and Alison Skipworth. Standing behind Rob Dow (Alan Hale), Billings was one of the villagers taking up arms in preparation for the arrival of soldiers in *The Little Minister* (1934), starring Katharine Hepburn and John Beal. *The Man Who Reclaimed His Head* (1934) included Billings as a newsboy selling a paper to protagonist Paul Verin (Claude Rains).

Billings played an old soldier in *Clive of India* (1935), starring Ronald Colman and featuring, among others, the title character's distant relative Colin Clive. Ted was a townsman in both *The Rustlers of Red Dog* (1935) and *Transient Lady* (1935), with Frances Drake and Henry Hull. He was barely noticeable as a little man in *Storm Over the Andes* (1935).

Billings' role of a bootblack was more substantial in *The Good Fairy* (1935), based on a Ferenc Molnar play and starring Margaret Sullavan. As Ted polishes shoes near a spiral staircase in a hotel, he is spun around by Frank Morgan, who is pursuing Sullavan and Reginald Owen. Billings maintains his balance and keeps on shining.

An item in "Film Daily" (2/8/35, p. 12) noted, "Teddy Billings, Universal's 'man about town,' gets a good role in *Return of Frankenstein*." Universal officially changed the title from *Return of Frankenstein* to *Bride of Frankenstein* in early 1935. As Ludwig, assistant to Henry Frankenstein (Colin Clive) and Dr. Pretorius (Ernest Thesiger), Billings' role represents his only on-screen credited (listed 16th) appearance in the sound film era.

In the latter portion of *Bride of Frankenstein* (1935), Ludwig is one of four men

The Prince and the Pauper (First National, 1937): At the Robbers' Roost Inn—Jimmy Aubrey, Frank Hagney, John J. Richardson, Bobby Mauch (with book), player, John George, and Ted Billings (holding mug)

Boy of the Streets (Monogram, 1937): Albert Murder (Billings, far right with walking stick) observes a street brawl in front of his tenement building.

carrying lanterns who approach the tower wherein the Frankenstein laboratory is housed. Ludwig closes the door after they enter, with all the men then climbing the stairs to the lab. Dr. Frankenstein summons Ludwig, who helps Dr. Pretorius position a table holding the heart intended for the "Bride." As the storm rises, Karl (Dwight Frye) calls to Ludwig to get the kites ready for launching. Ludwig turns one of the winches and then pulls a handle to open a hatch in the roof. He and Karl lower the connecting apparatus and then do the reverse process, raising the platform containing the "Bride" to the rooftop. Ludwig and Karl connect the cables and the creation process ensues. Later, when the Monster (Boris Karloff) comes up to the roof and hurls Karl to his death, Ludwig can do nothing but watch, not daring to intervene. Although Ludwig's death is not depicted in the film, it can be assumed that he perished when the Monster pulled the lever, blowing the structure to rubble. Billings has frequently and erroneously been credited as a grave robber in *Bride of Frankenstein*, but the role of Rudy, Karl's murderous colleague in the crypt sequence, was played by Neil Fitzgerald.

Bonnie Scotland (1935), starring Laurel and Hardy, showed Billings at his familiar pub locale. *Condemned to Live* (1935), an independent effort with a vampire angle directed by Frank Strayer (who also helmed *The Vampire Bat*), had Billings, attired in a Tyrolean outfit, as a bellringer. He sounds his bell in long-shot at three transition points of the film, the last two after vampiric slayings. Again, with James Whale directing, Ted portrayed a sailor in *Remember Last Night?* (1935). *The Calling of Dan Matthews* (1935) included Billings as a card player. Ted was one of a huge array of British supporting players in *Captain Blood* (1935), where he was a juror at the trial of Doctor Peter Blood (Errol Flynn) and the rebels. The 12-episode *Tailspin Tommy in the Great Air Mystery* (1935) featured Billings as an airport attendant.

The Invisible Ray (1936), showcasing the combined talents of Boris Karloff and Bela Lugosi, had Billings as a counterman who serves coffee and ladles hot soup. Dr. Janos Rukh (Karloff) approaches one of Ted's customers (Walter Miller), a derelict, whom he then murders, using the body to feign his own death.

Billings portrayed a convict laboring in the Blackfoot Coal Mine prison camp in *Road Gang* (1936), with Donald Woods. When the prisoners revolt, and the mine is tear gassed, Ted's character exclaims:

We can't last much longer. We got to have air. I'm for giving up.

Sunset Trail (Western Classics, 1938): Ted Billings (far back, right), William Boyd (man holding pistol, foreground right), and George "Gabby" Hayes (man in middle, holding gun)

Pacific Liner (RKO Radio, 1939): Ted Billings (second from left, holding hat), Adia Kuznetzoff, Alan Hale, Victor McLaglen, Barry Fitzgerald, Anthony Warde, John Bleifer, Cy Kendall, John Wray, and players

The convicts, however, blast their way to freedom and Billings stares down vile warden Charles Middleton, when he directs them to return to their quarters. A much smaller bit came with his enacting a man standing on the railroad platform in *Dodsworth* (1936). Ted had another minor bit as a saloon waiter in *Hopalong Cassidy Returns* (1935), with William Boyd taking on the Hoppy role for the seventh time.

Billings is first seen in *The Prince and the Pauper* (1937), drinking in a pub as the scene shifts to Henry VIII (Montagu Love), raising his glass upon the birth of his son Edward. Ted is later viewed wearing an eyepatch as a tinker in the streets witnessing the murder by John Canty (Barton MacLane) of Father Andrew (Fritz Leiber). The tinker then assembles with his fellow ragged beggars at the "Robbers' Roost," where they interact with Prince Edward (Bobby Mauch), pretending to be Tom Canty.

Soak the Poor (1937), an MGM "Crime Does Not Pay" (#11) short, had Billings as a citizen in the front row on-line at the Home Relief Bureau. Leslie Fenton played the head of a gang of racketeers out to exploit those already suffering during the Great Depression. Billings had small parts in two Westerns, *North of the Rio Grande* (1937), playing a waiter in a saloon, and *The Trigger Trio* (1937), as a spectator at a horse race. *Daughter of Shanghai* (1937), a tale of human trafficking starring Anna May Wong, had Billings again as a barfly, this time in an island honky-tonk, run by corrupt Charles Bickford.

Ted had perhaps his richest character name as Albert "Old Man" Murder, who lives in an old tenement building in *Boy of the Streets* (1937). Jackie Cooper, the leader of an Irish boys' gang in a New York City slum, has his boys place a crank call on Halloween to falsely report a murder in Apartment 5, where Albert lives. Cooper exclaims, "Old Man Murder is gonna be scared to death." When Police Investigator Craig (Edward Peil, Sr.) arrives on the scene, he spots Albert sitting on the stoop and enquires about the murder in Apartment 5. "A murder—that's me—Albert Murder," Billings tells the flustered homicide detective.

It was back to characters without names for Billings as an angry laborer in *Mr. Boggs Steps Out* (1938), a studio grip in a film-within-a-film in *The Goldwyn Follies* (1938), a waiter in *Sunset Trail* (1938), a pedestrian in *Prairie Moon* (1938), and as a barfly in both the serial *Flaming Frontiers* (1938) and *Panamint's Bad Man* (1938). Ted was referred to as "Harry" in *Reckless Living* (1938), featuring Nan Grey of *Dracula's Daughter* notoriety. He also was glimpsed as a man walking on the sidewalk in MGM's Reginald Owen version of *A Christmas Carol* (1938). Billings was among the legion of Parisian peasants in *If I Were King* (1938), starring Ronald Colman.

Billings played a stoker aboard the "S.S. Arcturus" in *Pacific Liner* (1939), with Victor McLaglen. While on the set of this film, shot in November of 1938, McLaglen reportedly overheard Billings and fellow bit player Shorty English discussing their difficult work and financial situations, anticipating being broke at Christmas time. Ted and Shorty had both been property men in the silent era and now tried to eke by with meager earnings from bit roles. In a kind gesture, McLaglen invited both actors to his ranch for Christmas dinner (the *Los Angeles Times*, 12/4/38).

Ted was once again a Western townsman in the Charles Starrett feature, *The Thundering West* (1939). *Mr. Moto's Last Warning* (1939), starring Peter Lorre as the sleuth, had Billings at the bar in "Connie's Place," smoking a pipe and nursing a beer, when he is pushed aside by aggressive George Sanders. Near the conclusion of John Ford's *Stagecoach* (1939), as

Rio (Universal, 1939): Portrait of Ted Billings as a convict

Rio (Universal, 1939): A convict (Ted Billings) collapses while helping move an enormous log, while Paul Renard (Basil Rathbone) confronts the sadistic guard (Paul Bryar).

the cavalry troops ride into Lordsburg, New Mexico Territory, where the stagecoach has also arrived, a pointing Billings, wearing a white cowboy hat, runs across the street. It was truly a "blink and you missed him" moment as he is on-screen for just a couple of seconds. In *Undercover Agent* (1939), Billings is in the background seated at the bar as bartender Lee Phelps contends with alcoholic J.M. Kerrigan.

In Billings' seventh and final film under director James Whale, Ted played a demented prisoner in the Bastille in *The Man in the Iron Mask* (1939). As D'Artagnan (Warren William) and his colleagues hide in the shadows, attempting to free Philippe (Louis Hayward), a jailer attempts to silence the screaming prisoners, including Billings, who stares out of the small opening of his cell, laughing and grunting.

As a foreshadowing of things to come, Billings was a pub customer in *The Adventures of Sherlock Holmes* (1939), 20th Century Fox's follow-up to *The Hound of the Baskervilles* (1939), which introduced Basil Rathbone as Holmes and Nigel Bruce as Watson to the film-going public. Ted would subsequently appear in four of the Universal Rathbone/Bruce "Sherlock Holmes" series, each time materializing in a British pub.

Rio (1939) provided Billings with a memorable scene as a slightly built convict who collapses while struggling to move a large tree, while being monitored by sadistic guards on Devil's Island. Billings was reunited with Boris Karloff (as Mord) in *Tower of London* (1939), as one of the army of beggars under the influence of Mord, the executioner. Billings does not speak but looks around for the reactions of others as Mord arrests Clarence (Vincent Price), when he disembarks from a boat landing at the Tower.

The Hunchback of Notre Dame (1939), featuring a bravura performance by Charles Laughton in the title role, had Billings as a short peasant attempting to gaze through the window to witness Quasimodo's arraignment.

Soon after the death of wife Margaret in 1939, Billings moved in as a lodger with the George family in Los Angeles. At this point, all the Ludwick/Billings stepchildren were grown and living independently. By 1943, Ted had reestablished his own residence at 1119 McCaddden Place, Los Angeles (according to his WWII draft registration). His draft material also noted a mole by his left eye and claimed his height at 5'1 and weight as 107 pounds.

Now a widower, Ted was determined to remain busy with extra and bit roles in films. He played a townsperson outside the House of Lords in *The Earl of Chicago* (1940), starring Robert Montgomery. Ted was one of the onlookers at the Lincoln (Raymond Massey)-Douglas (Gene Lockhart) debate, in *Abe Lincoln in Illinois* (1940). *The Light of Western Stars* (1940),

Captain Caution (UA, 1940): Billings (rear, center) is one of the ship's prisoners grasping for food, while Dan Marvin (Victor Mature, in white shirt) takes a fish.

Sullivan's Travels **(Paramount, 1941): Sullivan (Joel McCrea) and the girl (Veronica Lake) eat at the soup kitchen, with Frank Moran and Billings alongside of them.**

with Victor Jory in a rare hero role, included Billings as a waiter in a saloon, a role he repeated in *The Showdown* (1940), again opposite William Boyd as Hopalong Cassidy. Billings played a farmer in *In Old Missouri* (1940) and was a trapper in DeMille's *North West Mounted Police* (1940).

Set during the War of 1812, *Captain Caution* (1940) had Billings as one of many captured seamen aboard a British ship. The prisoners, including Ted, lunge for meager rations of fish. As the food situation worsens, the men share memories of meals at home, with Billings adding "… and pour your juice and vegetables all over your bread." Billings was seen both in a saloon and inside a courtroom in *Seven Sinners* (1940), with Marlene Dietrich and John Wayne. The musical *Tin Pan Alley* (1940), with Alice Faye and Betty Grable, had Billings depicted as a peddler on a recruiting poster during a montage sequence. *The Son of Monte Cristo* (1940), which included a brief speaking part for Dwight Frye, had Billings as a townsman outside the shop of Otto Mirbach (Charles Waldron).

John Ford utilized Billings in a brief bit as a Welsh villager in *How Green Was My Valley* (1941). Billings was a spectator at a wreck in *Horror Island* (1941), with Dick Foran and Peggy Moran. He popped up among the bidders at an auction in *The Lady from Cheyenne* (1941). Ted played a fisherman in *The Flame of New Orleans* (1941), starring Marlene Dietrich and directed by Rene Clair. In Fritz Lang's *Man Hunt* (1941), with Walter Pidgeon and John Carradine, Billings returned to the occupation of newsboy. MGM's remake of *Dr. Jekyll and Mr. Hyde* (1941), with Spencer Tracy in the complex role(s), included Ted as a customer in the pub in which Ingrid Bergman (as Ivy) is a barmaid. Billings was one of the air-raid refugees in the London underground in *Confirm or Deny* (1941). *Shadow of the Thin Man* (1941), with William Powell as Nick Charles, featured Billings smoking a cigar and wearing a hat as a spectator at a wrestling match.

Preston Sturges' poignant yet comedic *Sullivan's Travels* (1941) included Billings as one of the homeless individuals, whom director John L. Sullivan (Joel McCrea) encounters while trying to obtain real life experience for his upcoming film, *O Brother, Where Art Thou?* Ted is spotted in the front row of a mission listening to a preacher, as the camera pans further and further back to reveal Sullivan and "the girl" (Veronica Lake), blended in with all the poor folk in the congregation. In the next scene, set in a soup kitchen, an ema-

The Lodger **(20th Century-Fox, 1944): Billings as the news vendor, with the paper headlining the "Ripper Murders"**

ciated Billings is joyfully partaking in the free meal at the same table as Sullivan.

Sealed Lips (1942), with William Gargan and June Clyde, had Billings as a convict in San Quentin. Ted played a customer entering a tavern behind Clem Miniver (Walter Pidgeon), just before Clem's son Vin (Richard Ney) unexpectedly arrives in the Academy Award-winning *Mrs. Miniver* (1942), starring Greer Garson. Ted was a courtroom spectator in the scene in *The Gay Sisters* (1942), wherein the title heroines (Barbara Stanwyck, Geraldine Fitzgerald, Nancy Coleman) contest George Brent's claims on their estate. In Julien Duvivier's *Tales of Manhattan* (1942), concerning a custom-made tailcoat that brings bad luck to all who possess it, Billings was seen as a poor man at the city mission in the Edward G. Robinson sequence. *Pittsburgh* (1942), with Marlene Dietrich, John Wayne, and Randolph Scott, included Billings as a miner. Ted also was viewed as a townsman in *Juke Girl* (1940), starring Ann Sheridan and Ronald Reagan.

Virtually every entry in the Universal *Sherlock Holmes* series had at least one scene in a pub or bar. No wonder Billings would make multiple appearances in this series. In *Sherlock Holmes and the Voice of Terror* (1942), Ted was briefly on view as the bartender in the basement dive where Holmes (Basil Rathbone) and Watson (Nigel Bruce), after being approached by the burly Camberwell (Harry Cording), implore Kitty (Evelyn Ankers) to use her influence to help them solve a murder. *Sherlock Holmes and the Secret Weapon* (1942) had Holmes in the disguise of a longshoreman, going from bar to bar seeking information. Billings was a patron interacting with a barmaid in the first establishment ("Star and Dagger") entered by the master detective. Wearing a stocking cap, Billings was among the denizens of the "Journet Hotel Café" in the village of La Morte Rouge, in the atmospheric *The Scarlet Claw* (1944). In one scene he is viewed sitting at a table with Dr. Watson (Nigel Bruce), although he has no dialogue. Billings is seen during the café sequence, however, singing along with a man playing a concertina. *Dressed to Kill* (1946), the final entry in the Universal Rathbone "Sherlock Holmes" series, managed to include Billings once again as a pub patron.

The Scarlet Claw **(Universal, 1944): Inside Journet's Inn—Bob Burns, David Clyde, Jack Kenny, Nigel Bruce, Al Kunde, Arthur Hohl, Frank Austin, Ted Billings (in stocking cap), Phil Schumacher, and players**

In *The Song of Bernadette* (1943), after Bernadette (Jennifer Jones) is taken away for digging for spring water at Lourdes, Billings laughs and gestures to onlookers as the police commissioner (Charles Dingle) calls her a fraud. Billings was a man at the train depot as soldiers return in *Immortal Sergeant* (1943). He was seen as the janitor photo model in *The Powers Girl* (1943), a man at the inn in *Mission to Moscow* (1943), a Russian prisoner in *Jack London* (1943), and a townsman in *Jane Eyre* (1943), with Orson Welles and Joan Fontaine. Amid murder, dancers, and comics in *Lady of Burlesque* (1943), Ted was a regular and enthusiastic spectator, sitting in the front row two seats off the aisle at the Old Opera House, now converted for burlesque. Director Julien Duvivier's moody, *Flesh and Fantasy* (1943), had Billings on hand as a sidewalk artist. *The Woman of the Town* (1943), starring Claire Trevor, included Ted among the townspeople.

Billings was a Sydney pub patron in *The Man from Down Under* (1943), starring Charles Laughton, and was also a bar character in *The Kansan* (1943), with Richard Dix. Although Billings was still stuck in a bar, *Thank Your Lucky Stars* (1943) offered him the chance to partake in a musical number. Billings, singing and dancing, has his metal stein of beer commandeered by Errol Flynn, who leads all the pub patrons, including Charles Irwin and David Thursby, in the song "That's What You Jolly Well Get." In *Johnny Come Lately* (1943), Billings was Hiram Webster, one of three vagabonds (another being James Cagney) who are brought before the judge (Joseph Crehan) on charges of vagrancy in the town of Plattsville.

Shine on Harvest Moon (1944), a musical with Ann Sheridan and Dennis Morgan, had Billings as a man in the audience. In an equally short moment, he was a bystander in the crowd in the Edgar Bergen/Charlie McCarthy comedy *Song of the Open Road* (1944). Billings played a workman in *Meet the People* (1944), with Lucille Ball and Dick Powell. *The Mask of Dimitrios* (1944), with Sydney Greenstreet and Peter Lorre yielding colorful portrayals, included Ted once again as a bar patron.

The Invisible Man's Revenge (1944) had Billings, wearing a blazer, striped shirt, and striped cap, as one of the patrons of the "Running Nag Inn." When invisible Robert Griffin (Jon Hall) challenges boastful Ned Towle (Tom Dillon) to darts, it is the inept Herbert Higgins (Leon Errol) who is perceived to have issued the dare.

The Scarlet Claw (Universal, 1944): A screen grab with Nigel Bruce as Dr. Watson sitting at a table in the inn with villager Ted Billings.

Ted's character laughs as Ned makes fun of Herbert, who then presents Billings with a five-pound note to secure the bet. "Right-o," exclaims Ted, who receives another note from Ned, before turning to Jim (Yorke Sherwood) stating, "'Ere, you hold it!" Billings stares with amazement as Herbert's darts, thrown in eccentric ways, are all guided to the bullseye by the invisible Griffin.

None But the Lonely Heart (1944), written and directed by Clifford Odets, included Billings as a Cockney vagrant lying against a London slum building as Cary Grant walks by. Ted was one of the many grotesque looking citizens of Casa Rouge, observed by squeamish Bob Hope and beautiful Virginia Mayo in *The Princess and the Pirate* (1944). In *Belle of the Yukon* (1944), featuring Gypsy Rose Lee and Dinah Shore, Billings performed many functions, including bank teller, townsman, and barfly. Ted also briefly appeared as a racetrack spectator in *National Velvet* (1944), starring young Elizabeth Taylor. In *Nothing but Trouble* (1944), Laurel and Hardy's antepenultimate film together (and their last for MGM), Billings was viewed at a mission for the poor.

Billings had small roles in Laird Cregar's final two films for 20th Century Fox. Ted was briefly seen as a news vendor in the atmospheric Cregar starrer, *The Lodger* (1944). In the early scenes of *Hangover Square* (1945), featuring another bravura lead performance by Laird Cregar, a mustachioed Billings is viewed on Fulham Road, holding a placard for the *London Globe*, when a dazed George Harvey Bone (Cregar) nearly staggers into him. Billings turns, pointing to the blazing antique store (where a murder has been committed) exclaiming, "Look, you can see the fire from 'ere!"

Other parts for Billings at this time were: A fight spectator in *The Great John L* (1945), a barroom spectator in *Secret Agent X-9* (1945), a pub customer in *The Fatal Witness* (1945), the little man sleeping on a bench in *The Man in Half Moon Street* (1945), a barfly in the Universal serial *Jungle Queen* (1945), a vendor in *Scarlet Street* (1945), a party guest in *Salome Where She Danced* (1945), and a saloon sweeper in *Frontier Gal* (1945), the latter two starring Yvonne De Carlo. *Scotland Yard Investigator* (1945), with the villainous Erich von Stroheim, had Billings in another newsboy role.

Billings managed to find his way into two of the impressive, atmospheric RKO productions of Val Lewton. In *The Body Snatcher* (1945), Ted is walking on the street dressed in a top hat and coat, when he is passed by Dr. MacFarlane (Henry Daniell) and Fettes (Russell Wade), as they hurry toward "Hobbs Public House." Billings' scene in *Bedlam* (1946) is equally brief, as he is glimpsed, near the film's climax, among the inmates who grab hold of Sims (Boris Karloff), to conduct their own trial, passing judgment on the sadistic apothecary general of the hospital.

Tarzan and the Leopard Woman (1946), with Johnny Weismuller and Acquanetta, had Billings quickly glimpsed as a native passerby. Ted was a patron of the "Golden Rooster" in the musical *Two Sisters from Boston* (1946). Billings had another of his many "barfly" bits in *Renegades* (1946), was a Cockney man on the street in *Of Human Bondage* (1946), and he played a patron at the Mango Inn in Pago Pago in the Sidney Toler "Charlie Chan" *Dangerous Money* (1946). Ted was one of the miners in a Lens, France coal mine in *The Razor's Edge* (1946), starring Tyrone Power. *The Missing Lady* (1946), with Kane Richmond as Lamont Cranston "the Shadow," included Ted as a bum in a flophouse. Billings had a character name "Shorty" in *Two Guys from Milwaukee* (1946), with Dennis Morgan and Jack Carson.

Near the beginning of *Two Years Before the Mast* (1946), with Alan Ladd in the lead, Billings is seen on a Boston Street corner as a crimp involved in shanghaiing men to sail on the "Pilgrim." Billings calls to Hayes (Theodore Newton), who is walking by, "Hey gent, how would you like to see the California coast, sail on a fine ship, and fill your pockets with gold?" When Hayes balks that he is a farmer and not a sailor, Ted's accomplice slugs him over the head. Billings laughingly adds, "You're a sailor now!"

Despite having no lines, Billings has some prominent moments as a customer in Max's Café in *Nobody Lives Forever* (1946), starring John Garfield. A smiling and inebriated Ted, smoking a pipe and carrying a glass mug of beer, places coins in a juke-

Aladdin and the Wonderful Lamp (Fox Film Corporation, 1917): One of Ted Billings' earliest screen credits

box to hear an instrumental version of "Don't Fence Me In," before crossing the foreground of the scene, making his way back to the bar. This occurs just prior to when unscrupulous George Coulouris enters the establishment, seeking out Walter Brennan.

In a 1946 piece in the *Buffalo Courier-Express Pictorial* entitled "His Face is His Fortune," Billings was one of six distinctive-looking minor actors receiving a brief write-up. The article stated that Billings "has worked in pictures for the past 42 years, first as a 'prop' man, then as an extra and bit player." It went on to claim that "Ted makes from $5 to $35 a day doing extra work, averages $4,000 a year."

The Imperfect Lady (1947), starring Teresa Wright and Ray Milland, had Billings as a chimney sweep. Ted had the minor role as a huckster in the colorful fantasy *The Secret Life of Walter Mitty* (1946), with Danny Kaye as the titled daydreamer and Boris Karloff among his nemeses. Billings' final film was 20th Century-Fox's lavish Technicolor *Forever Amber* (1947), directed by Otto Preminger. In the movie, released four months after Ted's death, Billings, wearing a wide brimmed hat, is viewed seated in the background of the tavern of Mother Red Cap (Anne Revere), when Newgate Prison escapee John Russell and Linda Darnell enter to solicit her assistance. Billings had no lines, but the headgear he sported was perhaps the most unusual of the more than 100 different hats and caps he wore in his screen appearances. True to his training as a prop man who could come up with almost any small item at a moment's notice to complete a scene, Ted used hats, pipes, cigars, beer mugs, and other items to garner attention even in his briefest of roles.

Ted Billings died at his home at 1119 N. McCadden Place, in Sherman Oaks, California, at the age of 65 (or 67) on Saturday July 5, 1947. A funeral service for the actor was held on July 9, 1947, at the Pierce Brothers Memorial Chapel in Hollywood. Ted was interred in the Troupers Plot in Block F, section 5568, lot 4, at Pierce Brothers Valhalla Memorial Park in North Hollywood. Billings was survived by his stepsons Richard and Elmo Billings (and their families) and stepdaughters, Anna May Conk, and Catherine Dunn (and her son), in addition to his sister Emily.

Ted Billings labored in the motion picture industry for more than 40 years with only two on-screen credits and minimal recognition. By paying tribute to his career, it is my attempt to illustrate the plight of thousands of men and women who labored in obscurity in films in bits or as extras for so many years. Billings was more fortunate than most, mainly due to his appearances in classic horror films, in that contemporary movie fans now have some awareness of his work. Once one becomes attuned to Ted Billing's diminutive stature and gnarled countenance, there is the opportunity to focus on his costumes (mainly his varied collection of hats), his props (pipes, cigars, beer mugs, etc.), and the pieces of business he utilized to bring a colorful human element to the smallest of parts. By paying attention to minor players and the small details they can add to the picture, the director and cinematographer can paint a whole new dimension to the appreciation of the art of film.

SOURCES

"His Face is His Fortune," *Buffalo Courier-Express Pictorial*, 10/20/46, p. 13.

Heffernan, Harold. "Life of Hollywood Extras Better Now Than in Past," *Buffalo Evening News*, 11/12/46, p. 10.

Hoey, Michael A. *Sherlock Holmes & the Fabulous Faces: The Universal Pictures Repertory Company*, Albany, Georgia: BearManor Media, 2011.

Seymour, Blackie. "The Vigilant Villagers: Ted Billings," in *Classic Images #235*, January 1995, pp. C23, x.

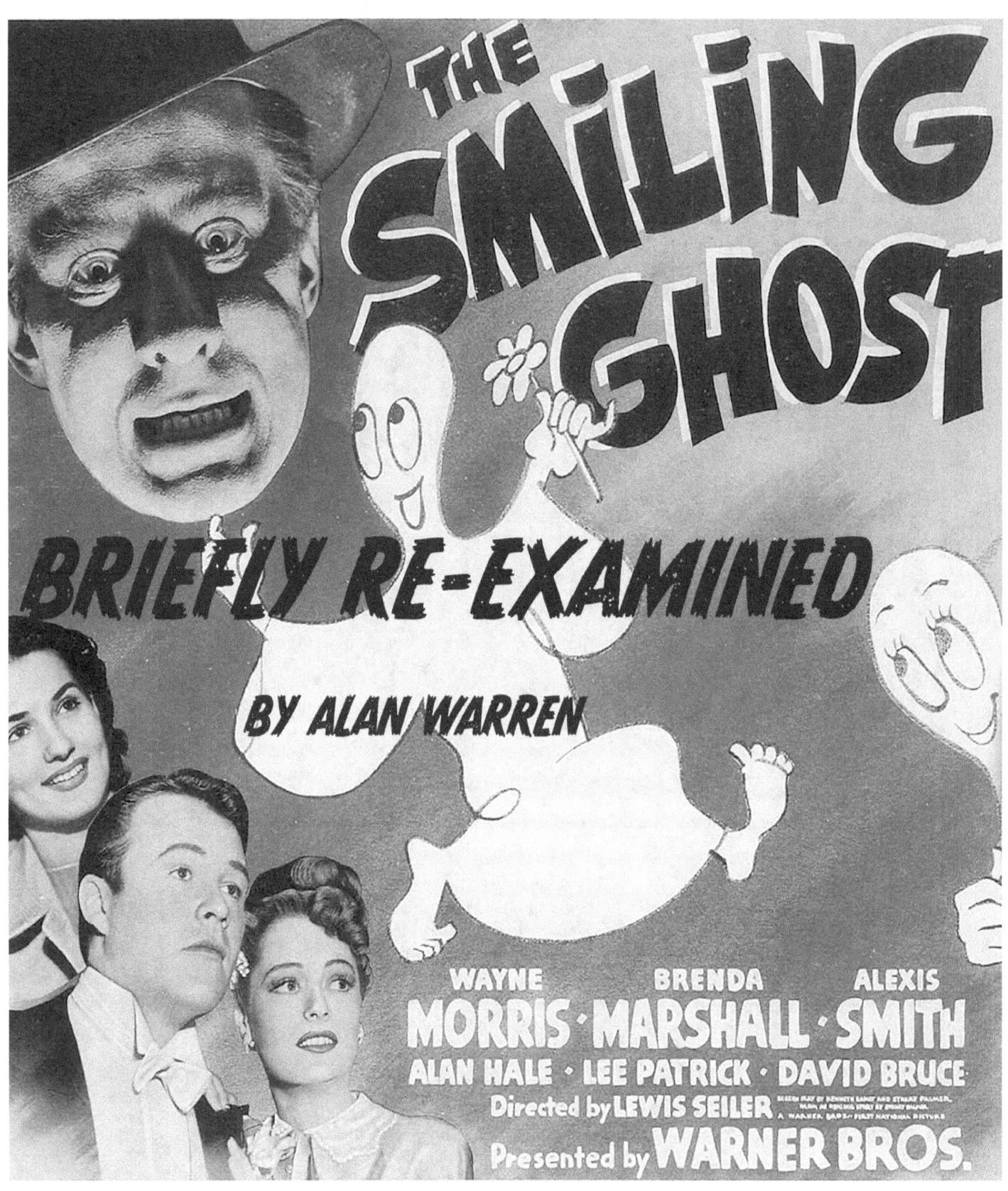

A close-up of the Smiling Ghost.

When Joe Dante, Jr. (as he was then called) listed the 50 worst horror movies ever made in *Famous Monsters of Filmland* #18 (July 1962), he included a perfectly enjoyable horror-comedy with this rather unkind review: "*The Smiling Ghost* of 1941 was another regrettable haunted house comedy, loaded with overworked gags, and trite situations." As one reviewer said, "If Wayne Morris had looked hard enough, he might have found the script among the ruins!"

To paraphrase Norman Mailer, we will now leave Mr. Dante behind to discover the truth.

In 1940 the enormous success of *The Ghost Breakers* did two things: It shot Bob Hope to fourth place in the annual box-office charts. Second, it ensured that any film with "ghost" in the title was likely to be successful. Thus, we had *Hold That Ghost* (1941), *The Ghost of Frankenstein* (1942), *Whispering Ghosts* (1942), *The Ghost and the Guest* (1943), *Ghost Catchers* (1944), *The Mummy's Ghost* (1944), *The Frozen Ghost* (1945), and several others. Among this group, *The Smiling Ghost* (1941) deserves at least an honorable mention.

The titles are superimposed over a grinning visage of the smiling ghost. Suddenly—a metropolis. A wealthy woman is seeking a young man to take on a job. The young man in question, "Lucky" Downing (Wayne Morris), is trapped inside his office, barricaded against a mob of bill collectors and various other impediments. He will be paid $1,000 to be engaged for a month to Elinor Bentley Fairchild. He agrees.

Along with his companion Clarence (Willie Best), he travels to East Haven, unaware that Elinor is known as the kiss-of-death girl, her previous beaus having met with death or disaster. At the train station he mistakes a homely woman (Renie Riano) for Elinor. "That face looks like seven miles of bad road," Lucky says, and promptly gets slugged by the woman's husband. The real Elinor (Alexis Smith) shows up and Lucky is whisked off to the family mansion. Meanwhile, reporter Lil Barstow (Brenda Marshall) is photographing the event.

This is a fine beginning: the breezy pace, the appealing characters, and spirited acting all carry the film along.

The family mansion is lavish, with all the accruements of wealth, including a butler named Norton (Alan Hale, Sr.), an unfunny characterization that becomes increasingly annoying as the film progresses, particularly his shtick of pulling out a gun and threatening everyone at the slightest opportunity and who has a collection of shrunken heads. Ames is immediately taken with Clarence,

Wayne Morris' companion Clarence (Willie Best) is good for comic relief.

Another victim of the Smiling Ghost is about to be chloroformed.

obviously wishing to add his cranium to the collection.

Other members of the family include the avaricious Rose Fairchild (Lee Patrick) and the alcoholic Tennant (Richard Ainley). Meanwhile, the family does not expect Lucky to be around for long.

In due course Lucky and Clarence move upstairs to accommodate Tennant. This brings on the film's first unnerving scene: A sliding panel rises to disclose the staring eyes of the Smiling Ghost, who mistakes Tennant for Lucky. He stalks his victim, brandishing a knife.

Meanwhile, Lil explains the situation to Lucky. So far, the Smiling Ghost has struck three times … the first, officially ruled a suicide; the second, an attempt on Paul Myron's life that left him in an iron lung, and the third, death by snakebite—on the 18th floor of a Boston hotel. "You are number four," she explains. "They're using you as a guinea pig, setting you up as a target, to tempt the killer to strike so they can nab him."

Lucky is set on decamping when he hears this, but Elinor pleads: "I don't suppose I'll ever break the jinx now. I'll go on being the kiss-of-death girl until I'm an old maid." She proclaims her love for Lucky, and he has a change of heart; he decides to stay, despite the danger.

Meanwhile, Tennant, bloodied but alive, is discovered and taken to a hospital. (The scene where he rises from a coffin-like box to frighten Clarence is one of the scariest in the film.)

"Lucky" Downing (Wayne Morris), Rose Fairchild (Lee Patrick), and Elinor Fairchild (Alexis Smith)

Pretend bride Elinor with reporter Lil Barstow (Brenda Marshall).

Then things turn grim. Lil Barstow visits Paul Myron (David Bruce), the only one of Elinor's suitors to survive. He is in an iron lung, a victim of the Smiling Ghost. Myron tells his story: "The night before Elinor and I were to be married—it was a foggy, rainy night—she kissed me goodbye, then, while I was driving home, something wrestled the wheel of my car out of my hands, and I went off the highway." And then the Smiling Ghost appeared: "The face all white, bloated and puffy-like, that of a corpse long drowned." He tells them it was the face of Johnny Eggleston, Elinor's first suitor. Is Eggleston still alive, preventing Elinor from marrying again? Myron tries to warn Lucky not to take the offer as he will surely die, but Lucky disregards his advice. This scene is eerily effective, helped by Bruce's deadpan delivery.

Lucky suspects Eggleston is still alive. They decide to make sure, by visiting the family crypt.

This is the film's best scene: the mood turns ominous, the cemetery is smothered in fog, with frogs croaking and the music providing an ominous chorus. Coming on the heels of Paul Myron's description of the Smiling Ghost, it is doubly effective. They are unable to open the door of the crypt, so Lil goes back to find the sexton (Clem Bevans) to let them in. Meanwhile, the Smiling Ghost is lying in wait. He opens the door to the crypt and Lucky goes in. The Ghost stalking and attacking Lucky is the high point of the film; all comedy is left behind and the suspense is overpowering. Director Lewis Seiler and cinematographer Arthur L. Todd evoke a gloomy atmosphere that is nicely sustained by Lucky's futile efforts to open the coffin.

Lil, Clarence, and the sexton return, find the door open, and enter, but find nothing. They are about to leave when Lil hears a rapping sound and discovers Lucky, very much alive, tied up in a coffin. (This begs the question: Why didn't the Smiling Ghost kill Lucky while he had the chance? Since he is determined to see to it that Elinor never marries, why leave him alive?)

Lucky is unhurt. He was chloroformed and identifies his attacker as Johnny Eggleston. He is taken back to the mansion. Tennant is found and rushed to a hospital.

Meanwhile, Lucky develops an idea to trap the Smiling Ghost: Have the pseudo-marriage performed at midnight,

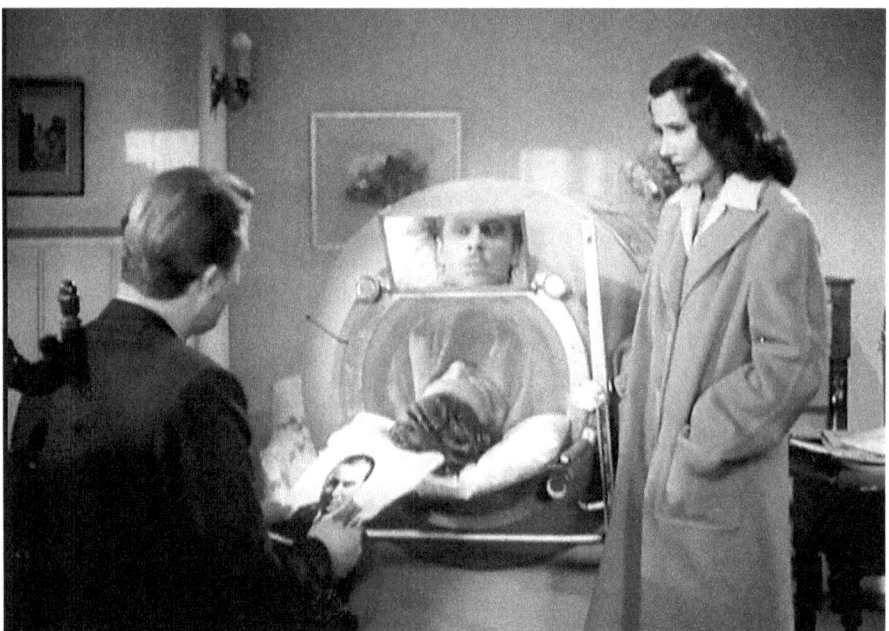

Lil Barstow visits Paul Myron (David Bruce), who is confined to an iron lung, being one of the victims of the Smiling Ghost.

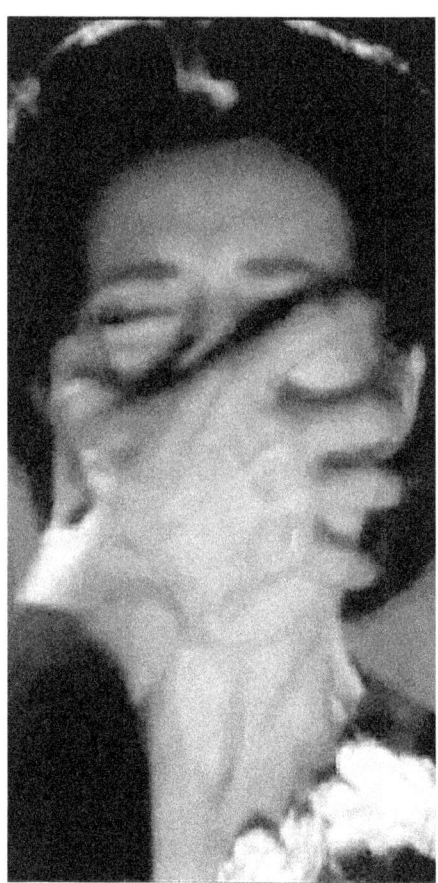

Lil Barstow appears to be getting smothered.

with detectives scattered about. The Ghost is certain to show up. Elinor takes it a step further, convincing Lucky to make the marriage real. He agrees, much to Lil's displeasure.

Midnight approaches. Just as the marriage ceremony commences, the Smiling Ghost douses the lights and kidnaps Lil. Meanwhile, there is some nonsense involving Lucky, Clarence, and a revolving door. Then Lucky discovers Lil, tied up in the cellar. The Smiling Ghost appears and starts shooting. After a fight, the murderer's identity, obvious to anyone over the age of 12, is revealed, and the film's running gag—Ames' obsession with Clarence's head—limps to a conclusion: "My collection is now complete," he gloats, while Lucky looks in horror at what appears to be Clarence's head, shrunk to the size of an orange. Unfortunately, the film spoils this shocking revelation, which would have made for a grisly finale, but far too macabre for 1941 audiences. Instead, Clarence is alive and well: the old man merely wanted his head for a model. Ugh.

The plot is resolved in the usual fashion: Lucky decides he loves Lil after all. But instead of ending on that note, the film shoots itself in the foot, very nearly destroying every bit of atmosphere and suspense that has been built up by a slipshod ending: Lucky dons the Smiling Ghost's mask and idiotically risks his life posing as the murderer, meanwhile dodging all the bullets the trigger-happy Norton fires at him. It's a forced, unfunny scene, and hard to overlook, coming so late in the film—it recalls the glaringly unfunny ending of *The Beast with Five Fingers*, which pretty much ruins everything that has gone before. An equally unfunny scene involving Clarence outrunning a racehorse closes the film.

The Smiling Ghost with Elinor in the background

If one can ignore the film's admitted shortcomings (the stereotypical cowardly black servant, the unfunny comedy of Alan Hale, the unsurprising revelation of the Smiling Ghost's identity), there are ample dividends: the palatial mansion, the utterly bizarre idea of a wedding at midnight, and all the gloss and pomp of 1940s Warner Bros. production values. And the Smiling Ghost is a pleasantly outré figure (make-up courtesy of Perc Westmore). In sum, it's the kind of pleasing horror-comedy that benefits from low expectations and tends to get ignored, coming as it did in the hectic War years, with *The Wolf Man* and the Val Lewton films following in its wake.

Wayne Morris is a likable leading man; he became a Navy flier in 1942, leaving acting temporarily behind. He engaged in 57 aerial sorties and was awarded four Distinguished Flying Crosses and two Air Medallions. His later career was undistinguished, aside from a supporting role in Stanley Kubrick's *Paths of Glory* (1957). He also had a leading role in Bogart's only horror film, *The Return of Dr. X* (1939).

The film's leading ladies, Alexis Smith and Brenda Marshall, both went on to stellar careers. Marshall, who appeared in *The Lady Eve* and *The Sea Hawk*, saw her career decline after she married William Holden in 1941, but Smith achieved stardom via such efforts as *The Constant Nymph* (1943), *The Horn Blows at Midnight* (1945), and two with Bogart, *Conflict* (1945) and *The Two Mrs. Carrolls* (1947).

Willie Best, also known as Sleep 'n' Eat, was described by Bob Hope as "the best actor I know." He and Hope made a splendid comedy duo in *The Ghost Breakers* (1940), the template for the suspiciously similar *Whispering Ghosts* (1942). Best enlivened many straight horror and semi-horror film, including *The Monster Walks* (1932), *Mummy's Boys* (1936), *Who Killed Aunt Maggie?* (1940), *A-Haunting We Will Go* (1942), *The Hidden Hand* (1942), *The Girl Who Dared* (1944), *The Monster and the Ape* (1944), and *The Face of Marble* (1946). A drug arrest curtailed his film career, though he continued in television. He died in 1962 at the age of 48.

Lee Patrick shines in a nicely understated role as the bitchy Rose Fairchild. That same year she played Sam Spade's secretary in *The Maltese Falcon*. She also appeared in *Vertigo* (1958), but she is probably best remembered as Leo G. Carroll's wife on television's *Topper*.

The Smiling Ghost hardly deserves its obscurity. It is much better than *The Body Disappears*, released by Warner Bros. that same year, and although not in the same class as the 1940s classics (*The Wolf Man*, *The Body Snatcher*, and *Dead of Night*), it is a pleasing diversion, if not subjected to close critical scrutiny. Hardly a guilty pleasure, it's more of an innocent amusement.

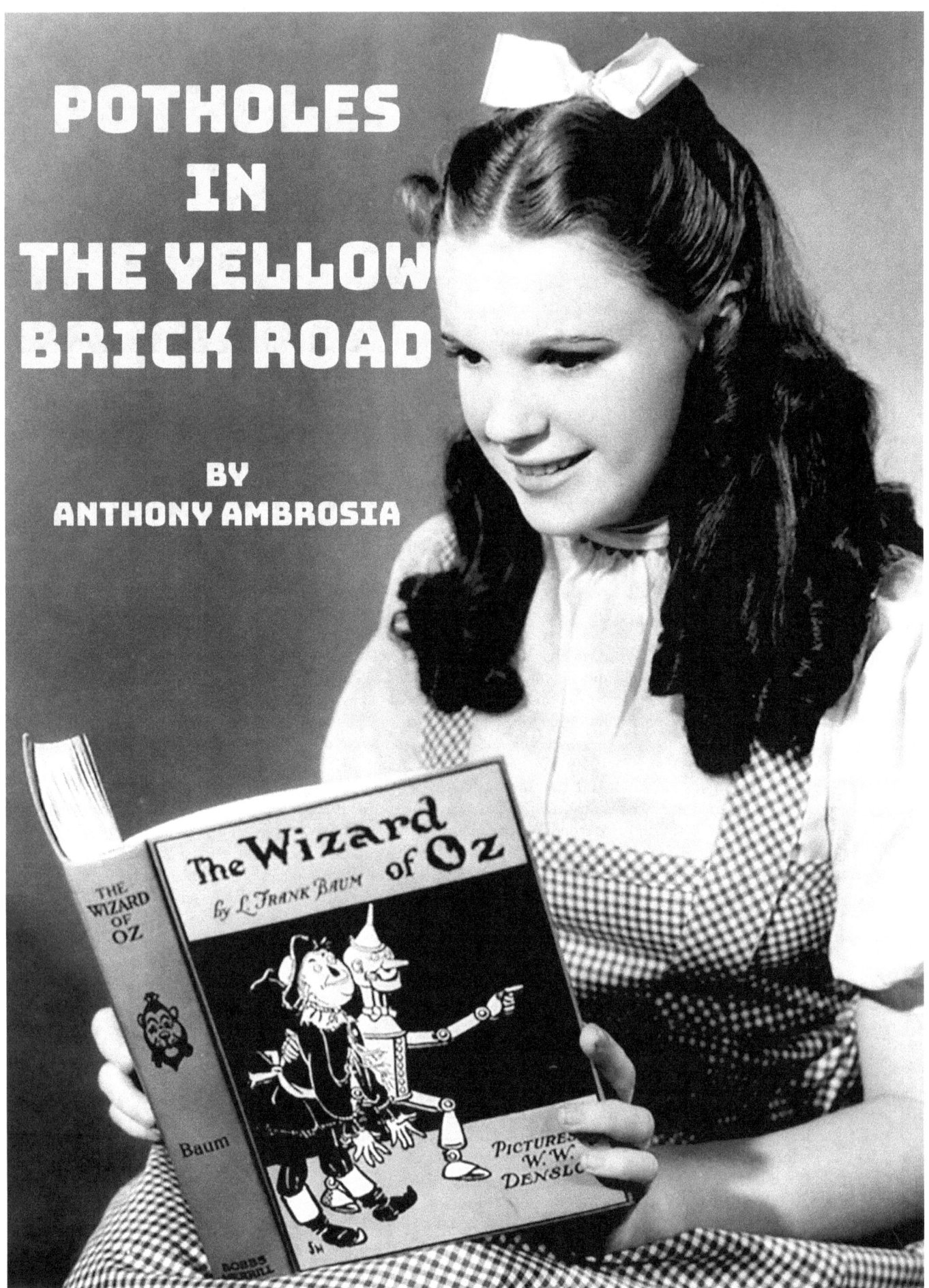

POTHOLES IN THE YELLOW BRICK ROAD

BY ANTHONY AMBROSIA

(Author's note: all quotes from L. Frank Baum's *The Wonderful The Wizard of Oz* come from a 1960 Dover Books "unabridged and unaltered republication of the first edition published by the George M. Hill Company in 1900.")

Disclaimer Before the Plunge

Let's talk about what's wrong with *The The Wizard of Oz* (1939).

First, I freely admit that I like the movie. I'm dating myself, but I'll tell you that I saw it when it was first broadcast on TV (Saturday, November 3, 1956); I had just turned eight. When it became an annual television event, starting in 1959, I, like many people, watched it year after year. When my daughter was five, in 1986, I took her to see a theatrical showing of the film. Now that I have a six-year-old granddaughter, I'm hoping to soon show her the *The Wizard of Oz* Blu-ray that I purchased.

So, it's obviously a film I enjoy. I like the songs, and I think all the performers are perfect in their parts. (But, after enough repeated viewings, I suppose it's inevitable that one should identify Bert Lahr with the Cowardly Lion, Margaret Hamilton with the Wicked Witch of the West, and so forth—just as everyone knows [or used to know] that Sherlock Holmes is always Basil Rathbone and no one's really Charlie Chan but Warner Oland.)

Okay. Now that I've sung its praises, we can talk about what's wrong with the movie.

Into the Foamy Brine

Among the various sins that can be laid at the feet of the film's writers is this most egregious misstep: They resorted to the old "It was only a dream" routine. The book itself has none of this.

In Baum's novel, when Dorothy taps her silver (not ruby) slippers, she goes home by magic. The scene doesn't blur and then suddenly dissolve into a shot of the girl waking up in bed. But the movie opts for the old baloney.

Compounding this sin is the screenwriter's attempt to "explain" all the characters in Dorothy's dream. Thus, mean old Miss Gulch (Margaret Hamilton), who wants to take Toto away, becomes the wicked witch (she metamorphoses before our very eyes, remember?); Professor Miracle (Frank Morgan), the fake mind reader who convinces Dorothy (Judy

The screenwriters try to explain Dorothy's dream by having real-life Kansas characters become essential characters who materialize in Oz.

Garland) to go back home when she's running away, becomes the (phony) wizard whose aid Dorothy seeks so she can go back home; and Hunk, Hickory, and Zeke (Ray Bolger, Jack Haley, and Bert Lahr)—the three farm hands who turn up as the Scarecrow, Tin Man, and Cowardly Lion—all exhibit the qualities that their fantastic counterparts possess (clumsiness, kindness, cowardice). This is all done, it seems, in the interest of unnecessary "realism" (unless the writers wanted to show what clever contrivers they were). None of these Kansas characters are in the book, by the way.

We Slice Up the Old Baloney

Everybody knows that the two *Alice* adventures turn out to be dreams—but one can excuse Lewis Carroll for this device because of the period in which he lived. At a time when Victorian realism reigned supreme, the dream endings for delightfully absurd novels like *Alice's Adventures in Wonderland* and its sequel must have been considered *de rigueur*, sort of the Victorian equivalent of the superficial happy ending or a later era's "redeeming social value" tacked on to the ends of films. (Also, because of the period in which Carroll lived, Freudians are all very happy that Carroll's *Alice* is a dream because then they can better apply to it the kind of symbolism found in the Interpretation of Dreams.)

I don't know why the writers of the Oz movie felt that they had to plagiarize from *Alice* and inject such a stupid "realistic"

A *The Wizard of Oz* American 1 sheet, style D

The Wicked Witch of the West (Margaret Hamilton) and Dorothy (Judy Garland)

explanation into Dorothy's adventure. For one thing, it detracts from the purity of the tale. It is easier to believe in a genuine ghost story than in one which turns out to be a hoax; the elaborate explanations and unbelievably intricate details about how it was all done with smoke and mirrors are much harder to believe than any ghost. Similarly, going to Oz is one thing, but having a dream about the place is quite another. Nobody's dreams are that good.

Thus, the dream ending serves to destroy our willing suspension of disbelief. We have gone along with the story thus far, credulously accepting the witches and wizards and magic—why pull the rug out from under us? Did the screenwriters think that their audience was so unimaginative that it couldn't accept a real Oz? I, for one, prefer a concrete Oz to some dream counterpart—and I'm sure that most children, at whom the book is aimed, do too. (If Oz is real, anybody can go there. But only her psychologist can share Dorothy Gale's dreams.) However, I have a sneaking suspicion that the movie is made for "adults"—or, more properly, for certain parents—who can precariously enjoy the fantasy of the film but then take their children home, secure in the knowledge that it was all only a dream and that the kids' minds won't be filled with any of that nonsense. I guess it never occurred to them to think it was all only a movie!

And That's Not All …

Besides impurifying the story, the writers also waste valuable screen time. Instead of the two reels set in Kansas, putting forth the "realistic" elements to be incorporated into the dream, the writers would have done better to tell the story proper. All of this "realistic" material in the long exposition takes time away from the Oz adventure itself.

In the movie, when the wizard accidentally sails off, back to Kansas, without Dorothy, and everyone seems on the verge of despair, along comes the Good Witch of the North who sets everything right and sends Dorothy home (or makes her wake up). In the book, things don't end so abruptly. The Good Witch of the North does not reappear. Instead, the Scarecrow suggests that they go to the Good Witch of the South for help. (Baum does not give short shrift to the fourth point of the compass, unlike the movie. I'm surprised that Dixie didn't complain. But the South had *Gone With the Wind* to watch in 1939, so maybe it didn't mind or notice.)

On their way down, Dorothy and her friends have a number of adventures—they pass through a country where everyone is made of china (and therefore very fragile); the Lion fights and defeats a giant spider (important because then he becomes king of the forest, just as the Tin Man has become king of the Winkies and the Scarecrow ruler of Oz); they encounter some belligerent people called Hammer-Heads, with long rubber necks and hammer heads, and finally reach the South, where the Good Witch there tells Dorothy about the power of her slippers so that she can finally go home. (Note: the movie calls the Good Witch of the North "Glinda," but in the book she has no name; Glinda is the name of the Good Witch of the South.)

All's Well That Ends?

The expedient ending of the film makes the dialogue inconsistent and causes the Good Witch of the North to appear less good. At the beginning of the film, when the Wicked Witch commands

The Motion Picture pressbook herald from the 1939 movie.

In this lobby card, the Tin Man (Jack Haley), the Cowardly Lion (Bert Lahr), and the Scarecrow (Rat Bolger) dress as Winkies to invade the Wicked Witch's castle.

A studio portrait of Dorothy looking frightened

Dorothy to give her the ruby slippers, the Good Witch tells her not to, for the shoes' power must be very great if the bad witch wants them so badly. This remark clearly implies that the Good Witch does not know what magical properties the footwear possesses. (The good witch in the book does not know.) However, at the end of the film, this same witch tells Dorothy that she's had the means to go home all along: Her ruby slippers are a miniature matter transporter, which can take her anywhere in a matter of minutes. This revelation represents a pretty-mean trick on the part of the "Good" Witch—since, from the moment Dorothy arrived, she kept begging for a way to go home, but the Witch sent her on a wild goose chase to Oz.

When Dorothy asks why the Witch didn't tell her about the slippers to begin with, the Witch offers some lame excuse that Dorothy "wouldn't have believed" her then. (Yeah, right. The kid is plopped down in the middle of a fairy-tale land with witches and various other supernatural elements, and yet she wouldn't have believed the witch about teleportation shoes?) So, the Good Witch, who apparently knew the truth about the slippers all along, chose to conceal it from Dorothy. Doesn't that make the witch complicit with the bad guys and exceptionally cruel, especially since she must have known—couldn't help but see—the mental and physical agony the girl was suffering? If it was just to teach Dorothy a lesson—as is somewhat implied at the end—that "there's no place like home," that's a silly lesson; Dorothy already knew that! Did the girl really display some inordinate wanderlust because she sang "Over the Rainbow" and wanted to run away merely to save her dog? Is this the foul secret that's lurking in her subconscious, and which manifests itself in the scriptwriter-created dream?

For goodness' sake, Dorothy's hardly been gone with Toto for 15 minutes before Professor Marvel (Frank Morgan) convinces her to go home, so the scriptwriters defeat their own purpose. And, in the book, Dorothy's Kansas home is described as gray and bleak—as someplace someone would want to leave. But, even so, in the book—and in the movie—all Dorothy does from the moment she gets to Oz is to try to go home. Of all the "moral lessons" the scriptwriters could have picked, "there's no place like home" is the most ridiculous. (Once again, I suspect the scriptwriters put this unnecessary device in for those parents who'd think the film was teaching their children how important it is to stay home.)

The truth is that the Good Witch is just a *deux ex machina*, illogically used by the screenwriters to quickly tie up loose ends and finish the story. L. Frank Baum wasn't such a sloppy plotter.

Phase II

I may be one of the few people born after 1939 who read the book before seeing the movie version of *The The Wizard of Oz*. Perhaps that's why my criticism of the movie is more vehement than most people's. That doesn't make my criticism any less justified, however. (Just more informed. So there!) My main complaint about the film version is that it alters the book's most important concepts.

In the movie, the Emerald City of Oz is literally green. Now, every reader of the book knows that (except for the walls and certain towers that could be seen from outside) nothing much in Oz was green. Both visitors to and citizens of Oz were all required to wear green spectacles ("Because if you did not wear spectacles, the brightness and glory of Oz would blind you," p. 117) so that everything would look green to them—this rather jaded deception being just another example of the Wizard's humbuggery. I can only guess that the film's producers felt that being faithful to the book would be—cinematically—too drab and difficult and therefore decided to exploit their expensive technicolor process rather than reinforce one of the major elements of the book.

Three Stalwarts into Three Stooges

Similarly, the movie does not do justice to the most important theme of the book. The whole point about the Scarecrow, the Tin Woodman, and the Cowardly Lion is that none of them is as brainless or heartless or cowardly as each—respectively—thinks he is. In the film, however, because there's a comic gold mine in screen cowardice, the fact that the Cowardly Lion is not actually cowardly is never made clear and is constantly undercut by some new outburst of fear from Bert Lahr.

The Tin Woodman is also given short shrift. Because of the exigencies of time (which is wasted on other things), his backstory is never told, and so the reason why he wants a heart remains a mystery to anyone who hasn't read the book. In the movie, the Tin Man (Jack Haley) comes off as some high-strung guy who's always crying and who seems like a dope because he wants a heart, when everybody knows that somebody smart would ask for money. (But then, he doesn't have the brains.)

The Unkindest Cut of All

The truth is that the Tin Woodman is not a dope. He used to be a flesh-and-blood man who had the misfortune to fall in love with a girl whose employer didn't want to lose her to any itinerant wood chopper. The employer made a deal with the Wicked Witch of the East, who kept enchanting the woodman's axe, which kept lopping off parts of his body—parts which a tinsmith replaced. Of course, when his torso was replaced, it didn't contain a heart; the woodman fell out of love with the girl and now needs a heart so that he can feel for her again. Therefore—although one may call it romantic—the Woodman's longing for a heart is a practical one. (I'll leave it to you, reader, to consider the sexual implications of his need to regain a vital organ.)

Though the Woodman cries a lot in the book, there are reasons for his tears.

A 1939 publicity photo of the main cast with the humbug wizard (Frank Moran) and dog Toto, in the middle of the shot.

At one point, he accidentally steps on a beetle—which greatly upsets him, so much so that he cries and rusts his jaw shut. (They must oil it.)

Thereafter he walked very carefully, with his eyes on the road, and when he saw a tiny ant toiling by, he would step over it, so as not to harm it. The Tin Woodman knew very well he had no heart, and therefore he took great care never to be cruel or unkind to anything.

"You people with hearts," he said, "have something to guide you, and need never do wrong; but I have no heart, and so I must be very careful. When Oz gives me a heart, of course, I needn't mind so much." (pp. 71-72)

This aspect of the Woodman's character (and Baum's sharp dig against human nature) is lost in the movie.

Straw Dog

The only character who comes close to his counterpart in the book is the Scarecrow (Ray Bolger). As in the novel, the movie shows that the brainless Scarecrow is smart nonetheless—he's always thinking up good ideas. However, some of the Scarecrow's positive characterization is achieved through the deprecation of his friends. The Scarecrow is always calm and rational when his companions are not—he is always in command of the situation (e.g., when things look desperate in the deadly poppy field, it is the Scarecrow who keeps his head and tells the despairing Woodman to stop crying before he rusts). The novel never builds up the Scarecrow at the expense of his comrades.

And this really irritates me about the movie: why should the Scarecrow be the most privileged character? In the film, when Dorothy is bidding a tearful goodbye to the trio, she tells the Scarecrow, "I think I'll miss you most of all." Why? What has he done to deserve this? Just because Dorothy has known him for a few hours longer than the others, there's no need for her to lavish such an inordinate amount of affection on him.

In the book, no one character out of the three is presented as more lovable than the others; each is equally nice, and Baum lets the reader choose his favorite. Apparently, the screenwriters preferred the Scarecrow, so they slighted the Lion and Woodman.

When I first saw *The The Wizard of Oz*, I was scandalized by the preferential treatment the Scarecrow received. I am not unbiased in this matter—I've always

The front and back cover of MGM's 1939 Campaign Book/Pressbook for *The Wizard of Oz*

liked the Tin Man. But that predilection doesn't invalidate my justifiable criticism of the film's strawman chauvinism.

And anyone who has ever favored the Lion or Tin Man should protest, too, for—imagine! —since 1939, at least four generations of children have grown up indoctrinated, with a falsely glorified image of the Scarecrow foisted upon them.

So, there!

There may be other, less egregious flaws in the film, but I think I have pointed out the worst of them. I'm of two minds about the movie's decision to have the Wizard provide the three comrades not with actual brains ("a measure of bran … mixed with a great many pins and needles" for "a lot of bran-new brains," p. 196), heart ("made entirely of silk and stuffed with sawdust," p. 197), and courage (the contents of a "square green bottle," which become courage once "you have swallowed it" because "courage is always inside one," p. 199). Instead, the movie's Wizard supplies them with testimonials or medals. But the Wizard's remarks about intelligence, heart, and courage represent some of the best writing in the film and improves upon the book.

The best are his words to the Tin Man: "As for you, my galvanized friend, you want a heart. You don't know how lucky you are not to have one. Hearts will never be practical until they can be made unbreakable." (Cf. the book: "I think you are wrong to want a heart. It makes most people unhappy. If you only knew it, you are in luck not to have a heart," p. 190) The Wizard continues: "A heart is not judged by how much you love; but by how much you are loved by others." (I admit it: not bad.)

Finally, don't take my word for it about the novel's superiority. Do me a favor: read the book for yourself before you watch the movie again; then—the next time you see Judy Garland and friends prancing down the yellow brick road—you'll see the potholes in that road, too.

CREDITS: An MGM film; 102 minutes; 1939. Producer: Mervyn Leroy; Director: Victor Fleming [and, uncredited, George Cukor, Mervyn LeRoy, Norman Taurog, Richard Thorpe, and King Vidor (Kansas sequences); Screenplay: Noel Langley, Florence Ryerson, and Edgar Allan Woolf (adaptation by Noel Langley), from the book by L. Frank Baum (IMDb lists 15 more uncredited writers, including actors Jack Haley and Bert Lahr for "additional dialogue"); Cinematographer: Harold Rossen; Editor: Blanche Sewell; Music: Harold Arlen (lyrics: E. Y. Harburg).
CAST: Judy Garland (Dorothy Gale); Frank Morgan (Professor Marvel/the The Wizard of Oz/the gatekeeper/the carriage driver/the guard); Ray Bolger ("Hunk"/the Scarecrow); Bert Lahr ("Zeke"/the Cowardly Lion); Jack Haley ("Hickory"/the Tin Man); Billie Burke (Glinda [the Good Witch of the North]); Margaret Hamilton (Miss Gulch/the Wicked Witch of the West); Charley Grapewine (Uncle Henry); Clara Blandick (Auntie Em); Terry (Toto); the Singer Midgets (the Munchkins).

A publicity shot of the Tin Man

HARRYHAUSEN IN ITALY
20 MILLION MILES TO EARTH
ON LOCATION

ARTICLE BY RAY AND GAIL ORWIG; CONTEMPORARY PHOTOS COURTESY OF PATRICK AND TINA FORD, CHAD FORRESTER, AND BONNIE NISHIHARA

Just off the coast of Sicily, the XY-21—the first U.S. spaceship to be sent to Venus—crashes in the Mediterranean on its return flight. Several small fishing boats in the area witness the crash, and one of the boats with two fishermen and a boy paddle over to the spaceship and rescue two men aboard the spaceship before it sinks (a third man was found dead).

Meanwhile, back in Washington DC, Dr. Uhl (John Zaremba) and Major General McIntosh (Thomas B. Henry) are glad to hear there are survivors and arrange to fly out to Italy. We find out that the local fishermen in the village of Gerra have been interviewed regarding the crash, and they speculate (for a ship that size) that there must have been more crew members to begin with than the three they saw (there were, but they died). The two rescued men, flight commander Col. Robert Calder (William Hopper) and Dr. Sharman (Arthur Space), are taken to the village hospital, but unfortunately Sharman succumbs to a Venusian disease. (Luckily, he hands over his notes to Calder before he dies). Calder is worried about a canister they had brought back with them: it contained an "unborn specimen"—an embryonic creature from Venus—and it was not known how long it could survive in Earth's atmosphere.

Unknown to Calder, the young local fisherboy on the boat that rescued him, Pepe (Bart Braverman) has found the canister and has removed its contents, wrapping the jellied specimen in a jacket. Pepe brings his find to local zoologist Dr. Leonardo (Frank Puglia). The Doctor has been procuring specimens of other local sea creatures from the entrepreneurial lad for small change. His interest piqued, Dr. Leonardo (like Pepe) can see something encased in the gelatinous material. Pepe hastily retreats to the village.

From here, things start moving quickly: an exquisite reptilian creature (that *we* come to know as an Ymir, but not called that in the film) hatches from the embryo in the gelatin. Dr. Leonardo is fascinated and sees that the creature isn't like anything he has ever studied before. He must find Pepe and get more details regarding the specimen. Meanwhile, Leonardo puts the creature in a cage—and by the next morning it has grown two feet in length.

Dr. Uhl and General MacIntosh finally make it to the village, and they meet up with Calder and Commissario Charra (Tito Vuolo) from the Italian government. During the briefing, the missing canister is again mentioned. It is hoped it didn't go down with the XY-21 and that it will eventually float to shore. When the local fishermen are again queried regarding the canister, cagey Pepe reveals that he has found the precious cargo, and—for a price—tells the authorities that the specimen is now in the hands of Dr. Leonardo and his granddaughter Marisa (Joan Taylor), and they are on their way to Rome via caravan, with the Ymir in tow. Calder has previously met Marisa at the village hospital when she helped to care for him (Marisa is in her third year studying medicine). Now Calder is dispatched to Rome to find the pair.

Unfortunately, Dr. Leonardo's cage will no longer hold the growing Ymir. When Leonardo stops to secure a loose rope on the cage, the Ymir (who has grown to the size of a man) breaks free. During its escape, Marisa is slightly injured. Calder catches up to the pair and finds out the Ymir has bolted.

On the trail of the Ymir, the three find out two things: the creature eats sulfur (the Ymir, being peckish after his escape, makes a sulfur discovery in a local barn, where the farmer housed bags of the stuff for fertilizing crops).

And the Ymir continues to rapidly grow larger. Calder, Dr. Leonardo, and Marisa must catch up with the Ymir—and soon!

LOCATIONS

Many scenes for *20 Million Miles to Earth* were shot on location in both California and Italy. Opening scenes were shot in Sperlonga, Italy.

To reach Sperlonga: Take SS7 out of Rome heading southeast. After you pass La Casina near the coast, look for SR213, and continue east. Look for a roundabout and Via Canzatora, then Via Cristoforo Colombo; this should take you into town and the beach.

PHOTOGRAPHIC LOCATIONS

LEFT: The fisherman on the beach at Sperlonga. RIGHT: Same view from the beach today. Many building survived from 1957.

The next part of the film takes place at Iverson Ranch in Chatsworth, California. To get to Iverson Ranch you need to take the Ronald Reagan Freeway (Highway 118) and take Topanga Canyon Blvd. South (exit 34). Follow Topanga Canyon Blvd. until you reach Santa Susana Pass Road. Turn right onto Santa Susana Pass Road and go west. When you reach Redmesa Rd., turn right and head uphill. The names for the rock formations at Iverson Ranch come from a website:
http://iversonmovieranch.blogspot.com

The creator of the blog knows the rock formations very well. He has named them for ease of keeping track of everything on site. We use the same names.

LEFT: The Ymir looks to hide in "Zorro's Cave." RIGHT: "Zorro's Cave" as it appears today. To reach this location you need to climb uphill from the end of Sun Ranch Ct. The court is at the end of Sierra Pass Pl., the first right you can make off Redmesa Rd. This site may no longer be accessible.

LEFT: The police try to chase down the Ymir around "Crown Rock." RIGHT: What remains of "Crown Rock" today. You can stop here on your way to "Zorro's Cave." After you turn right onto Sierra Pass Place, go past the second condo on your left. The rock formation is between the second and third condos.

Then we go back to Italy (specifically, Rome).

The Ymir is captured and transferred to the zoo in Rome (Bioparco di Roma). But that does not go well. He escapes and we now get a "Where Monsters Walked" excursion of major tourist sites in Rome.

LEFT: The Ymir battles an elephant as they move through the entrance to the zoo. RIGHT: The entrance as it appears today, virtually unchanged from 1957. The zoo is one of many upcoming sites that are almost literally in the center of the city. It is found between the V. le del Giardino Zoologico and the Via Ulisse Aldrovandi.

LEFT: They continue their fight in front of the Borghese Gallery and Museum. RIGHT: The Gallery and Museum today. As you exit the zoo, head southeast down the Viale dell'Uccelliera toward the Gallery. Colonel Calder drove down this road, which is not open to auto traffic these days. The fight finally ends after they go under the aqueduct. Ymir-1, elephant-0. Now the Ymir takes a quick stroll through the backlot of Columbia Studios in Burbank, California before jumping into the Tyber River. Col. Calder finds another phone booth to report the situation (the army then throws a few dozen hand grenades into the river).

LEFT: The Ymir finally comes up for air (or whatever) next to the Ponte Sant' Angelo. RIGHT: This is the same bridge today. You must be facing west to get this view.

The bridge and Castel Sant' Angelo are just a short walk west of Vatican City. The Ymir gets downright antisocial and punches a hole in the Pont Sant' Angelo (the castle is viewed in the background.) The emperor Hadrian built this bridge in 134 AD; he would be really upset!

Our next stop will be the Roman Forum. The Ymir strolls a quick two miles from the Castel to this next location.

LEFT: The Ymir confronts a squad of soldiers at the Roman Forum. RIGHT: The Forum ruins as they appear now, looking no worse for the wear. Continuing through a treasure trove of ancient ruins, the Ymir now makes his final stand at the Roman Coliseum.

LEFT: Soldiers prepare for the final battle against their Venusian foe. RIGHT: Look for the notch on the side opposite of the Piazza del Colosseo (northwest side).

The outcome: sadly, soldiers-1, Ymir-0

NOTES:

Ray Harryhausen related lots of interesting information regarding the production of *20 Million Miles to Earth* in his book, *Ray Harryhausen—An Animated Life* (Aurum Press, 2003), which he co-wrote with Tony Dalton. Harryhausen formulated his ideas for a possible story treatment for producer Charles Schneer, while they were working together on *Earth vs. the Flying Saucers* (1956). Schneer liked the premise: screenwriters Bob Williams and Chris Knopf fleshed out the outline, but Harryhausen didn't get any story credit for his part in the development. Ray said he and Schneer only disagreed on one point: Schneer wanted the film to be in color, and Ray preferred black-and-white: Harryhausen won—but a colorized version came out on DVD for the 50th Anniversary in 2007, and Harryhausen did give it his blessing.

As far as the Ymir design goes, Harryhausen wanted the creature to be humanoid "because I wanted audiences to sympathize with it, and you can't do that if it is totally alien." Three models were eventually made (their use depending on the scene) and Ray's Dad was pressed into service to build the armatures. Harryhausen's rocket design (for the spacecraft in the film's beginning scenes) was an amalgam of a WWII Nazi V2 Rocket, an early design of a NASA rocket, and other rockets as seen in popular culture at the time.

Ray Harryhausen's early story outline included scenes to be shot in California, but he also wanted to take a European vacation (he'd never been) and his fifth treatment included locations in Italy. He really looked forward to scouting out these locations and the shooting of parts of the film there. And (of course) the film became a fan favorite.

20 Million Miles to Earth (Columbia, 1957): Directed by Nathan Juran; Produced by Charles Schneer. Music: Mischa Bakaleinikoff. Starring William Hopper, Joan Taylor, Frank Puglia, John Zaremba, Thomas Browne Henry, Tito Vuolo, Jan Arvan, Arthur Space, and Bart Braverman.

On Sunday February 16, 1964, I attended the ABC cinema in Falmouth where an enticing double "X" bill comprising *Terror in the Midnight Sun* and *Lust of the Vampire* (the British title for Riccardo Freda's *I Vampiri*) was the presentation. Almost a year later, on Thursday January 21, 1965, *Invasion of the Animal People* was being shown at The Cameo, South Roskear, teamed with Lon Chaney, Jr.'s ever-popular *Indestructible Man*. Both were rated "X." A little way into *Animal People*, I thought, "Hang on a minute. Haven't I seen this before?" Well yes, I had, in February of the previous year. But that had been the Swedish uncut original, and much to my surprise, I thoroughly enjoyed it. Today, we had the Jerry Warren Americanized version, chopped up and sliced-and-diced for public consumption (but not for those discerning fans!), a real hatchet job to rival Kenneth G. Crane's mutilation of Toho's *Half Human* and Jerry A. Baerwitz's similar desecration of the same company's *Varan the Unbelievable* (the author details both versions of these movies in *Atomic Age Cinema* [Midnight Marquee Press, 2014]). Warren's U.S. edit was a 55-minute stinker of the first order, leading to restless bums on seats, whether it was an "X" or not. American John Carradine, who had appeared in the butchered *Half Human*, was brought in by Warren to star as the principal narrator, mainly because the cheapo film producer/director apparently despised (or couldn't afford) dubbing foreign actors' speech, even though in this case, the Swedish cast all spoke perfect English! In retrospect, Warren's ham-fisted tampering has given *Midnight Sun* a bit of a bad press over the years, and an unfair one at that; being a relative sci-fi obscurity doesn't help its cause, either.

However, we jump the gun a bit. Let's have an in-depth look at the original 73-minute cut of Sweden's one-and-only (for the period: copyright 1958, released August 1959) sci-fi/monster movie and see how it bears up to the American bastardization, and whether, like all classic and semi-classic fodder from those far-off exciting cinematic days, the picture has stood the test of time. We're not talking *Horror in the Midnight Sun* here (some reviewers mistakenly refer to the film under this title), or a mix of the Swedish print *Space Invasion of Lapland* (*Rymdinvasion i Lappland*), and the Jerry Warren travesty (again, many buffs trip over themselves when it comes to forming an opinion or describing the film as it *should* be)—we're talking *Terror in the Midnight Sun*, directed by Virgil W. Vogel (*The Mole People*; *The Land Unknown*), the bona fide Swedish version released by AB Fortuna Film/Gustaf Unger Productions as I caught it way back in 1964, unedited, and featuring, for its day, a *very* risqué nude scene!

It's winter in Sweden. The movie's main credits appear after a crystal-like glowing globe has materialized out of the night sky, accompanied by an unearthly whistling sound, scaring Laplanders trekking over the snowfields, plowing through a snow-laden valley floor, and coming to an abrupt halt at the base of a cliff (Universal's *It Came from Outer Space* was the inspiration behind this effective scene). The credits are backed by a mournful song, "Midnight Sun Lament," based on an old Swedish folk melody ("Värmlandsvisan") with lyrics written by Gustaf Unger (English lyrics by Frederick Herbert), performed by The Golden Gate Quartet. A manned weather station transmits the news of the other-worldly visitor to Stockholm, where newspaper headlines proclaim, "Meteor Lands in Lapland." At the Royal Academy of Science, scientists

Two foreign posters from *Terror in the Midnight Sun*

Poster for Jerry Warren's recut/re-edited American version

Robert Burton (Dr. Frederick Wilson), Aka Grönberg (Dr. Henrik), and Gösta Prüzelius (Dr. Walter Ullman) are puzzling over pictures of deep parallel ruts left by the inexplicable object ("It left skid marks on contact."), when they are joined by a womanizing geologist, played by Swedish heartthrob actor Stan Gester (Erik Engström), complete with lipstick smudges over his face, a sign of his latest conquest. Could magnetic attraction (not Gester's magnetic attraction!) from rich mineral deposits in the mountainous region have forced the "meteor" to land? Flying out to a village, the party meets a Laplander who states that reindeer have been killed by "a fireball as big as a mountain" before taking the plane over rugged terrain to the site accompanied by Bengt Blomgren (Colonel Robert Bottiger) and a few soldiers. On the 13th minute, they spot the object buried in a crater at the end of a wide shallow valley floor. Even this early in the proceedings, cinematographer Hilding Bladh's stark black-and-white footage of the sweeping Lapland snowscapes (shooting took place in Lapland, Northern Sweden, above the Arctic circle) imbues the atmosphere with an air of mystery and foreboding, no bad thing in a modest production such as this. One minute later, sexy brunette Barbara Wilson (Diane Wilson), Burton's niece, shows off her Olympic skating skills to a small group of admirers including Gester who mutters, "Now there's championship form—with or without skates!" "That lad has left a string of broken hearts all over Europe," warns Burton to Wilson, which only inflames her curiosity (and desire) for the handsome geologist even more. At 16:48 we get that much-vaunted nude scene: Wilson strips off, back to camera, and steps into the shower stark naked, full frontal, the shower curtains allowing us a clear glimpse of her curvaceous body. Fifty-five seconds of pure titillation, extremely daring for the time it was made, guaranteeing, in Britain at least, the prohibitive "X" certification. No wonder any underage schoolkids who had sneaked in to see the flick probably thought, "Blimey. So, *this* is what women look like without any clothes on!"

Matters then calm down (and needed to!): Gester and Wilson flirt ("Some of us like wolves," she smiles coyly at Gester) and go skiing, have a drink, attend a dinner party, dance to a band playing the film's main title theme, and afterwards drive out to a remote location with the scientists and the Colonel where numerous reindeer have been slaughtered, their bodies mutilated and violently ripped apart. Vogel then ups the pace, jettisoning the Gester/Wilson romantic angle (we all know she's going to fall between the sheets with the good-looker eventually): Wilson sees huge footsteps in the snow, made by a creature "20 feet tall." Studying more photos of the crater, the scientists are convinced that the so-called meteor landed on purpose so the next day the group fly out to the site a second time, troop through the snow, and arrive above the globular object (33:46). Using a rope ladder, they descend to investigate, monitored by several hairless aliens inside the partly buried ship. "Colonel, we are standing before some kind of craft from

John Carradine was edited into the American Jerry Warren version.

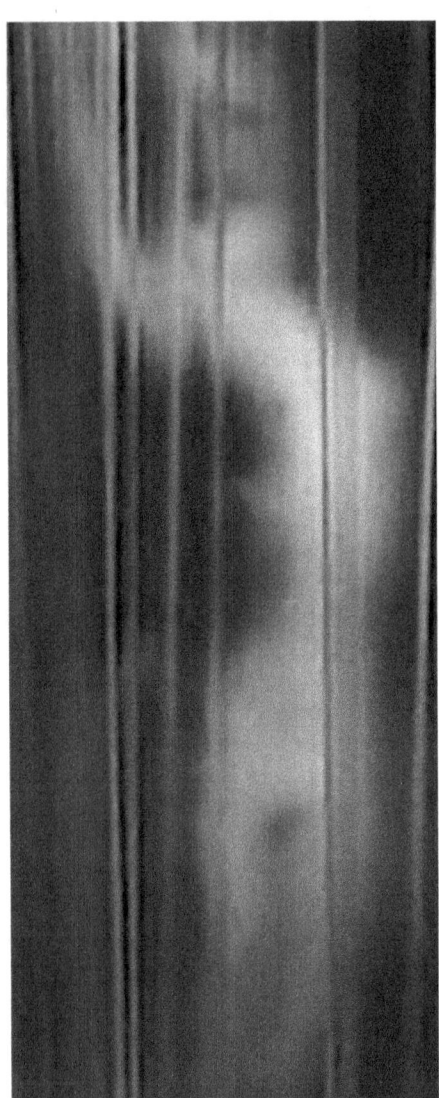

Behind the shower curtain occurs the infamous nude scene of Barbara Wilson.

outer space," announces Burton. Lights inside the ship begin flashing on and off, and the nervous team beats a hasty retreat. Back at the plane, the solitary guard shoots at something very big and is later found dead under the wrecked aircraft, those odd footprints are imprinted in the snow. Wilson and Gester decide to ski to the nearest village for assistance; she takes a tumble against a tree and twists her knee while, back at the crater, Grönberg, retrieving some equipment, notes that the craft is radioactive. Descending into the crater, he runs the Geiger counter over the vessel's surface, becomes alarmed at the sight of shadowy figures inside the globe, climbs the ladder, and is hit by a ray (or flash of light), falling backwards to his death.

Gester and Wilson chance upon a rescue cabin where she discards her damp clothes (her alluring shadow is cast on the cabin wall; this is one girl who loves to flaunt her goods!) and wears only a wraparound towel, while Gester places a compress on her swollen right knee, trying his hardest to avert his eyes from her ample thighs, the lass grinning in undisguised glee at his discomfort. "Couldn't the creature be one of their animals?" Gester muses. He then decides to leave for town and get help: alone. Wilson hears disturbing noises outside, goes to look through an open window, and at 49:38, we finally get to see what's behind all the occurring mayhem, a giant shaggy growling Yeti-type monster sporting two upward-curved tusks set in powerful jaws, massive double claws for hands, and of course those padded feet. Gester hears her screams and returns to the cabin in a hurry, just in time to behold the monster, shambling up an ice ridge and appearing rather lost, creating an avalanche that smashes the cabin to matchwood. The geologist is struck on the head by a falling beam while Wilson, exiting the cabin, watches the creature lurching toward the wreckage and, frightened, runs off (with that damaged knee?); Gester regains consciousness in a howling blizzard, collapsing by a pole in the snow. In the morning, the hairy giant appears above her (Vogel shoots most of the monster action from ground level, accentuating the beast's height); there's a brief interlude depicting the Laplanders in their fancy costumes before the alien beast, carrying Wilson in its arms, places her beside an ice cave near the spaceship. A metallic voice is heard (the aliens never speak) and Wilson, now awake, is confronted by the pasty-faced humanoid beings from another world, dressed from head to toe in black, who are attempting to communicate with her by telepathy. All this does is to make her faint.

At 58:12, we are treated to over three minutes of splendid monster-on-the-loose destruction: The woolly biped, on a rampage attacks a Sami village, demolishing two huts, hurling the roofs at the plane, and smashing down tepees which burst into flames; it's noted that the beast carries Wilson's scarf in its claws. Come night (although the sun is still out, this being the land of the midnight sun), the Laplanders, armed with torches (much like the villagers in the old Universal *Frankenstein* pictures), pursue the monster across the frozen wastes. Wilson awakes to see the creature hovering over her; the thing again carries her away, but with a certain degree of gentleness; is it being mind-controlled by its masters in the ship? Lumbering along the edge of a snow cliff, the animal carefully places her down, as the villagers toss their flaming torches at it; its dense fur catches fire and the monster goes up in a fiery blaze, toppling into the crater beside the ship, viewed by the aliens on their screens. The craft then takes off towards the heavens, a bemused Burton wondering, "… if they found out what they wanted to know." "Well," he adds, "Let's hope for better luck when we set foot on some other world." The final shot is of Gester and Wilson wandering

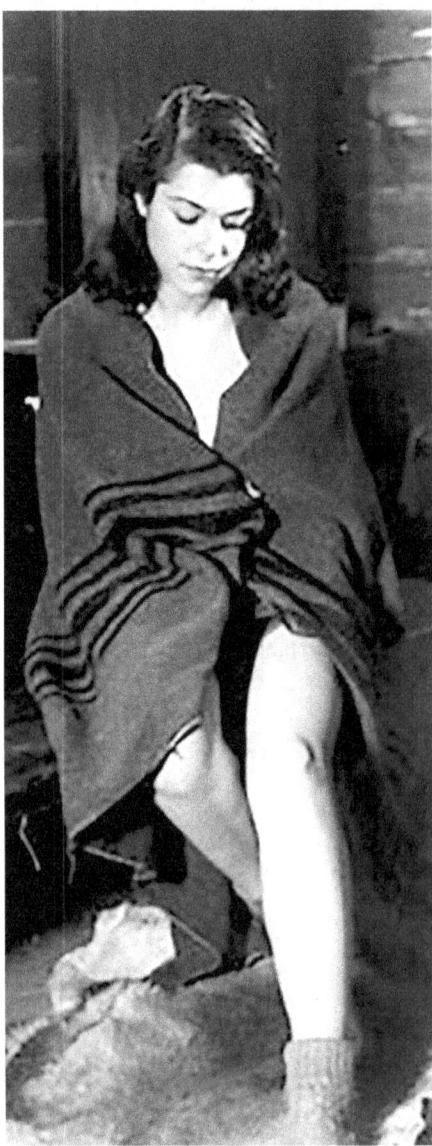

Wilson, in a wrap-around towel, is about to have a compress applied to her right knee.

The Yeti attacks the cabin.

off arm-in-arm toward the midnight sun, no doubt to locate a cosy cabin in which to consummate their relationship!

All-in-all, *Terror in the Midnight Sun* is no better or worse than much of the sci-fi/monster fare emanating from America during the 1950s. In fact, it's a sight classier than *Phantom from Space*, *Robot Monster*, *Killers from Space*, *The Astounding She-Monster*, *The Cosmic Man*, *Plan 9 from Outer Space*, and others of their grade Z ilk, including Jerry Warren's tatty output (more on Warren in a minute). Full marks to special effects supervisor Odert von Schoultz for conjuring up a believable spaceship and a beguiling big dumb scowling monster: the icy landscapes are at least different, Vogel directs with panache, Harry Arnold and Allan Johansson provide a quirky score, Arthur C. Pierce's screenplay commendably steers clear of sci-fi clichés, the aliens are creepy, and Wilson is darkly and seductively attractive. Okay, there are questions to be answered: the ending is enigmatic, the spaceship zooming off as quickly as it had arrived; why did the extra-terrestrials come to Earth anyway and what did they hope to achieve? And was their gigantic "pet" some kind of hunter-gatherer? Did it escape, or was it let loose with the intention of simply panicking the local populace? But, overall, Sweden's spiffy little gem, made on a $40,000 budget, has a lot going for it—the movie certainly didn't deserve the shoddy treatment meted out by Jerry Warren when co-producer Gustaf Unger sold the rights to Warren for American distribution in 1962, claiming Paramount might be interested, and (according to producer Bertil Jernberg) high-tailed it with the money made on the deal.

After Warren got his hands on the film, he restructured it, changed the title, and released the finished product (*his* finished product) in 1962, paired with his own 1962 effort *Terror of the Blood Hunters*. The producer/director cut 28 minutes from *Terror in the Midnight Sun*'s 73-minute running time and added 10 minutes of his own footage, shot in the States, to concoct a 55-minute version that bore little resemblance to the original; he even had the gall to award himself a co-director's credit alongside Virgil Vogel! Gone was the lovely title music over the credits. We now have John Carradine in the opening minutes sitting at a desk spouting all things scientific, strange phenomena, the great mysteries, the cosmos, the planets, and so on. Fair enough, Carradine's fine in the role, a figure of authority, and his name (at that period) was a box-office draw with buffs, but what's he doing in this picture? Then we had the "new" scenario showing a traumatized Barbara Wilson escaping from a sanatorium in her nightdress, a circular light in the sky (a UFO?), and a high-pitched, ear-splitting sound; she runs in terror down a dark street and is picked up by the police, the chief cop ringing a psychiatrist. "She's mentally ill," narrates Carradine, the girl "seized by a mystery force." "Is there a link between the sky object and the girl?" state the newspapers. Wilson then quickly recovers from her catatonic state, leaves the hospital, and goes to Switzerland (not Sweden), and it's somewhere around this point that the genuine article kicks in, scientists convening in Stockholm to discuss the meteor/spaceship that has landed in Lapland.

But Warren clumsily opted to pick and choose what sequences to use (and what *not* to use) from *Terror*, leading to a disjointed feel hindered by moments of silence, then Carradine's expository narration, then actors' speaking the dialogue muffled and occasionally out-of-sync. As an example of scenes juggled haphazardly around: the first entrance of the monster is of the beast walking slowly towards Wilson (but you don't see her lying in the snow), *not* Wilson observing the monster through the cabin window, as in the original. And when the scientists first fly over the crash site, you don't see them peering down at the craft, a soldier filming it; Warren intercuts with Wilson skating on the ice, a lousy piece of editing in anyone's book. At least half-a-dozen scenes are repeated twice (particularly the inside aircraft shots, the skiing incidents,

The Yeti hovers over a cabin.

the plane taking off, the Laplanders going about their business, and aerial views of the wild landscapes), some are out-of-order (but you would only really notice this if you had sat through the original), Wilson's nude frolic is regrettably missing (blame it on the U.S. censors, a rare case of the States being stricter than the British censor's office), as are many of her amusing flirtatious spats with female-hungry Gester, two men crop up, ham radio operators trying to contact Lapland, and are never seen again, and the print has lost its pristine sheen, looking grainy, ragged, and messed-around with, as it most certainly was!

However, horror of horrors, *Invasion of the Animal People* was, at 55 minutes, deemed too short for U.S. television viewing (as far as I am aware, it's never been screened on British TV in my area), so Warren padded the narrative by adding another 25 minutes, thus increasing the running time to 80 minutes, the major additional sequences being: (a) at eight minutes in, a doctor is talking to Wilson's mother, played by Katherine Victor, about her daughter's mental state. Another doctor enters the room to yap on about flying saucers, and a *third* doctor appears clutching a human skull, lecturing to all and sundry about the complexities of the ear and surgery. Unfortunately, there's nine minutes of this incomprehensible stuff to contend with. As if that isn't bad enough, (b) three men are introduced, at 48:32, babbling on about losing contact with Lapland, even when looking at the large wall map, they're pointing at Greenland; there's a two-minute pause, then they reappear again for a few more minutes; they disappear and return for a third time, the monster looming above their shack, but *not their* shack—it's the rescue cabin from the original, which turns up at 56:20. Even more scenes have been introduced twice (and thrice!) and the continuity, when compared to the original, is all over the place. *Terror* is there, all right, but buried under layers of Warren's interference and ineptitude, unrecognizable for what it once was. This 80-minute edit is a crazy patchwork of the original Swedish picture, the U.S. theatrical release, and the television syndicated release which will even have seasoned lovers of grade Z schlock scratching their heads in total bewilderment.

Warren's intervention and his unskilled re-editing of *Terror in the Midnight Sun* turned a decent little sci-fi/monster movie into something excruciatingly awful, an absolute chore to sit through. In England, although I caught *Invasion of the Animal People* with *Indestructible Man*, it played elsewhere with another Warren stinker, *The Incredible Petrified World*. I thank the Lord above that I missed out on this double bill—two Jerry Warren features (well, *Invasion* wasn't strictly his, was it?) would test the patience and endurance of even the most hardened fan. As it stands, avoid, at all costs, both cuts of Warren's *Invasion of the Animal People*; the Swedish *Terror in the Midnight Sun* remains a highly satisfying (and quite unusual) slice of late '50s monster fodder with the additional bonus of a very juicy nude scene! How many films of this genre, produced over 60 years ago, can boast *that* in their repertoire!

The two alien visitors

A DOUBLE BILL OF TELEPORTATION TERRORS!

CURSE OF THE FLY AND THE PROJECTED MAN

BY BARRY ATKINSON

Two movies released in the mid-1960s, *Curse of the Fly* and *The Projected Man*, proved conclusively that if scientists persisted in playing God by experimenting in transporting matter from A to B via the fourth dimension, whatever the distance involved, they were asking for trouble, big time! To begin with, we go back to July 1958 when 20th Century Fox's *The Fly*, produced on a $400,000 budget, was released, becoming one of the decade's top-grossing horror hits, racking up nearly $4,000,000 worldwide. Soon-to-be top horror actor Vincent Price was in it, on the side of good this time, and the unmasking of David Hedison, revealing his freakish fly-features, caused English females to faint in droves, as had similar scenes in *House of Wax*, *The Quatermass Experiment*, *The Curse of Frankenstein* and [*Horror of*] *Dracula*. A year later, *Return of the Fly* hit the screens, in CinemaScope and again starring Price, but not as in the previous film, in color, and it was not quite the success of Kurt Neumann's classic. But ironically, *Return of the Fly* was the most-seen out of the two in the United Kingdom, a profitable screening on the Sunday one-day circuit where it could be found sharing the bill with Fox's *The Alligator People*, also in CinemaScope and black and white. Two first-rate X-certified horror movies shown in widescreen was a big draw for buffs of that period (I caught this double bill in a packed house in June 1964), representing outstanding value for the price of a three-shilling ticket, value that, unfortunately, is totally missing from today's sanitized and costly trip to the cinema.

Adapted from George Langelaan's 1957 short story published, of all places, in *Playboy* magazine, the *Fly* movies were based on scientists and physicists teleporting matter, human and otherwise, from one machine to another and the inherent problems in doing so—if something else inadvertently entered the transmitter pod with a human being (such as a common housefly), a person's molecular structure would be altered and the atoms mixed up, with hideous consequences. It was this still saleable idea that prompted Robert L. Lippert, boss of Fox subsidiary outfit Regal Pictures, to consider a third chapter in the *Fly* franchise in 1965, six years after *Return of*. Lippert was ensconced in the United Kingdom, taking advantage of 1949's Eady Levy, a government tax on British box-office receipts, introduced to assist producers of modest-budget films to get their pet projects off the ground; the American was busy producing a string of medium-budget horror movies (*The Cabinet of Caligari*; *The Last Man on Earth*; *Witchcraft*; *The Earth Dies Screaming*) to foist onto the British circuits. He wanted to make a third *Fly* movie, reckoning there

A studio publicity shot of Brian Donlevy from *Curse of the Fly*

was further mileage in the scenario, and told screenwriter Harry Spalding to handle the script, even though Spalding was hesitant in taking it on. Don Sharp was hired as director, the budget was set at $90,000 (as were Lippert's other British productions), Jack Parsons co-produced, and Brian Donlevy was brought in as the main lead, Lippert reasoning that Donlevy's association with Hammer's *The Quatermass Experiment* and *Quatermass 2* would boost box-office takings. Spalding later claimed that Donlevy was the wrong choice (he thought a Claude Rains-type actor would have been ideal), even though Lippert disagreed, and this in turn affected Sharp's confidence in the material. But, on the positive side, the movie would be shot in CinemaScope and the music supplied by Bert Shefter who, alongside composing partner Paul Sawtell, had provided some stirring scores for many a horror/sci-fi outing, most notably *It! The Terror from Beyond Space*, *Kronos*, and *The Lost World*. Strands from the first two *Fly* pictures would be included in the narra-

Henri Delambre (Brian Donlevy) and Martin Delambre (George Baker)

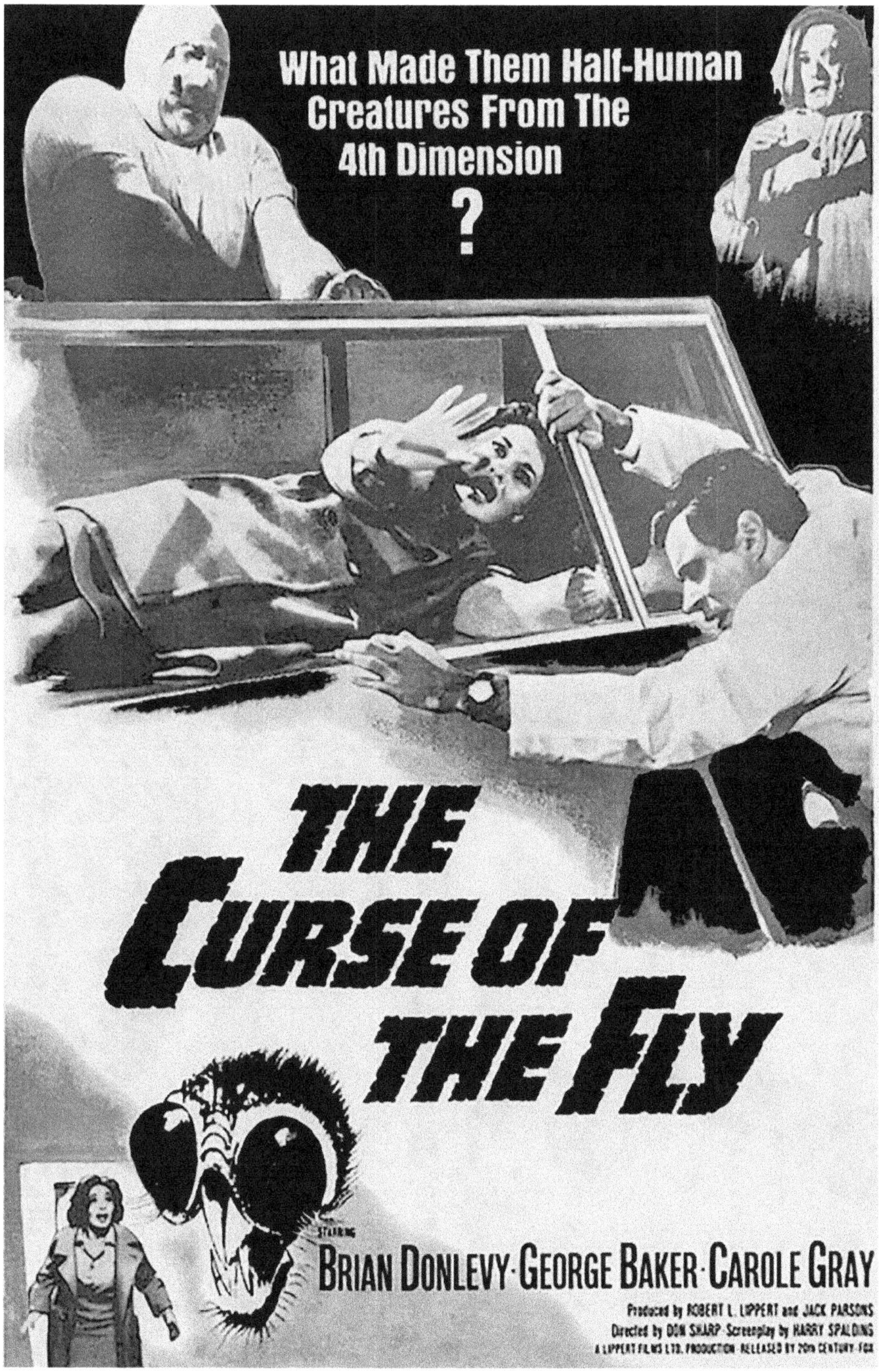

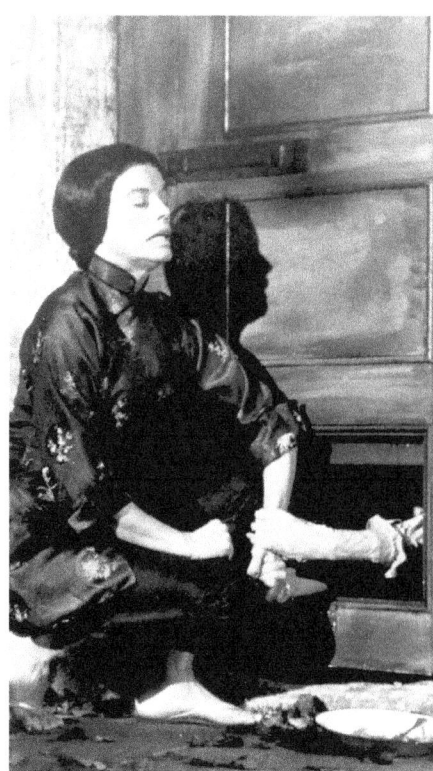

The Chinese housekeeper Yvette Rees is grabbed by the arm by one of the teleporation mutants behind the door.

tive, as would references to the Delambre family, but the film would not be a direct follow-up to the 1958 and 1959 movies and, more importantly, there would be no fly-monster in it. The production would also be shot in England, not Canada, where the story takes place. Did the end product work? Let's find out.

First and foremost, Bert Shefter's rich title music, played by the New Philharmonia London Orchestra, belongs to movies of a far higher caliber than this one, but if it was the wish of the producers to have a lush soundtrack running through the action, so be it. Following the credits, glass cascades from a window in slow motion as Carole Gray (Patricia Stanley), attired only in bra and panties, escapes from the Fournier Mental Hospital at night, negotiates the gates, flees through dark woods, and encounters George Baker (Martin Delambre, the grandson of André Delambre in *The Fly*) out on the open road (Sharp later said that he rated this opening sequence as one of his best pieces of work). He's driving from Quebec to Montreal on business. Taking a shine to the girl, he takes her to Montreal, puts her into an hotel room, and gives her money to buy some clothes. She has no friends, no family, and no job, she tells her benefactor. At Baker's plush residence, assistant Bert Kwouk (Tai) is telephoning Michael Graham (Albert Delambre, the second grandson) in London, informing him of the imminent arrival of new equipment, prompting director Sharp to quickly cut to London where, in his lab, irascible Brian Donlevy (Henri Delambre) is resting on a bed, his bandaged torso hiding gruesome radiation burns, the result of too much teleportation. It's made quite obvious that Graham has a different, and rather low opinion of his father's experiments and ethics in teleportation, because major slip-ups have been made, resulting in a string of "mistakes." "Three generations of Delambres have devoted their lives to this work ... the teleporter will replace every known means of transportation," barks Donlevy. "What about the failures?" asks his son. "No greater advance was ever made without sacrifice," is Donlevy's blunt response. He's then teleported to Quebec (the authorities are on his tail because he hasn't a passport) to find out how Baker is getting along with the fresh equipment.

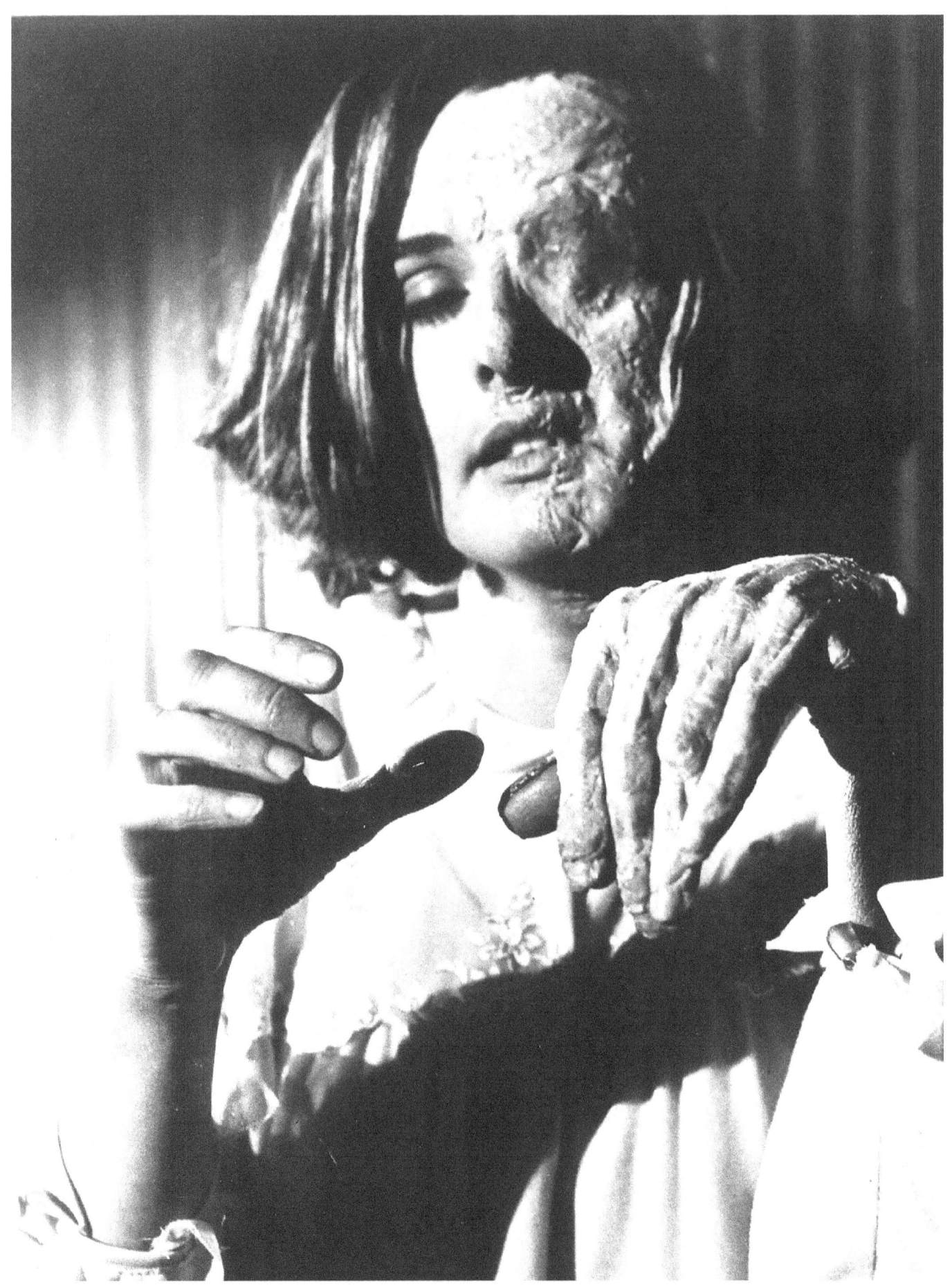

The mutant woman, Judith, (Mary Manson) stalks the mansion playing piano.

In Montreal, Baker and Gray impulsively get married after a seven-day whirlwind courtship, neither of them knowing much about the other, and it's just as well she has little inkling about what her new husband is up to. Feeling unwell, he retires to his room and collapses on his bed, his hands horribly swollen and wrinkled, his face aging rapidly, the recessive fly genes in his body causing periodic reactions that require injections of serum to straighten him out. In the morning, he's back to normal; they decide to motor back to his country manor in Quebec. Meanwhile, cop Jeremy Wilkins (Inspector Ronet) is questioning the mistress of the asylum, Rachel Kempson (Madame Fournier), over the disappearance of her inmate. Apparently, she was a promising concert pianist who suffered a nervous breakdown after the death of her mother. We then switch to Baker's Gothic stately home (Old Manor Lodge, in Shepperton, was the location) where Baker introduces Gray to Donlevy (his father), the domineering scientist seeming a touch perturbed over the new addition to his family. Baker claims to his new bride that animals form the basis of their experimentations, not humans, a direct lie to stop her from being over-inquisitive about his activities.

Curse of the Fly is a well-constructed mix of suspense, romantic tragedy, mystery, and science gone wrong, blessed with diamond-hard black-and-white photography and artful lighting courtesy of Basil Emmott, Shefter's beautiful score, Spalding's intelligent screenplay, Sharp's professional roving camerawork, and believable acting from all concerned. These elements all gel perfectly a third of the way into the picture, viewers intrigued as to what lies beyond those four wooden doors in the garden. Who is the oft-

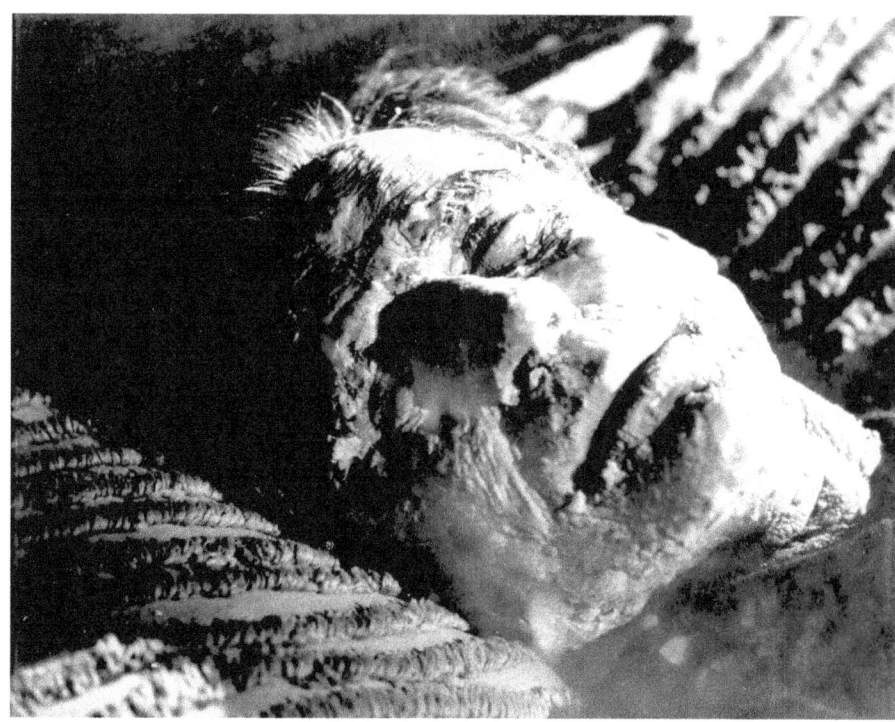

Martin Delambre suffers terrible radiation burns from too much teleportation.

mentioned "Judith" and why does shifty Chinese housekeeper Yvette Rees (Wan) hold her close to her heart, at the expense of Gray's fragile mental state? Will snooping Wilkins gain any further information about the Delambre family from his former boss, Charles Carson (Inspector Charas), now hospitalized? (At one point, Carson relates the story from the first *Fly* movie but the photo he shows Wilkins is of the monster from *Return of the Fly*); and will Baker and Donlevy's experiments in teleportation succeed? "Well, travel is so much quicker these days. One can get anyplace almost in a flash," grins Donlevy to Gray to her enquiry over the short time it took him to journey from London to Quebec. Gray expertly tickles the ivories, creating a lovely melody on the piano, and investigates those mysterious doors, screaming in terror as a disfigured face stares back at her, Baker letting on about the mutants, the experiments that went wrong. She then hears the piano being played off-key during the night. In a chilling sequence, she slowly goes downstairs, enters the room, and sees Mary Manson (Judith) sitting at the keys, the left side of her body—face, hand, and foot—deformed. Rees grabs Gray from behind and she faints. Next morning, accused of having a nightmare, Gray yells at Baker, "I did see it. You're lying. She (Rees) was there—with that thing!"

Carole Gray appears to be stuck in the teleporation chamber, while George Baker helps her.

Matters escalate, the Delambres, exhibiting a combination of madness and guile, producing a wedding certificate to Wilkins and Kempson as proof that Baker and Gray are indeed married, and then deciding to teleport the evidence of their "failures" to London, much to Graham's disgust. A couple of the insane mutants, Samuels and Dill, are taken out of their cages, drugged and sent to London ("Reintegrate and dispose of them," Donlevy orders his son), where they materialize, transformed into one writhing inhuman ghastly mass; Graham, appalled, taking an axe to this monstrosity, "We're scientists. We have to do things we hate and even sicken us," moans Donlevy to Baker, who spills the beans to his wife about his *former* wife. "You did see her (Judith). She's one of our experiments that went wrong. It isn't animals—it's people. This machine could be a great and wonderful gift," he adds as a form of moral compensation for all his lies.

The frenetic climax has loony homicidal Manson breaking loose from her cage, and Kwouk killing the woman with a blow from a hefty spanner after she has stalked Gray through the house. The Chinese couple place Manson's body in the teleportation machine and send her into the ether, afterwards driving off in panic. Wilkins, search warrant in hand, drives up, determined to sort things out. In Baker's spartan lab, Baker phones his brother in London to tell him that his father is being teleported ("You've got to save your father!"). Too late! Donlevy climbs into the transporter machine, dons goggles, there's a blinding light, and he's gone—but where? In London, Graham, distraught and revolted at the mutated mess in the machine, has wrecked the equipment beyond repair, meaning that in the fourth dimension, a meld of Donlevy and Manson hovers for all eternity, something too terrible to contemplate. No happy ending here either for the newlyweds: Baker drags Gray outside, convulses in pain, and tumbles into his car, turning old and wizened by the second, Gray screaming in revulsion. Wilkins runs up and stares at a hollow, ghostly dusty skull in the driver's seat, leading Gray away from the Delambre house of horrors.

In America, *Curse of the Fly* was released in May 1965, paired with Planet's limp vampire opus, *Devils of Darkness*.

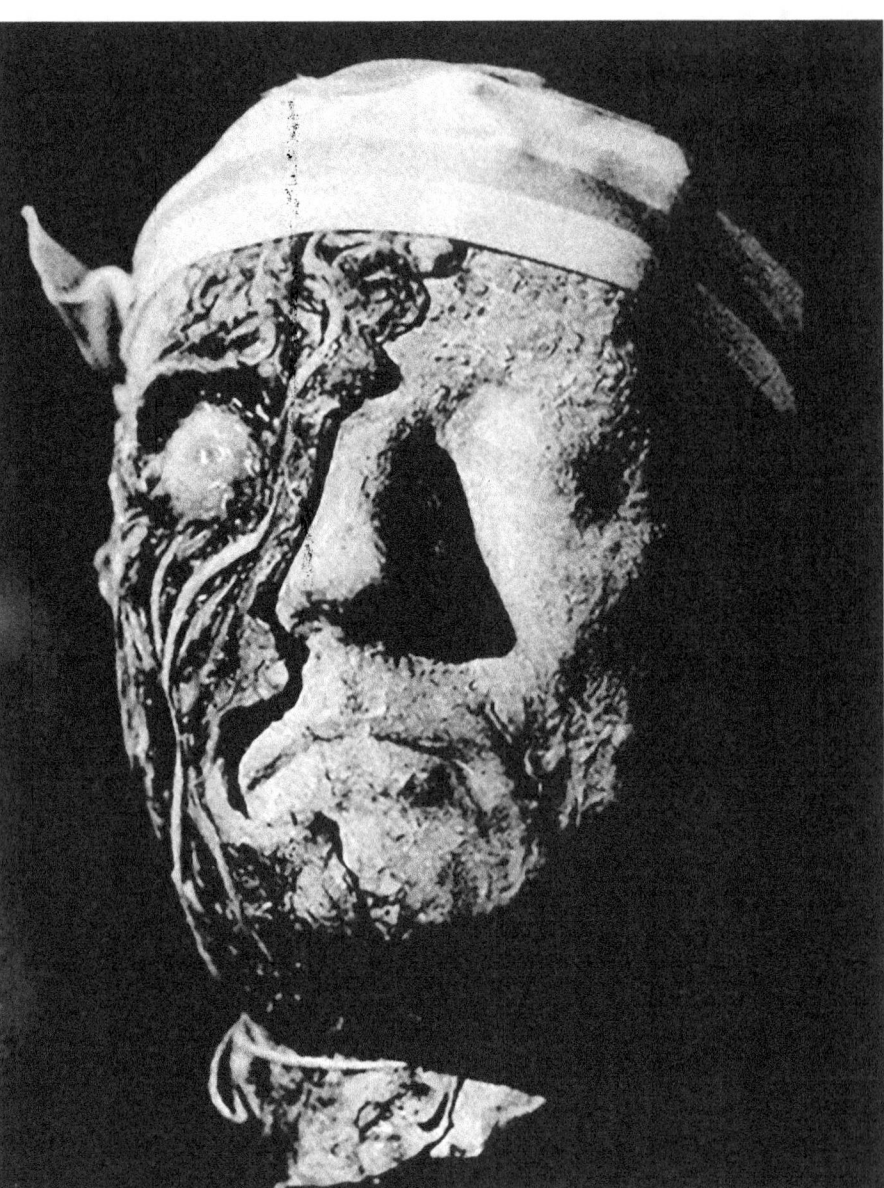

At the 40th minute, Bryant Haliday's inside-out face is revealed. Here is the mask used, created by make-up artist Eric Carter.

In the United Kingdom, it appeared in January 1966 where it played in some selected theaters (not on the main circuits) with Futurama's dire *Duel of the Space Monsters*. The picture failed to make an impact, even though it was promoted as the third fly movie, mainly because fans felt let down by the absence of an insect-type monster. But was it needed here? Years later, on re-evaluating the picture, the answer is "No." The film stands by its own merits as a truly adult-orientated 86 minutes of fast-paced, well-made meaty shock sci-fi thrills, with enough grotesque shocks on display to satisfy all diehards. Out of the three *Fly* movies, it's also the one with a bit more depth and bite, thanks in no small part to Harry Spalding's incisive script, rising admirably above its budget restrictions. *Curse of the Fly* is a highly credible slice of good-looking mid-'60s horror that deserves further recognition by fans and critics alike.

The Projected Man, "Britain's answer to *The Fly*" (*sic*), began life when producer Alex Gordon discovered an unproduced script written by Frank Quattrocchi, a Hollywood screenwriter. The action was originally to be set in the States, but Richard Gordon, Alex's brother, on receiving the draft, decided to shoot the proposed movie in England. Television writer/director Ian Curteis was hired at the insistence of producer/writer John Croydon, and the project would be 50% financed by Compton Productions, the company run by Michael Klinger and Tony Tenser, the budget coming in at £100,000. Curteis, lacking any experience of cinema work, quit (or was pushed out) when the film ran overschedule and over budget, Croydon, who co-wrote with Peter Bryan, completing the direction, although he didn't receive a credit (this was to be Curteis' one and only feature film). In England, the movie was passed with an "X" rating and released in March 1966, paired with *Island of Terror*; it ran for 90 minutes, 13 minutes longer than the U.S. cut, which was distributed by Universal-International in February 1967. Shot in Techniscope and Technicolor, widescreen prints are available from gray-market dealers but some come in the edited 77-minute version, with muddy color; the full-length British cut is crisper and has much more vibrant color, containing those missing 13 minutes omitted for American release, for better or worse.

The Sinfonia Orchestra of London plays Kenneth V. Jones' title music over the credits, proving that 60 years ago decent movie scores *did* matter. In a very noisy laboratory, lit by garish color (cinematography by Stanley Pavey), scientists Bryant Haliday (Dr. Paul Steiner) and Ronald Allen (Dr. Christopher Mitchel) are busy on their matter transmitting machine, "sucking up" objects, storing them in a cell as pure energy, and projecting them via a laser to a cradle (this laser device cropped up a year later in Avco Embassy's awful pair of sci-fi outings *They Came from Beyond Space* and *The Terrornauts*). The trouble is (as it was in those *Fly* flicks), the process works okay on inanimate objects, but not on flesh and blood. A guinea pig is teleported, lives for a few minutes, and expires after giving out an electric shock. Bellicose Director of The Farber Research Foundation, Norman Wooland (Dr. L.G. Blanchard), wants results fast, so pathologist Mary Peach (Dr. Patricia Hill) is contacted in the hope that she can determine why the subjects are dying after being transported—she's also Haliday's ex-lover, although when she sets her eyes on good-looker Allen, her allegiances rapidly change (Allen gained popularity in England starring in two long-running TV soaps, *Compact* [1962-1965] and *Crossroads* [1969-1985], and died tragically from a heart attack at only 60). Haliday carries out a demonstration on Peach's watch,

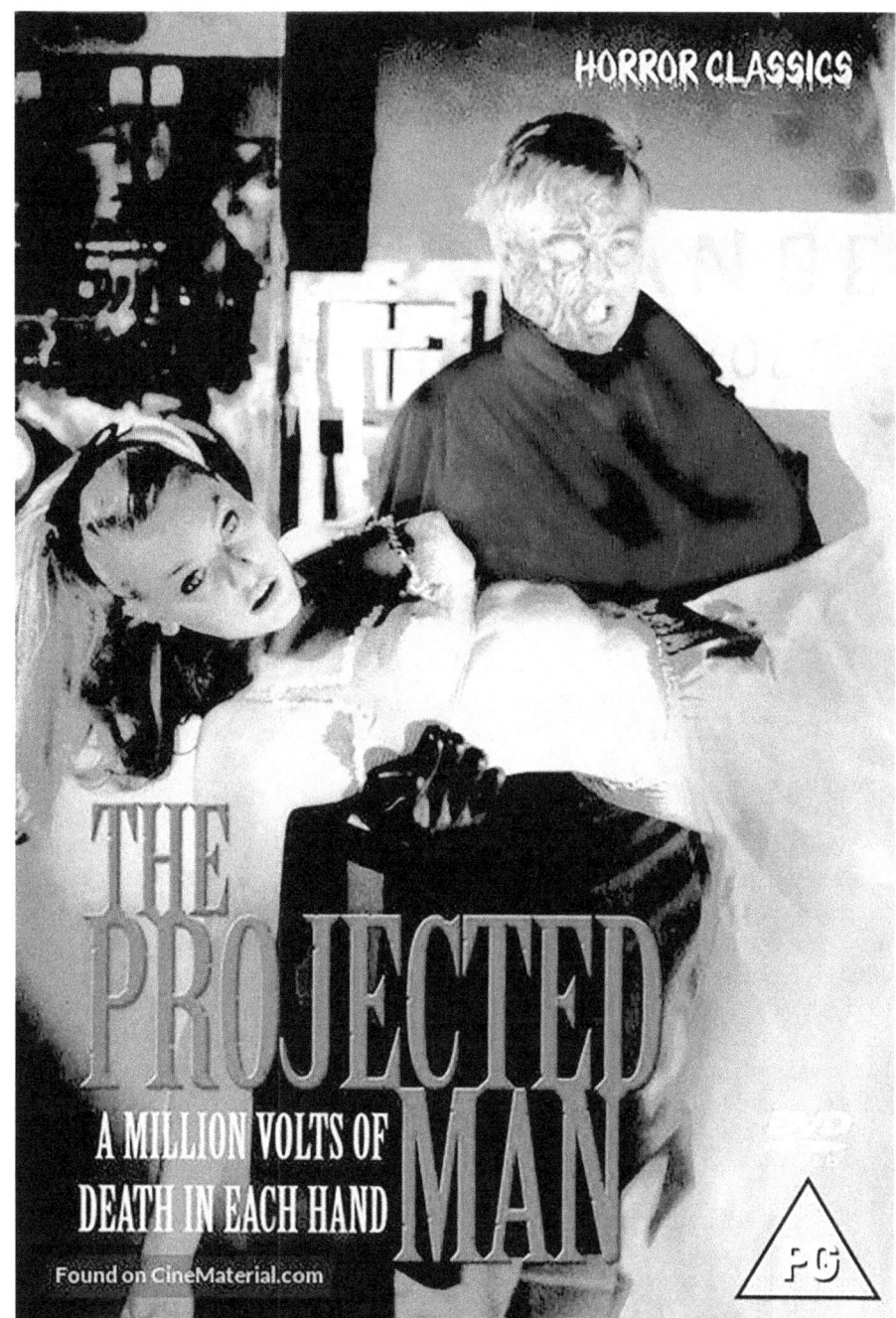

which emerges unscathed but goes haywire, giving out an electric shock.

So far, so good, although the film is rather talky and pedestrian in places. But at this point, *The Projected Man* dips its toes into sub-James Bond territory, as did so many features made during the sixties, the heyday of the spy thriller. Oily Wooland, being blackmailed by Derrick De Marney (Latham) because of his fondness for young girls, is bent on sabotaging Haliday's experiments, thus enabling Gerard Heinz (Professor Lembach) to take up the reins. A demonstration is arranged in front of Wooland and Lembach, with a mouse the subject. There's an explosion and the laser malfunctions. "Your experiments will be abandoned ... dismantle your laboratory," sneers Wooland to Haliday, who has discovered that acid was the culprit, corroding leads in a vital component due to Wooland's tampering. "I will give you evidence that will force you to acclaim my discovery," Haliday storms back! The man's under stress, not only at having his cherished project thwarted but annoyed at Peach's interest in Allen. Back at the lab, he instructs his secretary, Tracey Crisp (Sheila Anderson), how to use the various devices, clambers into the cradle, and, scared out of her wits, she mishandles the machine, causing Haliday,

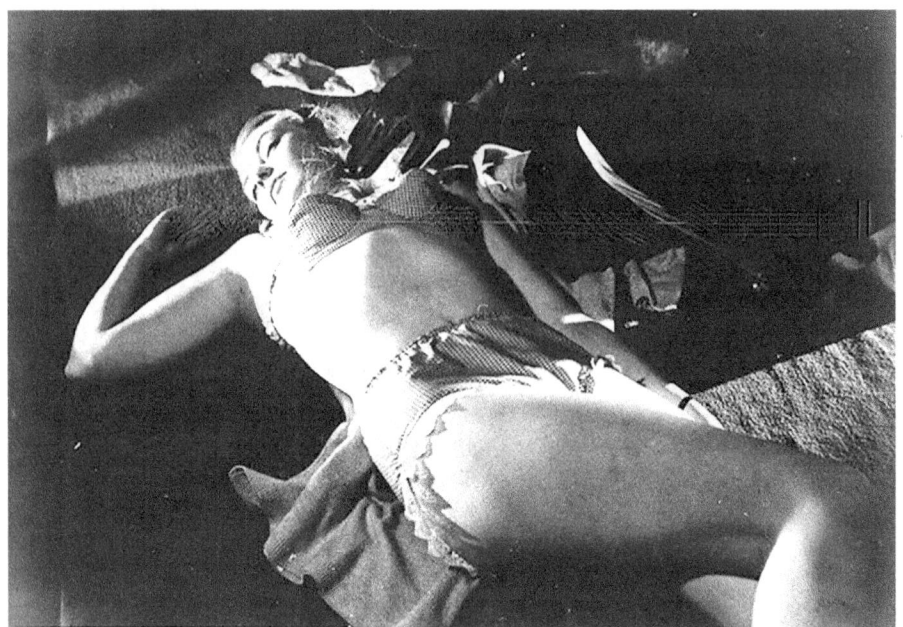

Another victim of Dr. Paul Steiner, the Projected Man.

screaming in pain, to fade from sight but *not* to reappear.

We finally get to see Haliday's inside-out face on the 40th minute. He's been teleported to a construction site where three thieves are killed by his lethal, electrically charged fingers, the camera closing in on his features as he emerges into the light; the right side resembles a half-cooked pizza, one bulging white eye staring out amid facial tissues, sinews and ragged teeth, a decent make-up job by Eric Carter, one of the '60s more memorable efforts. Derek Farr (Inspector Davis) enters the scenario as Haliday, growling like a wounded beast, busts into a store, grabs a pair of large rubber gloves and some bandages, and goes on a revenge-fueled rampage. We are now in standard "deformed madman on the loose" territory and the rather plodding pace, evident in the earlier laboratory sequences, speeds up, as does the tension. Haliday murders De Marney at the institute, just as he's about to run off with the tapes of the experiments; those are destroyed by Haliday's high-voltage right-hand touch. Next, Crisp is interrogated by Haliday about De Marney's shady involvement with Wooland, the terrified girl's apartment set on fire (she recovers in hospital). Allen and Peach stop playing house for a minute and join Farr in the hunt for the once brilliant research scientist, now transformed into a deranged, horribly deformed, and electrically charged monster; Wooland, being the fifth victim, slain in his home after trying to dispose of incriminating evidence. "I need power to think clearly," groans Haliday to Peach, bursting in on her and Allen canoodling on a bed, then entering the London Electricity Board Power Station to obtain that much-needed energy, the cops converging on the place and shooting at him wildly, bullets having no effect.

Eventually, Peach corners Haliday in a garage where he's thumping car batteries to drain their power into his body, but to no use; he drops to the ground exhausted and then follows her to the laboratory, where he turns the laser on. The machine goes berserk, devices and equipment short-circuiting and rendered useless, tapes burnt, and in the reversal process, the deadly laser beam hits Haliday directly in the chest, making him vanish into the nether world, as the fire rages on in the lab; Allen and Peach depart into the night to resume their romance.

British critics over-all reacted favorably to *The Projected Man*, commenting on the strong characterizations, a script mercifully free of clichés, the vivid colors, and Haliday's unique ravaged features, which would "scare the pants of any child today." Comparisons with *The Fly* and even Universal's *4D Man* were inevitable, given the subject matter. It was also a moderate success at the box-office; being teamed with *Island of Terror*, which had the pulling power of Peter Cushing, helped in this respect. And, like *Curse of the Fly* before it, the film firmly reinforced the fact that if men monkey around with voyages in and out of the fourth dimension, the repercussions will not bear thinking about. The warning is clear—you enter those teleportation devices at your peril; stay out at all costs!

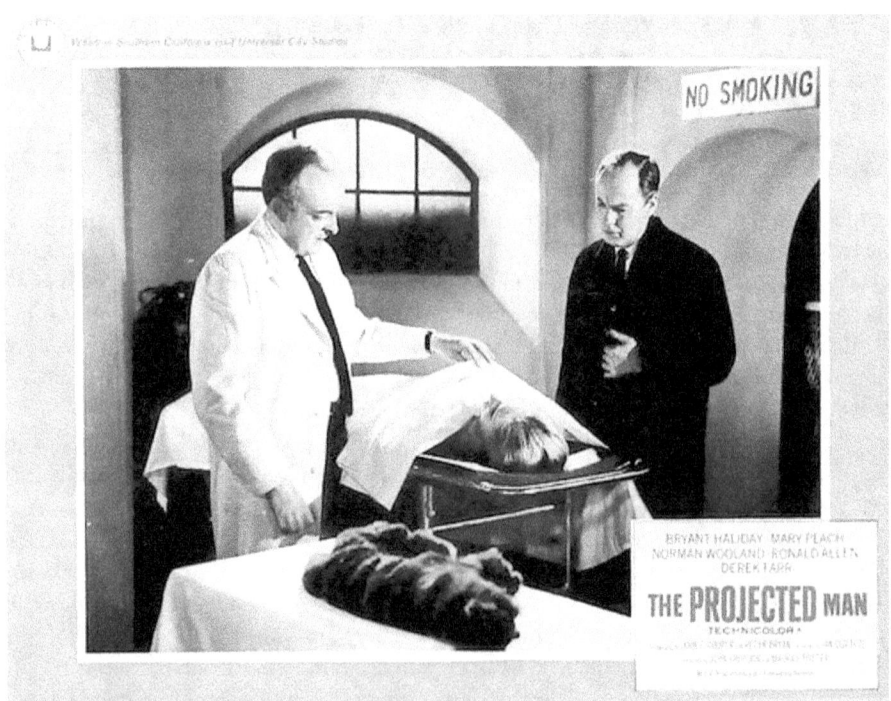

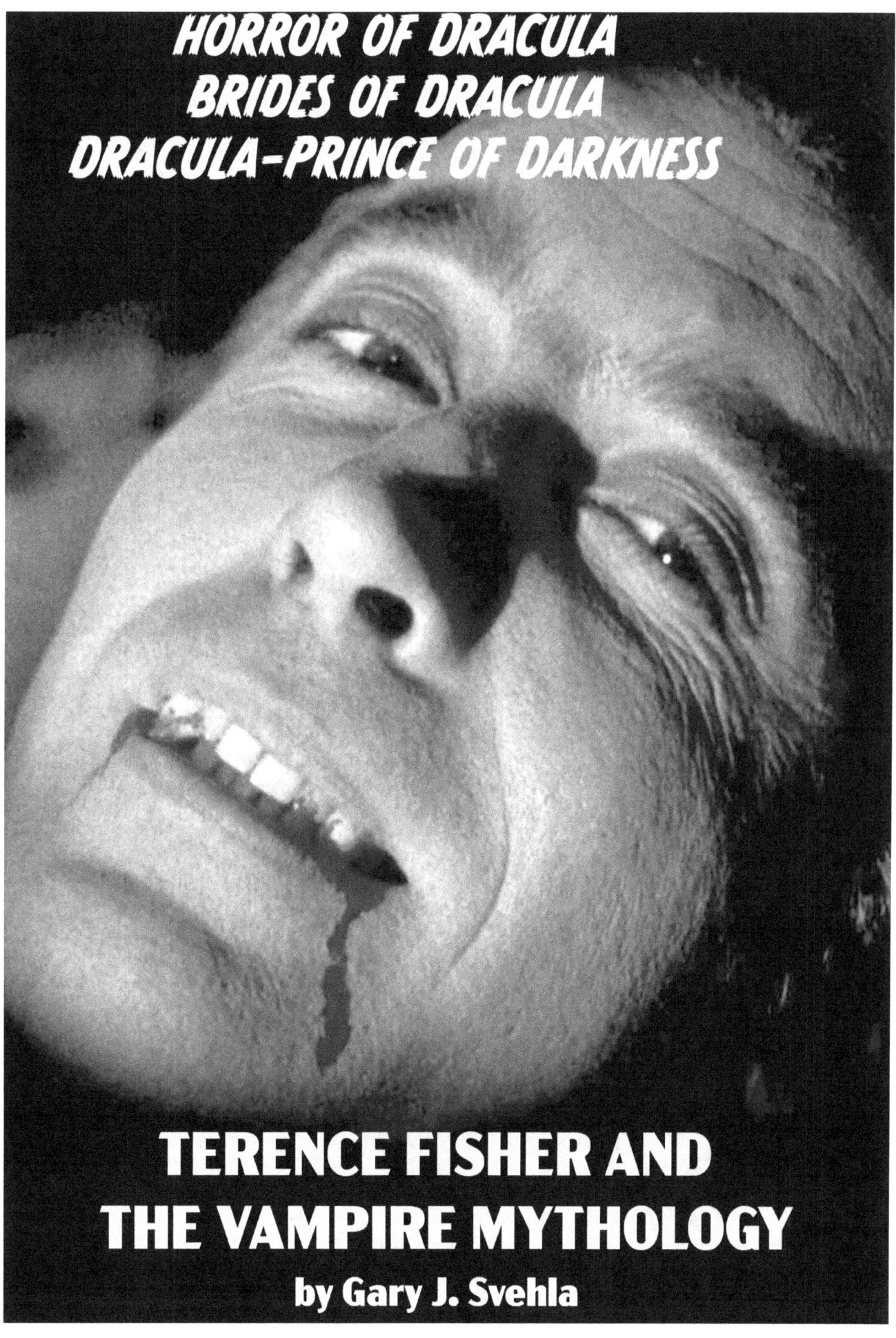

HORROR OF DRACULA
BRIDES OF DRACULA
DRACULA-PRINCE OF DARKNESS

TERENCE FISHER AND THE VAMPIRE MYTHOLOGY
by Gary J. Svehla

Being second is generally considered being a loser—a copycat, inferior, and lacking in innovation. But such wasn't the case with director Terence Fisher and Hammer Film Productions in the late 1950s. Though Universal was first with *Dracula, Spanish Dracula,* and *Dracula's Daughter* in the 1930s, Terence Fisher was first to single-handedly create a detailed vampire mythology with specific rules. Rules which were followed closely in *Horror of Dracula* (1958), *The Brides of Dracula* (1960), and *Dracula—Prince of Darkness* (1966). Other Hammer directors in their vampire films such as Freddie Francis, Don Sharp, Peter Sasdy, Alan Gibson, etc. have attempted a similar mythos in their Hammer films, but they were derivative of Fisher's already established lore or half-heartedly created with more and more hyperbolic silliness, and no other film featured the carefully thought-out mythology that Fisher established in his three vampire films. Let us carefully study these films to determine his vampiric rules and to see how this vision plays out in his films.

HORROR OF DRACULA

His first vampire epic, *Horror of Dracula* 1958 (UK, *Dracula*), is perhaps Hammer's most important film, the one that put Hammer on the map. With rich, saturated Technicolor hues, powerful James Bernard soundtrack, stand-out performances by Peter Cushing (Dr. Van Helsing) and Christopher Lee (Count Dracula), and cheaply made but impressive

As he picks up a dropped tray, Jonathan Harker (John Van Eyssen) is atonished to see a beautiful woman (Valerie Gaunt) plead for help.

period décor provided by Bernard Robinson, further aided by a succinct screenplay by Jimmy Sangster, make-up by Phil Leaky, and cinematography by Jack Asher, *Horror of Dracula* was a modest-budgeted film that looked like *Masterpiece Theater.*

"*The Diary of Jonathan Harker*, third of May, 1885. At last, my long journey is drawing to its close. What the eventual end will be, I cannot foresee, but whatever may happen, I can rest secure that I have done all in my power to achieve success. The last lap of my journey from the village of Klausenberg proved to be more difficult than I had anticipated, due to the coach driver's reluctance to take me all the way. However, as there was no other transport available, I traveled the last few kilometers on foot, before arriving at Castle Dracula. The castle appeared innocuous enough in the warm afternoon sun, and all seemed normal except for one thing ... there were no birds singing. As I crossed the wooden bridge and entered the gateway, it seemed to become much colder, due, no doubt, to the icy waters of the mountain torrent I'd just crossed. However, I deemed myself lucky to have secured this post and didn't intend to falter in my purpose." This opening narration began the tradition of including a moody monologue to begin all three Terence Fisher vampire films.

The splash of blood closing the opening credits 2:21 minutes in, dripping blood on the nameplate of Dracula's stone sarcophagus is a wonderful touch, but it is not part of the vampire mythology. However, Valerie Gaunt's role of the vampire woman most definitely is. At 6:40 not long after Jonathan Harker's arrival, he is approached by a brunettec wearing a white nightgown. As Harker bends over to pick-up a metal tray, her sensuous form approaches from his rear, the musical score calmly accents her swaying, "You will help me, won't you? Say you will, please ..." She looks frightened and runs away as music builds and swirls in the background. Count Dracula (Christopher Lee) makes a dramatic entrance at the top of the staircase at 7:36,

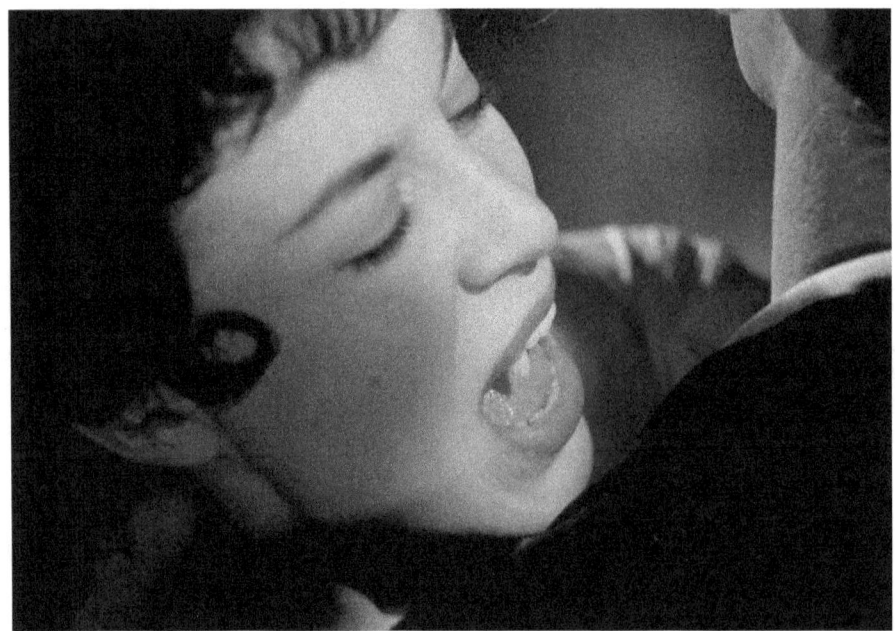

Valerie Gaunt plays her vulnerability card too well, as she drives for Harker's neck.

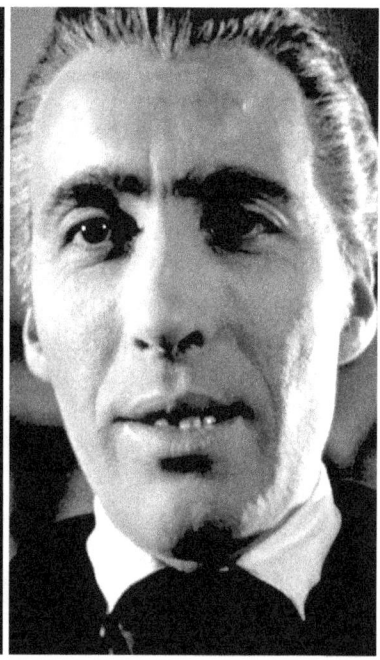

Top two left: In the library scene Count Dracula, enraged by the vampire woman, turns into a feral beast; Top Right: Count Dracula as the distinguished nobleman, the regal count

silhouetted in black shadows, music builds to a crescendo as James Bernard's leitmotiv for Dracula fills the air. The Count descends the many steps and introduces himself. "I am Dracula … and I welcome you to my house." As 13:56 Harker wanders into the ornate library accented by the deep tones of the oboe setting the mood as the troubled woman comes into the room from behind the library door pleading, "Mr. Harker, you will help me!" When she is unwilling or unable to tell him why Dracula keeps her prisoner, she only becomes more frantic. "You're my only hope," and she reaches out to touch his coat lapels. She realizes her appeal to the male ego is successfully manipulative. Smiling, he tells her he will help at 15:09. She snuggles into his upper shoulder, eventually reaching his neck. Music suddenly grows sinister as a menacing look comes over her face as she opens her mouth, fangs appear, and she quickly dives for his neck. Harker forcefully shoves her back, but he has been bitten. The vampire woman has been successful in her sexual vulnerability and male manipulation.

This is a significant part of Fisher's vampire mythos. Within the same individual, we contrast vulnerability and inherent evil, the will to survive. She does not desire Harker to save her for a moment, she only wishes to play her vulnerability

Above left: The vampire woman lies in her sarcophagus, blood dripping from her lips; Above right: The vampire woman moments after she is staked by Jonathan Harker, showing her actual age

Dracula, the horror from outside, comes into Lucy's bedroom, invited by Lucy herself (Carol Marsh).

card to assuage his male ego and appeal to his sense of protectiveness, to attack him when he least suspects it. And it works. Her sensuousness and playing the vulnerable heroine traps Harker into letting his guard down, and she enslaves him.

As is true with the vampire woman, we contrast the beautiful young woman who inside is the vampire beast, almost seeming like split personalties, one pure innocence and one corrupted by evil. Terence Fisher constantly shows us disparate sides of the individual. Continuing the sequence that started at 15:09, as the vampire woman bites Harker, Dracula appears, the classic close-up of his blood-smeared face as he emits an animalistic guttural growl with mouth open wide. Dracula leaps over the table and grabs his vampire mistress and shoves her to the floor. Harker, holding his bleeding neck, watches in horror. Dracula, his eyes staring at the girl, take on a predatory menace. She attempts to run to Harker as Dracula grabs her arm and growls. Harker bravely attempts to attack Dracula from behind, but the enraged vampire turns and holds Harker at arm's reach before throwing his body backward. A scream pierces the night and Dracula leaves the library carrying the limp body of his bewitched minion. Dracula glances at the grimacing Harker as the wounded man falls backward and passes out.

Again, and more dramatically, we have the contrast between the regal Count who welcomes Harker to his castle and majestically descends the staircase vs. the animalistic blood-smeared beast snarling fearfully, the now revealed apex predator comes to claim his female accolade. This contrast becomes essential in Fisher's mythos, showing the difference between the human and undead version of the same individual.

Another example of this is between the innocent Lucy, fiancée of Jonathan Harker, and the ungodly monster she has become, attempting to seduce Greda's daughter Tania (Janina Faye) into the cult of vampirism, here we see her evil persona in all its glory. At 50:30, Tania says, "I heard you call me, Aunt Lucy." Lucy, at first trying to hide her fangs, says, "Yes dear!" And tells her to "Come along," grabbing her hand, Tania noticing, "Your hand is cold," when Aunt Lucy tells Tania, "We are going for a little walk." Contrast the vampiric Lucy trying to lure little Tania into the night to the peaceful soul she was after 54:50, when Holmwood (Michael Gough) refuses to al-

Vampire Aunt Lucy takes young Tania (Janina Faye) for a little walk.

Lucy is held transfixed by the power of the crucifix, which burns its impression in her forehead.

Lucy is once again beautiful, and at peace, after she is staked.

low Lucy to become a pawn used by Van Helsing to lead him to Dracula. Van Helsing (Peter Cushing) explains to Arthur Holmwood about freeing her soul with the stake through her heart. Holmwood asks, "Is there no other way?" The doctor shakes his head no and Holmwood, very distressed, says, "But its horrible!" Van Helsing tries to reassure him by saying, "This is not Lucy the sister you loved, but it's only a shell … possessed and corrupted by the evil of Dracula." Van Helsing continues, "We must destroy that shell for all time." We then watch as Van Helsing stakes Lucy, blood spurting, the vampire squirming and moaning in pain, as she soon expires. When Van Helsing shows Lucy's corpse to Holmwood, she looks radiant, like her former healthy self, finally

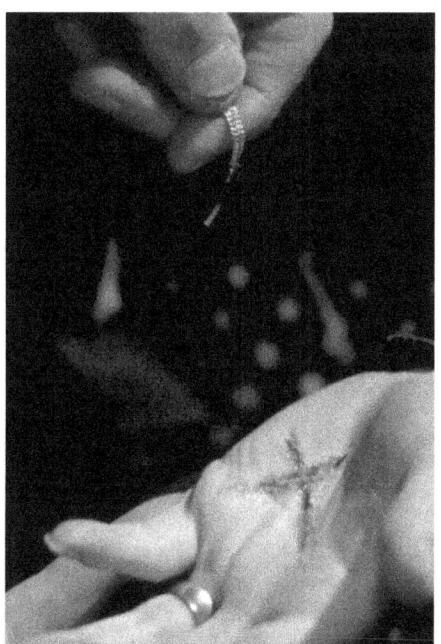

Mina's hand is burned by holding a small crucifix, after a few attacks by Dracula.

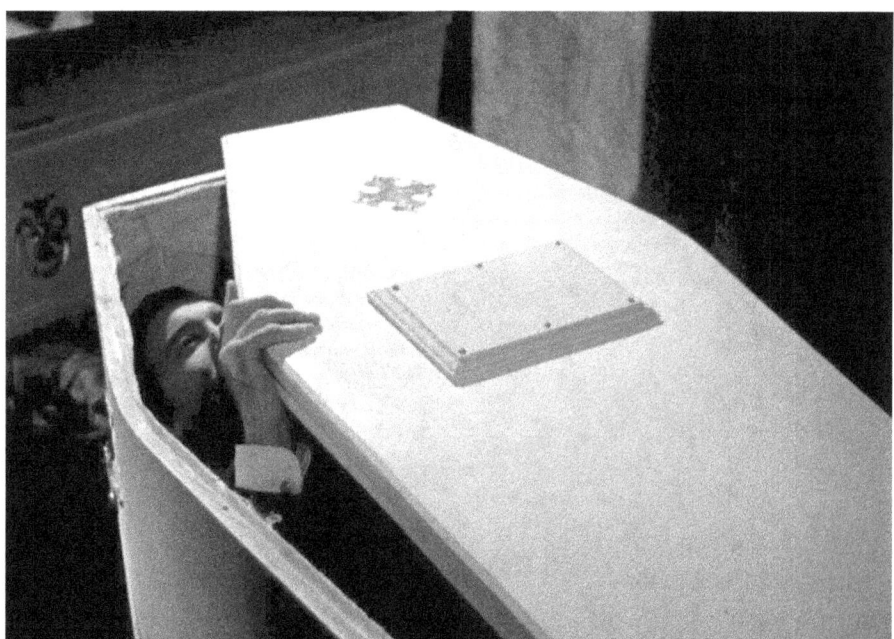

Mina (Melissa Stribing) is told by a messenger to meet her husband at J Marx, Mortician, but all she encounters is Dracula emerging from his coffin.

at peace, her head shrouded in peaceful blue. Again, the vampire beast's shell is always contrasted to the former uncorrupted human entity, showing the effect of vampirism upon one's appearance.

Another aspect of Fisher's mythology is the contrast between evil that lurks outside and inside the home. The evil inside is the most elusive and difficult to battle. First, we have the evil of Dracula prowling outside, trying to get inside, which is exhibited by Lucy leaving the French doors open and inviting Count Dracula to enter her bedroom. The tinkling, anticipatory music enhances Count Dracula's sudden appearance inside the French doors. As he slowly advances, Lucy slightly rises in her bed as music erupts. The mythos typically does not allow the vampire to cross a threshold until they are invited inside. This is exactly what occurs as Lucy silently beckons Dracula into her room.

At 1:05:37, Van Helsing and Holmwood return home after a night spent outside the house guarding Mina (Melissa Stribling), who collapses when Holmwood gives his wife a small crucifix to wear, she reacts as if the holy relic were poison, but it does sizzle and burn an impression in her palm. When Holmwood fetches a blanket for the good doctor to use that night, a frantic cry of "Mina" carries downstairs, Holmwood has found Mina sprawled face up on the bed, blood covering her neck and shoulder. Van Helsing scrambles up the stairs, and finds Mina near death. An emergency blood transfusion conducted by Van Helsing saves her life. At 1:14:23, Van Helsing scurries down to the basement, where he discovers Dracula's white coffin contain-

Count Dracula, already inside the Holmwood house, asends Mina's staircase.

Dr. Van Helsing (Peter Cushing) finds Dracula's coffin in the Holmwood cellar, while Dracula finds Van Helsing.

The innocent Mina waits for the kiss of Dracula.

ing his soil, into which Van Helsing drops a crucifix so the dreaded vampire cannot return to his resting place. This evil which exists within the house is the most shocking and most difficult to defend against because of the element of surprise.

In other words, the evil conducted by Dracula from outside is horrible enough, but the erstwhile heroes expect such an invasion and prepare for it. But they do not expect the evil from within their very home. At 43:05 Van Helsing orders pots of garlic flowers for Lucy's room for her own protection. However, Lucy can manipulate Gerda the maid to remove the garlic pots. "Please Gerda, they stifle me," Lucy pleads, and Gerda removes the plants. There is a distinct smile on Lucy's face as the music swells. Unknown to the vampire hunters, Dracula has been easily gaining entrance. Next morning, Lucy is discovered dead. In other words, the vampire hunters can never adequately prepare for evil which has already seeped inside, in this case, the half undead Lucy. One is never prepared to face evil so close to home.

The most tantalizing aspect of Fisher's vampire mythos is the sexual component, making the act of the vampire attacking another human akin to the sexual act. At 1:08:07 this is illustrating both the concept of evil within (other members of the family being unaware of evil's presence) and the sexual nature of the vampire's kiss while the men are outside the house sure they are protecting Mina. Mina opens her bedroom door to see Dracula below, already in the home. Dracula slowly climbs the stairs as Mina

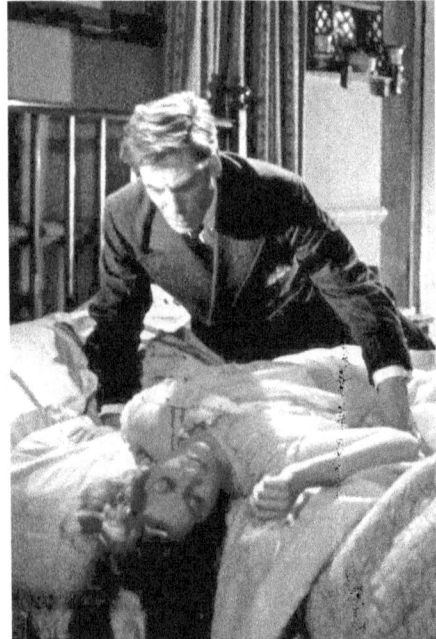

Arthur Holmwood (Michael Gough) finds his wife Mina sprawled on the bed and bleeding from the neck.

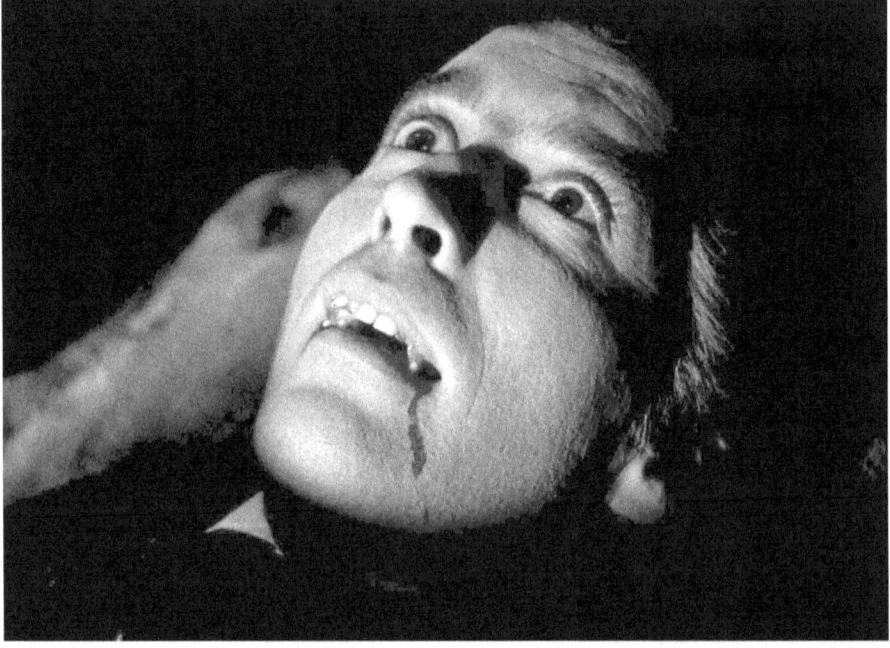

Dracula's eyes bolt open in his sarcophagus, a scene duplicated in *Dracula—Prince of Darkness,* but not as successfully.

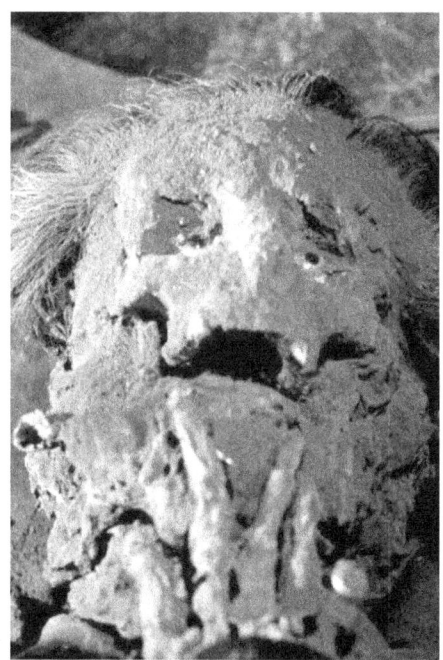

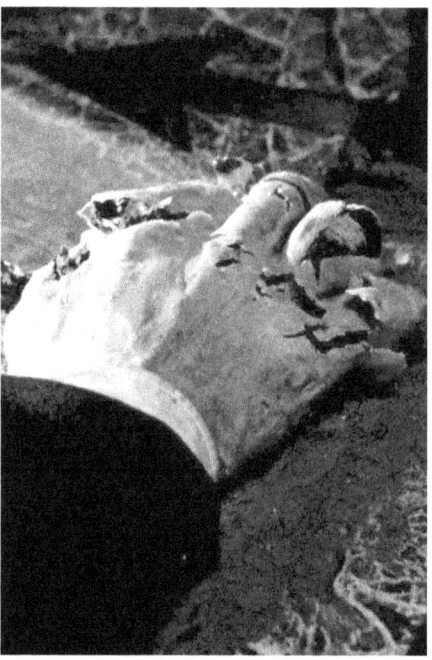

watches with both fear and anticipation. As he enters the door he forces Mina backward. Mina falls back on the bed, Dracula sinisterly smiling. He lowers himself to nuzzle her face, passionately kissing her. After arousing her, he goes down for the vampire's kiss, as an owl screeches outside. The vampire's phallic fangs, which mostly remain hidden, soon penetrate the tender flesh to suck her life's blood. An act akin to sex has occurred. Outside the men think they are defending Mina.

Another twisted example occurs at the 51:27 point in the film, as Lucy and Tania are returning to Lucy's tomb, Lucy encountering Arthur Holmwood, who is waiting for her. Lucy, looking like a sly predator, stops dead in her tracks and says, "Arthur, dear brother." She comes nearer and adds, "Come, let me kiss you" at the exact moment Van Helsing's arm, holding a crucifix, abruptly enters the frame, Lucy's terrorized breathing dominates the soundtrack. Van Helsing comes closer, forcing Lucy back, touching the crucifix to her forehead, its metal sizzling and burning an impression onto the skin, much like Mina's necklace similarly burns an impression onto her hand. Even if one is still alive, or undead, once the victim is corrupted by the vampire's kiss, holy relics leave a lasting, burning impression. In Fisher's mythos once the victim is corrupted by the vampire's bite, holy relics leave a burning impression on the bloodsuckers' prey.

Now we can see another aspect of Fisher's vampire mythos, the perversion of the family through vampirism. Consider Lucy's stalking of the family maid's daughter Tania, hoping to lure her to her tomb. We also find Mina willingly consenting to Dracula's seduction under her husband's very nose, he who is trying to protect her a few yards away. We have the vileness of Dracula contaminating the family, coming between husband-and-wife Mina and Arthur. We also find Lucy's vampirism horrifying trying to corrupt little Tania, who loves and trusts her "Aunt" Lucy. Of course we have Dracula coming between Jonathan Harker and his fiancée Lucy. As Van Helsing notes, Jonathan Harker destroyed Dracula's mate. Dracula retaliated by quickly vampirizing Harker and claiming Mina as his new mate, thus sowing seeds of evil within the Holmwood family. But this is what Dracula's evil does, corrupts and disintegrates families. That is the ultimate evil. Remember at 1:01:15, Dracula lured Mina to the mortican J Marx by sending word that her husband has sent for her. Arriving alone, she finds a pure white casket with a hand slowly extending outward. Later, when Van Helsing and Holmwood meet mortician J Marx, the white coffin is gone, only its catafalque remains. The coffin and its occupant are now in the cellar of the Holmwood home.

But for me the most terrifying sequence of the movie and one that adds to the mythology is at the 20:37 point when Harker, mortally bitten by the vampire woman, stakes her in the crypt located just outside the castle. Here is where Count Dracula and his vampire mate sleep during the day, fresh blood usually dripping from their lips, the blood of their latest victims. Harker knows he does not have much time before being reborn as an undead. Unpacking his compact bundle of wooden stakes and a mallet, he eyes the crypt, noticing stone sarcophaguses

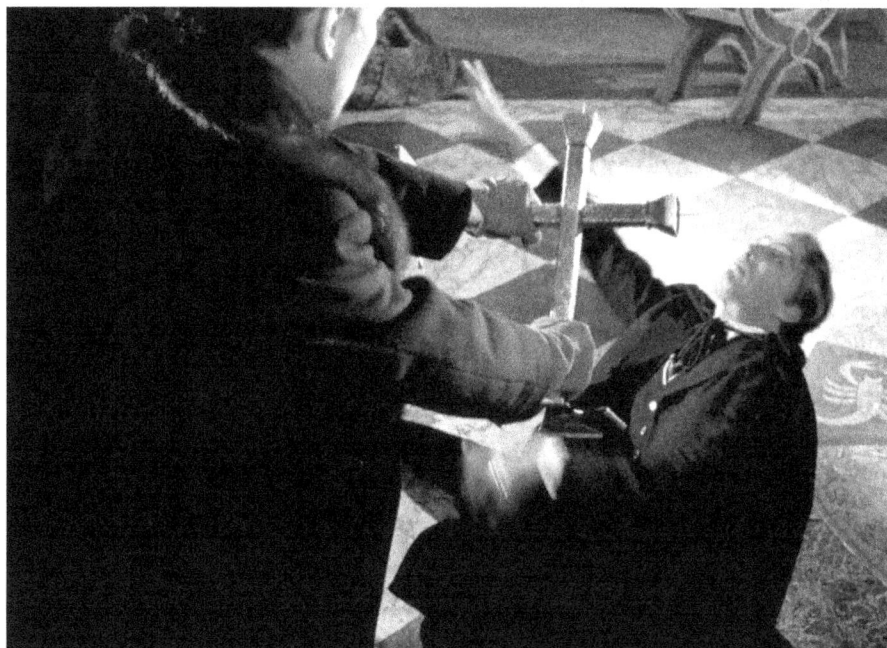

Dracula is held paralyzed by the power of the crucifix (actually two candlestick holders held together), as he turns to dust by the rays of the sun.

A novel touch ends the opening credits of *Horror of Dracula* by having blood drip onto the name plate of Dracula's sarcophagus.

for both Dracula and his mate. Only moments before daylight, he has the choice of destroying either the vampire woman or Dracula. He chooses the vampire woman simply because she seems the most dangerous to him, and his decision probably bothers every audience member who ever saw a Dracula film. Why not destroy Dracula when one has the chance? When Harker approaches the coffin of the vampire woman, she has been transformed from vulnerable woman to sneering animal, blood dripping from both sides of her mouth. Background music soars as he prepares his weapons of vampire liberation. In silhouette we hear the woman scream as he drives the stake in. We cut to Dracula's coffin, the Count's eyes spring open and then he looks downward. A look of animalic rage appears on his face as he looks to the windows of the tomb, and we see the sun setting. The camera cuts back to Dracula as he smugly smiles and flares his nose. We cut to the mate's coffin as we view an elderly white-haired woman with a wooden stake in her heart, blood oozing from her chest. Harker is too late as he turns to Dracula's coffin, his shocked face revealing it is empty and the Count is gone. Harker, in mortal terror, looks upward to the crypt's door. He sees nothing for several seconds, this elapsing time creates suspense for the viewer. Harker finally sees Dracula's form fill the doorway which is his only means of escape. Harker recoils, knowing he is trapped as Dracula approaches and closes the door behind him.

What does this have to say about vampire mythology? First, the corruptive evil of Dracula is usually confined to an area outside but attached to the castle. He is the supreme noble Count inside his castle, but his vile evil is confined to outside the castle, even though there are exceptions (such as the blood-smeared library scene). Also, the supremacy of evil is illustrated in this scene. Christopher Lee's mute acting inside his coffin shows why he probably did not have any lines in *Dracula—Prince of Darkness*. He plays here the high holiest of evil, realizing he holds all the cards and is undefeated. His confident demeanor clearly shows he is in charge. Human beings and his minions are easily toyed with and easily outsmarted, as the vampire woman showed.

This air of superiority is more clearly illustrated at the 18:25 mark, when the climactic chase at the end shows Van Helsing storming the castle looking for Dracula. Dracula holds open a trapdoor in the floor, while Van Helsing catches up to him. Dracula throws a convenient candle holder at Van Helsing and charges him, struggling to overpower the vampire hunter. With Van Helsing on his back, Dracula attempts to choke him to unconsciousness, as he then swoops for his neck. Van Helsing almost passes out as Dracula has the look of ultimate victory written on his face, as he slowly rises and towers over him. Dracula, smiling triumphantly, goes in for the kill, that superior look upon his face. Harker suddenly gains consciousness and pushes Dracula backward. Both men straddle one another, Van Helsing momentarily pausing to rub his neck. He eyes the closed curtains, which block out the morning sunlight. He runs across the long rectangular table and dives for the curtains, ripping them down. As the sunlight reaches Dracula, the dreaded vampire cowers in fear and pain. Dracula slowly turns to dust, only his clothes and ring remain. Van Helsing holds Dracula at bay, forming two metal candlesticks into the shape of a crucifix to prevent him from escaping. Meanwhile, Mina's burnt markings on her hand begin to vanish, freeing her from the control of Count Dracula. This is another aspect of the mythos, holy relics will burn the victim's flesh, but once the vampire predator is destroyed, so is the influence of evil.

Terence Fisher has created a remarkable mythology which will be expanded in his second and third film. Working with serviceable scripts, first-rate casts, and his vampire mythos, which perhaps serves him best as he portrays the vampire as a multidimensional character filled with depth.

Jonathan Harker looks on in horror as Dracula violently grabs the vampire vixen.

The Brides of Dracula

Horror of Dracula was such a hit for Hammer Film Productions that a sequel was warranted and released two years later. But not necessarily a true sequel (Christopher Lee did not play Count Dracula … he wasn't asked), but rather an extension to Hammer's vampire lore. *The Brides of Dracula* used most of the same talent—Terence Fisher, director; Jimmy Sangster, screenplay (along with co-screenwriters Peter Byran and Edward Percy); star Peter Cushing; Jack Asher, cinematography; Bernard Robinson, production design—but new talent also came aboard: Roy Ashton, chief make-up artist; Malcolm Williamson, music (with a score that nicely complements the first one by James Bernard); and Bill Lenny, film editing. While *The Brides of Dracula* contained many of the high points of *Horror of Dracula*, it also contained more flaws—however, Terence Fisher's mythology carried on, repeating the last film's mythos, but also adding to it.

"Transylvania, land of black forests, dread mountains, and black unfathomed lakes. Still the home of magic and devilry as the 19th century draws to its close. Count Dracula, monarch of all vampires, is dead. But his disciples live on to spread and corrupt the world." This is the narration which opens the movie, and it establishes an eerie mood which carries throughout the film.

Baron Meinster (David Peel) plays a very different kind of vampire compared to Christopher Lee. As the *Brides* narra-

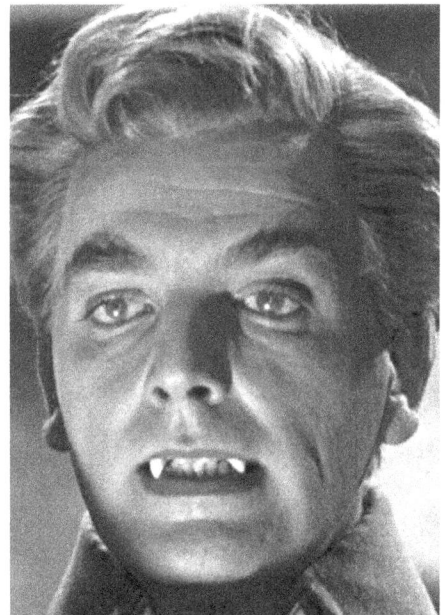 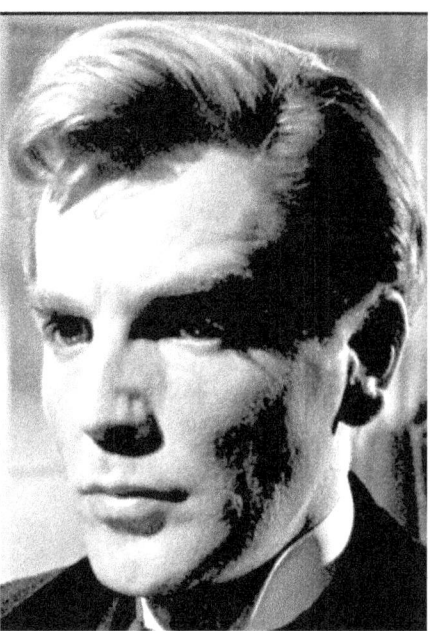

The vampiric David Peel is shown left; The rich landowner/landlord David Peel is shown right. Once again Terence Fisher loves to starkly contrast both entities.

tion says, he is a disciple having been vampirized more recently than Dracula so he lacks the ancient ancestry and breeding that the 500 year-old Count Dracula possessed. Meinster is the son of a deceased landowner—who is basically a landlord. He is youthful and more interested in feeding off the pretty female locals for their blood, essentially making him a "dandy," mainly interested in vulnerable females. He is social with the proper clientele and is referred to as a cult member, basically being seduced by his evil friends, as the Baroness refers to them. Count Dracula is more a brooding loner, happy to co-exist with one vampire mate, who seems to satisfy most of his needs. Dracula and his mate do regularly venture out of the castle for additional victims. David Peel was about four years older than Christopher Lee, but Peel was made-up to look youthful with curly red hair and a fat face, while Lee was made to appear as the distinguished elder statesman, having been made a vampire years before.

When it comes to writing, we secondary English teachers have a saying, show us don't tell us! This is not so much a sin in movies, but in *Horror of Dracula*, Van Helsing has an odd scene where he is spouting vampire lore into a Dictaphone-style machine. Here, in *The Brides of Dracula* at 42:35, he is sent for by a priest of a small village, when a local village girl (Marie Devereux) dies by a mysterious cause. He must get the priest up to speed about vampire lore quickly. So, he simply tells him the facts. The priest asks, "What is this vampirism, should I call it?" Van Helsing answers, "It's a survival of one of the ancient pagan religions in their struggle against Christianity." The priest further questions. "And there's first, as it was, the vampire, the undead?" Van Helsing says, "That passes on … yes, the vampire, by its kiss, the taking of blood from its victims, makes of their victim another vampire. So, the cult grows, infinitely slowly, but it grows. The vampire rests in the day, usually in his tomb, issuing as a living form only at night. And that means they need

Prisoner Baron Meinster (David Peel) is shackled and alone on the balcony, in his own wing of the Chateau Meinster.

Marianne (Yvonne Monlaur) is a surprise dinner guest at Chateau Meinster, being served by Greta (Freda Jackson) and entertained by the Baroness Meinster (Martita Hunt).

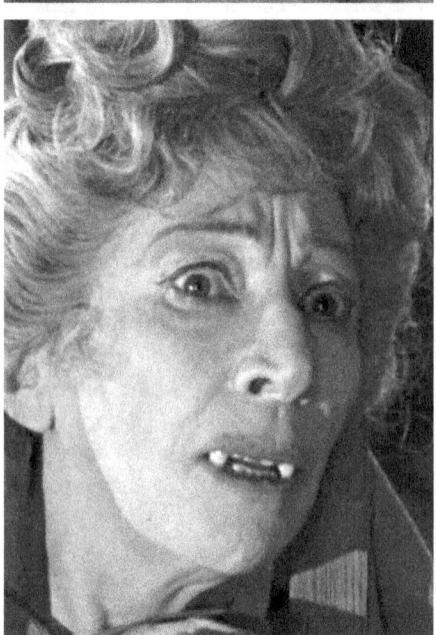

After Baroness Meinster has been vampirized, here are two shots, one she covers her fangs, the other she shows them.

the help, the protection of a human being during the hours of the daylight. A mother who may hide an infected son or daughter, or a servant, either hypnotized or so devoted to the master, they don't realize the evil they're doing. If it wasn't for this protection during the day, these vampires could be tracked down and destroyed." The priest asks how they can be destroyed, and Van Helsing says, "By driving a wooden stake through the heart or by burning. The tormented soul is then released to return to the peace of death. These colonies, such as you have here, must be wiped out. Only then will this bondage of hell be lifted from the world." Then the priest asks, "Are there ways of telling these undead from the living?" Van Helsing answers, "They're repelled by holy things and Christian images. They're thin. They have an air of hunger about them. They cast no reflection. And some have the power to transform themselves into bats." Van Helsing was disputing this fact, about transformation into bats, in the first movie, but here the three screenwriters probably had the power over the script and the director could not overrule them. In one short sequence, everyone in the theater is up to snuff on vampirism.

In his mythology, Terence Fisher speaks through Dr. Van Helsing (Peter Cushing) and in the next movie Father Sandor (Andrew Keir). Continuing with the mythology, Van Helsing stresses the need for a human servant who will protect the vampire during the daylight hours, when the undead creature is at his or her most vulnerable. In *The Brides of Dracula*, we have vampire Baron Meinster's (David Peel) old nurse, the faithful and half-crazy, Greta (Freda Jackson). We first meet Greta after Mariannee (Yvonne Monlaur) is stranded by her coach driver (Michael Ripper) at the Running Boar Inn. The Baroness (Martita Hunt) invites her to spend the night at Chateau Meinster. At 3:04, we have a mysterious man climb out of the dense forest, careful to stay unseen as he sneaks onto the rear of the carriage, getting a free ride to the inn. But after Mariannee goes inside, we see the mysterious man being paid off by the coach driver (this mystery man will later drive off in the carriage, stranding Mariannee). Inside the inn, the innkeeper advises Mariannee to get into her coach right away, but it is already too late, as the coach is driving off. Baroness Meinster miraculously arrives by coach and seems to be the solution to Mariannee's dilemma, but she is there to procure another victim for her son.

The scene where Mariannee first sees Baron Meinster proves once again that romance is the vampire's greatest power. Mariannee at 13:00 looks outside her bedroom window, sees a balcony, and witnesses the proverbial Byronic hero walking around, deep in thought. When Mariannee returns inside, Greta will not answer any of her questions about the young man. We have what will turn out to be the living space of pure evil, again sectioned off from the rest of the castle, just like the vampires' tomb was in *Horror of Dracula*. But the Baroness is not an old woman living alone. At dinner at the 14:50 mark with the Baroness, Mariannee is told that the Baron Meinster is her son. "My son is ill. His illness has destroyed my peace of mind in these last years. You may not believe it, but we have had gay times here. Balls, dinners. Life. People used to come from all over Europe, even from Paris, to be my guests, until he ruined it all. It

The Baron Meinster is released from his prison by Marianne and he appears wearing a drab gray cape, looking more and more like a disciple of Dracula.

Greta realizes her little boy has escaped but that he'll have to return here to his coffin.

hurt me too much not to be able to present my only child to my friends, to keep him locked up. I never see him myself. Greta looks after him. She's his old nurse. He has made me suffer so appallingly. He has his own rooms apart from the rest of the castle, only reached through that door. But all that's nothing, nothing. The vital thing is that you discovered his existence and I have explained the situation. Are madmen happy? We pray for death, he, and I. At least, I hope he does. The people around here think he's dead already. So, I'm told, and I encourage that belief. I see you are passing judgment on me, my child. Sleep before you pronounce sentence." The Baroness says she is tired and retires. Mariannee says, "God bless you." The Baroness answers, "If only he could."

Later at 18:16, Mariannee wakes up and gets out of bed, looks toward the lower balcony as the Baron steps onto the outer ledge, as if to jump. "Don't do that," Mariannee yells. She scurries down to the balcony, first entering the Baron's living quarters, where he asks her, "Who are you?" repeatedly and inquires, "Why have you come here?" Mariannee says, "I have come to help you, if I can." The Baron tells her to approach him, to not be afraid. "I want to look at you." He tells her that she is very beautiful, "So you have come to help me, have you?" He asks her, "No one can do that." He instructs her to come closer, "I can't come to you" and he stares at the leg manacle on his left lower leg. Mariannee says its inhuman, and the Baron responds, "My mother thinks of me as inhuman, doesn't she? I suppose she's told you that I'm mad, that I must be locked away like this for everyone's sake." The Baron tells Mariannee that all this, the castle, the valley, the mountains below, all are his inheritance. "But my mother is a vicious, evil, jealous woman. She let people believe that I'm dead." So, in other words, the Baron's inheritance has fallen to her. Mariannee smiles and tells him she will help him, "If you confide in me, I am sure I can." The Baron asks her to find the key that fits his manacle. He tells her where to find the key, and says, "There are grave risks you know," but Mariannee says, "I dare." Fisher creates a character whose naiveté unknowingly helps the vampire. Baron Meinster uses his brooding sexuality to lure Mariannee to his chamber. She believes his story that his mother is the evil one, so she steals the key to help him escape.

At 24:35 the Baroness confronts Mariannee trying to get her key back, but it's much too late for that, "You little fool, you don't know what you've done!" Mariannee runs down the staircase, into the waiting arms of the Baron. "Don't worry, she can't harm you." The Baroness appears at the head of the staircase, visibly shaken. We see a full body shot of the Baron wearing a full gray cape over his suit, looking more and more like a disciple of Count Dracula. "Mother, come

Once freed, Marianne runs into the waiting arms of the Baron.

here." The Baroness turns her back to the Baron, and whispers, "No." The Baron with a kind but dramatic inflection demands, "Mother, come *here*." She turns back around with a look of terror and slowly descends the staircase, the Baron ordering her to come with him.

But back to Greta, the Baron's nurse. She first rants, "Oh god … He's gone. Oh, good heavens. Oh, God help us. He's free! Oh, God help us, he's gone. He's gone. He's free." Then she cackles and laughs loudly as though she were a mad woman. "He's free, he's gone … the cunning devil. Who got him the key? Was it you? Gone into the night … bats are about … there's

Van Helsing (Peter Cushing) is called to come to the aid of a priest who is studying the case of a village girl (Marie Devereux) who died by mysterious means.

The dead village girl is soon reborn as a vampire, one of the undead.

a wolf howling down there … you don't know what you done, but I know." Mariannee asks about the Baroness, "Would you like to see her? Would you like that?" Greta leads Mariannee to a large chair, with the Baroness leaning back, dead. Calming down, Greta talks to the unhearing Baroness. "Don't blame me, mistress. It was none of my doing. Nay, I always kept faith with you. Twenty years since I first saw you come to the castle here with the old Baron and your little son. A fine handsome little imp he was, too. But you spoiled him. Oh, yes. He was always self-willed and cruel, and you encouraged him. Aye, and the bad company you kept, too. You used to sit and drink with them, didn't you? Yes, and you laughed at their wicked games. Till in the end one of them took him and made him what he is. Well, you've done what you could for him since then, God help you, keeping him prisoner, bringing these young girls to him, keeping him alive with their blood. But the powers of darkness are too strong. They've beaten you. He's free. But he'll come back here. It's certain, aye. He'll come back to his old Greta." Greta walks to a curtained partition, aside from his regular living quarters, housing a simple black empty coffin. "He's got to come back here before cock crow." This sequence reveals the closeness of the Baron and Greta (an actual family), since she literally raised him from childhood, knowing him before and during the time he became a vampire.

At 45:22 Van Helsing goes to the local village girl's grave, hoping to put her to peace before she rises from her grave, a vampire. Eerie organ music swells, as Van Helsing hears, "Wake up! Wake up! My dear, wake up. It's time you awaken. Come on, the master's waiting to see you." We see Greta hunched over the grave, actually lying on it, gently speaking to it. Van Helsing watches the spectacle. "Are you about ready? You've got to be strong … yes, I know it's dark, but you got to push … there's my little beauty."

Greta returns to cackling and smiling as the village girl's hand twists and extends out of her grave. Greta laughs more hysterically. Suddenly the coffin creaks and the lid is slowly pushed open. The organ music grows louder. She sits up, out of her grave, smiling with fangs gleaming in the darkness. Greta pulls the garlic flowers off her as she stands and savors the night air. Suddenly the village priest appears, yells, "Stop!" as he confronts the duo of evil. The priest charges forward bellowing, "In the name of the Almighty," as

The half-crazed Greta acts as a midwife who helps to "rebirth" the village girl as a vampire.

Greta coaxes the village girl to rise anew!

Van Helsing comes out of hiding to hold back the priest. Greta says, "Go, little one, quickly!" The vampire scurries away as the two men grab Greta. A major part of Fisher's mythology involves having a midwife help to give birth to the undead, first rising from the grave or casket to a new life as the reborn vampire. It's a metaphor for birthing an undead life.

At 1:17:07, Van Helsing is carefully exploring the old windmill where the vampires are supposedly hiding. Finding an empty coffin, he is ready to plant a crucifix there, to prevent the vampire from returning to its resting place. Suddenly he hears the wild laughter of Greta breaking the silence. She is surrounded by the smiling vampires, Gina (Mariannee's colleague), and the village girl. Greta says, "Go on, get him. Obey your master, take him," Greta demands. Van Helsing pulls the crucifix out of the coffin and points it toward the two female vampires, and they flee. Greta charges toward the doctor and struggles to knock the crucifix out of his hand. She grabs the holy relic but is unable to maintain her balance, falling to her death on the first level below, clutching the crucifix to her, it falls halfway down. Van Helsing tries to reach the holy cross while holding onto to a rope, but he cannot grasp it, and it falls even

Top: The Baron cowers in fear as he confronts Van Helsing's crucifix; Panicking, Meinster is about to throw a candlestick holder at Van Helsing

further away. The Baron is watching as the crucifix falls, baring his fangs, hissing. The Baron wields a swinging chain and attempts to quickly dispatch Van Helsing. But the erstwhile vampire killer athletically swings on a rope knocking the Baron onto a pile of hay. They struggle back and forth, and the Baron finally chokes Van Helsing into unconsciousness with a chain. Dr. Van Helsing falls to the ground and the wild-eyed Baron bends down, spreading his cape, for the vampire's kiss. When his head comes back up, his smiling lips are covered in blood.

At 1:18:59, the good doctor awakens, groaning in pain. He feels around his throat and finds the vampire's kiss, deep in thought, realizing what he must

Baron Meinster appears unexpectedly at Chateau Meinster.

Mariannee unknowingly escapes the wicked intentions of Baron Meinster but Gina (Andree Melly) isn't so lucky.

Gina is reborn quite supernaturally as a blood-lusting vampire.

do immediately. He reaches for his flask of holy water and puts an iron into the blacksmith's pit, waiting for it to heat up so he can burn the vampire's mark from his throat. As he applies the red-hot iron to his neck, the vampire's bite disappears with the aid of the holy water. The Baron finally returns to the mill, along with Mariannee, whom he has captured. "Beautiful, isn't she? What a pity such beauty must fade unless we preserve it. She's going to join us, Doctor. And you are going to watch her initiation." A closeup of the Baron reveals bloodshot eyes, red veins clearly showing. (All of Fisher's vampire films show those raging red eyes, when aroused.) While the Baron is momentary distracted, Van Helsing reaches for his flask of holy water and flings it twice into the demon's face, the blessed water acts like acid and burns him. The vampire backs up and screams. His face smokes. The Baron kicks the burning coals over, and sets fire to the mill. Van Helsing and Mariannee rush to the top floor, while the disfigured vampire rushes outside. Mariannee uses the ladder to climb below, but Van Helsing jumps heroically onto a blade of the windmill, falls upon all its blades to form the shadow of a crucifix, which catches the Baron. The Baron gasps, turns, and faces the crucifix shadow. He collapses and dies. Terribly undramatic. The mill goes up in flames.

In the original screenplay, Van Helsing evokes an evil spell which raises an army of bats to fight and destroy the vampires, but Peter Cushing objected to evoking evil forces and thus, rejected doing the scene (which ultimately was used for the climax of Don Sharp's Hammer film *The Kiss of The Vampire*). So we have a rather bland sequence where the giant shadow of a crucifix causes the destruction of the Baron Meinster. Compare that ending to the rousing chase sequence and disintegration in *Horror of Dracula*, one of the most riveting climaxes ever to grace a horror film.

After *Horror of Dracula*, Hammer vampire scripts usually employ a "Klove" who is a human servant, essentially a slave, who serves vampires, protects them, or re-animates them (a male Greta), showing the vampire is vulnerable to humans who seek to destroy them. Surprisingly, in *Horror of Dracula* Christopher Lee and mate (Valerie Gaunt) were never challenged by human vampire hunters until Jonathan Harker came along, although the crypt sequence shows the extent of their vulnerability.

Almost humorously, Baron Meinster, once freed from the chateau, reassumes his position as estate holder for the peasants living in the shadow of his chateau. The vampire finds himself getting into a heated argument with Herr Jang who cites his strict rules of fellowship (he does not approve of the relationship between Mariannee and the aristocrat, not realizing it is actually the new Baron). Once Meinster introduces himself, he smugly

Mariannee is shocked when the coffin lid of Gina (Andree Melly) flies off.

Van Helsing uses a blacksmith's iron to burn away the vampire's kiss.

At the old windmill, Greta gathers with the village girl and Gina, awaiting the return of Baron Meinster.

tells Lang that he is the landlord that collects Lang's rent, at a rather low fee (insinuating the rent might go up because of Lang's insults). As the vampire he bleeds victims dry, and, metaphorically, as landlord he also bleeds victims dry. But this is a British film, and it relies upon the age old conflict between the rich aristocracy and the working class, always making the gentry the villains and perhaps establishing a reason why vampires are often called "Count" or "Baron."

At 35:50, while being driven in the coach, Van Helsing asks Mariannee about her luggage, and she says she left it at the chateau. She intends to send for it, but Van Helsing advises against that saying, "I've been asked to make a study of a strange sickness. A sickness partially physical, partially spiritual. Have you heard of the cult of the undead? It is most prevalent in Transylvania and the lower Danube." Van Helsing says it could spread unless it's "stamped out." Vampirism is both a physical and spiritual disease, the physical representing all the traits of the undead predator and the spiritual representing the corruption that destroys the soul.

At 48:19 Van Helsing approaches the Chateau Meinster after dark. He comes across the table where Mariannee and the Baroness ate dinner, he pauses, only a ticking clock filling the soundtrack. Van Helsing, holding an ornate cruifix, opens the Baron's chamber door, the hinges creaking loudly. Roaming around the Baron's wing of the chateau, he finds and examines the vampire's manacle, and then opens the red-curtained chamber where the Baron's coffin formerly rested, its outline marked in dust. Dramatic music plays. Behind him creeping closer and closer is the image of the former Baroness, now garbed in dull gray, the same as the Baron. She sneaks nearer to Van Helsing, raising her cloak to hide her fangs, a look of guilt expressed on her face. Van Helsing tells the Baroness he's come to find her son. Suddenly the curtains are flung open and the Baron appears in the archway, cape fully spread. A maniacal sneer is on his face. The Baron hisses at Van Helsing, showing his fangs. Van Helsing produces his crucifix, causing the vampire to writhe in pain and close his cape upon his eyes. The Baron runs to throw a candlestick at him.

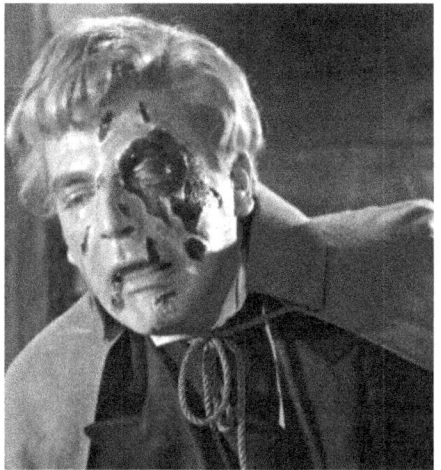

Baron Meinster is burned by holy water and escapes outside the mill.

Van Helsing reaches for the crucifix, which is about to fall from Greta's hand, as Baron Meinster looks on.

Using his chain, Baron Meinster is about to render Dr. Van Helsing unconscious.

Falling to the floor but quickly getting up, Van Helsing slides the crucifix down along the dinner table, the Baron cringes at its sight. The Baron pushes the table trying to crush Van Helsing behind it. The vampire rushes from the chateau, ancient candlesticks knocked down behind him as he flees. The Baron narrowly escapes into his coach. This sequence clearly shows the effects of holy relics on ultimate evil.

The Baroness confronts Van Helsing and asks if her son has escaped. Van Helsing says yes, and the Baroness says, "You'll never catch him. He's too clever." Van Helsing says, "He has taken the blood of his own mother." The Baroness says, "It was all my own fault. I loved his wildness. I encouraged it. And when this monstrous thing took possession of him, I didn't send for a priest or doctor. I hid him and helped him to live. And now there's no release from this life, which isn't life or death. And now I know I'll have to do any hideous thing he asks me to do." Van Helsing says there is one release, and the Baroness smiles. And we all know what that means.

Just as we stressed in *Horror of Dracula*, the vampire attempts to corrupt and ultimately destroy the family from within. Here the highest contamination occurs, the vampire giving the kiss of the undead (and we stressed it has sexual connotations) to his very own mother. Another case of incest has occurred. The ultimate evil wreaks havoc on the family, the Baroness finally paying for enabling her son and his evil ways for all these years. And the promise from the release of evil is strongly represented in Fisher's vampiric world view and mythos.

Comparing the physical appearance of the Baron in the chateau after his release can be contrasted to the Baron who is courting Mariannee at the Lang School, where he wears a neat haircut, a fine suit, and a countenance properly appropriate for the courtship. No wild-eyed, fang-filled monster here. Gina describes his appearance at 56:30 as, "Isn't he handsome. He's just like I imagined Prince Charming was to look at. So noble and with such wonderful eyes. Such tenderness in them and humor, too. I must be careful, or I'll be falling in love with him myself." This contrast between appearance is essential in Fisher's world.

Gina is vampirized when Mariannee goes downstairs to get fresh bread for toast for Gina and herself. The two are student teachers at the academy. Gina sits alone in the room, as eerie organ music swells. A bat swoops outside Gina's large windows, so she shuts most of them and closes the curtains. Sitting at her vanity, terrified, she silently waits as Meinster, in full vampire regalia, stands behind her, barring his fangs. Her Prince Charming image of the Baron now destroyed, Gina is still transfixed by his gaze and comes nearer the

A disciple of Dracula

Baron Meinster is perhaps the most perverted vampire of all time.

Young lovers at the Lang Academy

Undramatically, and inferior to *Horror of Dracula*, Baron Meinster dies by the shadow of the windmill blades, forming a crufix.

vampire He spreads her collar as she bends her neck to the side, making it easier for the vampire's kiss. He goes in for the kill.

At 1:09:10 dead Gina is chained inside her casket. Van Helsing has ordered that her body be held far away from the house in the stables, guarded by two adults until nightfall (the separation of evil from the main domain is evident again). Frau Lang and servant Severin are currently keeping watch. "No horse can abide a corpse nearby," Severin utters. The horse appearing in the background is very nervous. Mariannee comes to relieve Frau Lang before Van Helsing's return, and the woman is so grateful. Suddenly one of the two locks falls off the coffin, strangely still locked shut as it falls on the ground. Mariannee asks Severin to fetch Herr Lang, suspecting something's very wrong. But as soon as he exits the stables, a bat swoops down to attack, Severin screams. The casket lid thuds and flies open as Mariannee gasps, Gina rising in her coffin. She sits erect, smiling, showing her fangs. She slowly gets out of her coffin. Once again, the physical difference between the living Gina and the undead one is striking, the human façade mousey and quite literally an old maid in the making, while the vampiric one is all sexual sizzle. Mariannee cowers in fear, walking backward, horrified. "Mariannee, my darling Mariannee. You haven't forgotten your little Gina? Put your arms around me, please. I want to kiss you, Mariannee. Please be kind to me. Say that you forgive me for letting him love me." Van Helsing finds Severin's facially disfigured corpse lying just beyond the stables. "We can *both* love him, my darling. He's up at the old mill now. We can go there together. Come with me, Mariannee." The vampire reaches out to her just as Van Helsing bursts through the door. He eyes the empty coffin and rushes to the fainting Mariannee, grabbing her as she falls. Gina runs away. Van Helsing forces Mariannee to tell him the Baron's location and gives her a rosary to wear. He tells her to lock all her doors.

After the incest that occurs between the Baron and Baroness, we now have even more socially unacceptable behavior as Gina tries to appeal to lesbian seduction and a three-way sexual relationship, stressing the unholy togetherness of the vampire cult. In such times, this was considered very depraved behavior, even if it is more accepted today. Vampirism is the utter corruption of everything good.

Director Terence Fisher was most thorough in his creation of vampire mythology and seemed to have spent a great amount of time developing it. He was interested in the cultish ways of vampirism in this movie and what motivated their behavior, besides blood. His mythology was much more than good vs. evil, more than a Pagan religion against a Christian one. It primarily dealt with a

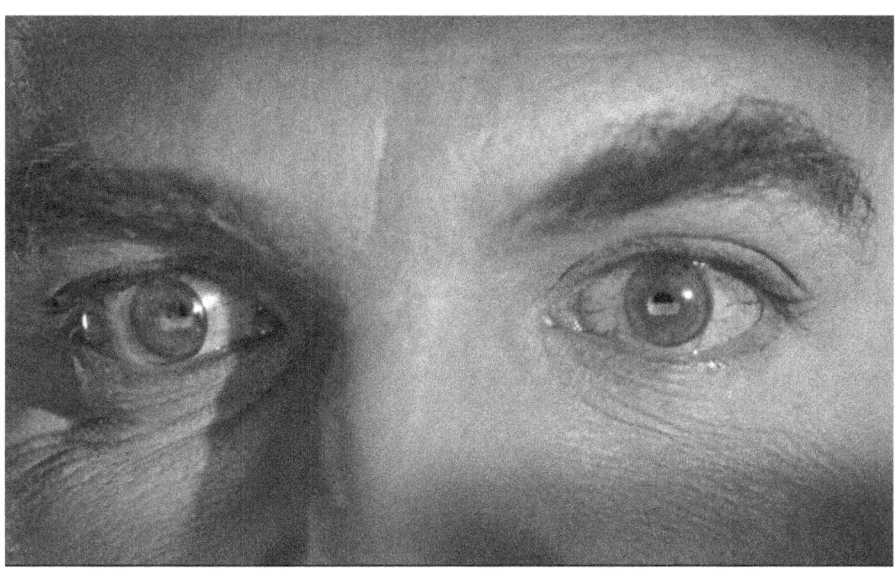

Director Terence Fisher loves to show close-ups of his vampire's eyes.

corruption of the soul, and family values. As the undead vampires attempted to copy these familial values—loyalty, attraction, and even love—they attempted to corrupt these forces in the human world, trying to prove vampirism was the way to exist eternally in the most satisfactory of ways. In the ultimate war, vampires were fighting for the most hedonistic existence possible, and sold their bill of goods rather well.

Dracula—Prince of Darkness

But what about a proper sequel to *Horror of Dracula*, one that would again star Christopher Lee (who along with Peter Cushing were now Hammer's major stars) and carry on from the exciting climax of *Horror of Dracula*? Fans were clamoring for this sequel for almost eight years when *Dracula—Prince of Darkness* finally appeared in 1966. By this time, the magic of Hammer Film Productions was transforming from making servicable art to delivering marketable product, and the crew that made this sequel must have realized that this film was basically a step down, but in parts it was still inspired. Terence Fisher was much older when directing this sequel, and most likely, far less inspired, but when it came to the mythology of vampirism, he still had new aspects to share. *Dracula—Prince of Darkness* reused some of the same talent—Terence Fisher, director (for his final *Dracula* entry); Jimmy Sangster, screenplay (from an idea by Hammer producer Anthony Hines … but Sangster wrote under the pen name of John Sansom, so this means he did not wish his real name used); star Christopher Lee; new co-stars Barbara Shelley, Andrew Keir (the new vampire hunter/expert), Francis Matthews; Michael Reed, the latest cinematographer; Bernard Robinson, production designer; Roy Ashton, chief make-up artist; James Bernard, music (returning to the series after *Horror of Dracula*); and Chris Barnes, the new film editor. And this was one of the first Hammer's to be photographed in widescreen/Techniscope.

In his third entry, director Fisher focuses on the contrast between proper Helen (Barbara Shelley) and the undead version … husband Alan (Charles Tingwell) is on the right.

Our main cast meets in a tavern: Father Sandor (Andrew Keir), Diana (Suzan Foster), Helen, Alan, and Charles (Francis Matthews)

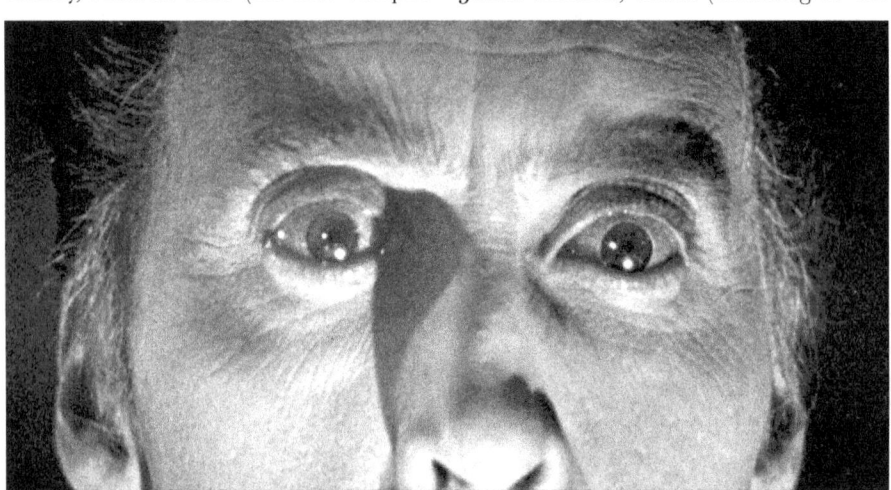

Another close-up of Count Dracula's (Christopher Lee) blood red eyes.

Charles enters the room with Dracula's sarcophagus and his eyes bolt open.

Helen trembles in fright as Count Dracula approaches her.

"After a reign of hideous terror spanning more than a century, the king of the undead was finally traced to his lair high in the Carpathian Mountains. Through the decades, many had sought to destroy him. All had failed. Here at last was an adversary armed with sufficient knowledge of the ways of the vampire to bring about the final and absolute destruction … This then was his fate. Thousands had been enslaved by the obscene cult of vampirism. Now, the fountainhead himself perished. Only the memory remained. The memory of the most evil and terrible creature who ever set his seal on civilization." (Cut to the opening credits with James Bernard reprising his *Dracula* theme.) This opening narration, like those which introduced the first two films, creates a somber mood. And as the visual backdrop for the narration, we have the reprise of the climax of *Horror of Dracula* to remind us of what has gone before.

The million-dollar question is why Christopher Lee had no dialogue in the movie? Many different answers have appeared since the film's release, trying to explain this controversial decision, everything from Christopher Lee rejecting a script which contained bad dialogue, to the non-dialogue sequences in *Horror of Dracula* featuring Lee being so superb and resulting in this entry being written entirely without dialogue. My own response is closer to the second answer, but it is a little more complicated. In both *Horror of Dracula* and *The Brides of Dracula*, director Fisher liked to contrast the distinguished nobleman, the rich landowner, the courtly suitor to the feral beast, the inhuman predator, the animal-like vampire. After illustrating this formula in both films, why the need to repeat the concept? *Horror of Dracula* more than aptly illustrated the difference between vampire and nobleman, so *Dracula—Prince of Darkness* only needed to build upon the feral beast aspect, the vampire predator. In Fisher's first two vampire films, only the nobleman spoke or had any need to do so. Christopher Lee had no need for dialogue in the library scene, the ferocious chase at the climax, or the various vampire's kiss seduction sequences. The same was true with *The Brides of Dracula*, David Peel only needed dialogue in his love scenes with Marianne or his scenes with his mother. When he was the vampire beast with Peter Cushing in the chateau, or in the windmill at the end, no dialogue was called for, even though David Peel did have a few lines

Dracula stands at the top of the stairs, ready to descend for Helen.

during the mill sequence. Now, in *Dracula—Prince of Darkness*, the filmmakers omitted any scenes of Lee as the distinguished Count and featured only those scenes with Lee in either seduction mode or feral beast mode. Those scenes had no dialogue in the first two vampire films, so they needed no dialogue here, since all of Lee's appearances are portraying the feral beast and not the distinguished Count. His mime performance here is superb, and he is only let down by the repetitive script and inferior cinematography.

Helen is resurrected as a vampire.

Helen is stopped dead in her tracks by the sudden appearance of Dracula.

Dracula's human servant is actually called Klove in the film.

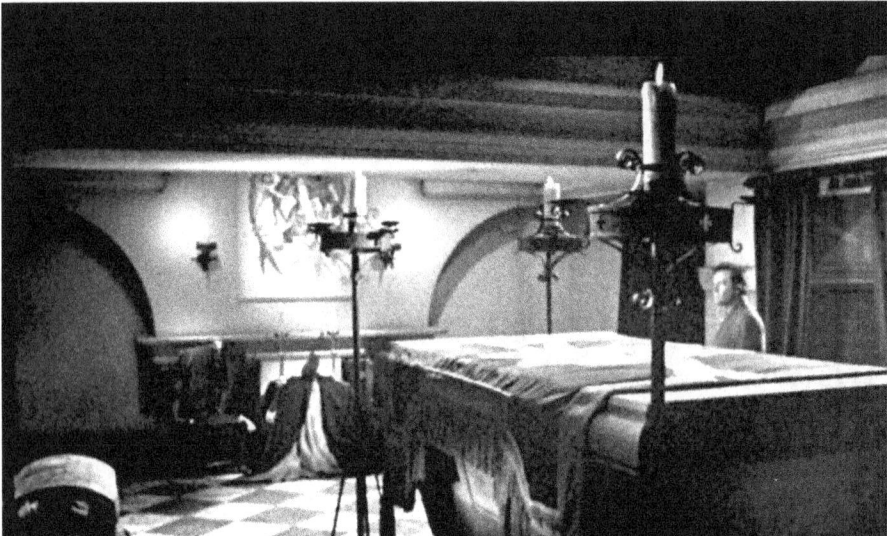

Alan ventures past the tapestry and finds the room where the sarcophagus of Dracula lies. The glorious color highlights the red-lined cape in back.

But director Terence Fisher's vampire mythology is primarily focused in his third vampire film on the contrast between the prim and proper Elizabethan Helen (Barbara Shelley) and the vampire free spirit, whose sexuality and appetite for blood completely changes her personality. At 8:24, we first have the four travelers convene in a tavern as they await their journey to Carlsbad. Charles (Francis Matthews) indulges in a drinking game for fun and buys everyone a round, for the third time that night. His wife, the youthful and pretty Diana (Suzan Farmer), seems to understand her husband and lets him have his fun. Prudish Helen thinks Charles' behavior is "far too extravagant" and looks disapprovingly at the entire scene. Helen tells Charles, "They just think you are a fool." And Charles retorts, "What I do, I do for my own satisfaction." His brother Alan (Charles Tingwell) remains neutral but assumes Charles will do as he pleases. Helen states, "Foolishness is foolishness."

At 14:26, the next day, the coach is at Carlsbad and the coachman refuses to go near the castle and furthermore refuses to even look at it, dumping their luggage and stating he will return two hours after dawn the next morning to take them to Carlsbad, two kilometers away. (Jonathan Harker made the same complaint during the opening narration of *Horror of Dracula*, when his coach driver leaves him stranded.) Within a minute or so, a driverless coach arrives to seemingly rescue them. Without being able to control the two horses, Charles the driver and the others inside veer down the wrong road and arrive at the mysterious castle where four places are already set for dinner, their luggage strangely laid out in two bedrooms, and a fire burns in the fireplace for them. But Helen suddenly changes mood, citing they must flee the castle at once, something threatening is occurring. "I am just frightened!" Helen proclaims later at dinner. In her bed chamber she tells husband Alan, "This place is evil."

So far Helen has been established as a strong-willed individual, having a mind of her own, but one that is very conservative, judgmental, and critical of her family. There is no sense of frivolity or being willing to become spontaneous and change plans when a priest, Father Sandor (Andrew Keir), warns them not to go near the castle in Carlsbad. Basically, she is again a proper Elizabethan who knows what is best.

But after Helen is vampirized at Castle Dracula at Carlsbad, she completely changes her personality. At 48:27, Helen is told by the manservant, Klove (Philip Latham), to go past the tapestry and venture downstairs to find her husband Alan, but she finds herself face-to-face with the recently resurrected Count Dracula, who stands atop the stairs. Dracula slyly smiles, baring his fangs, and slowly descends the staircase. As he approaches her, he raises his cape and bends down for the vampire's kiss, as the music swells. The *Dracula* theme sounds as we find Dracula asleep in his saprophagous, his blood needs satisfied.

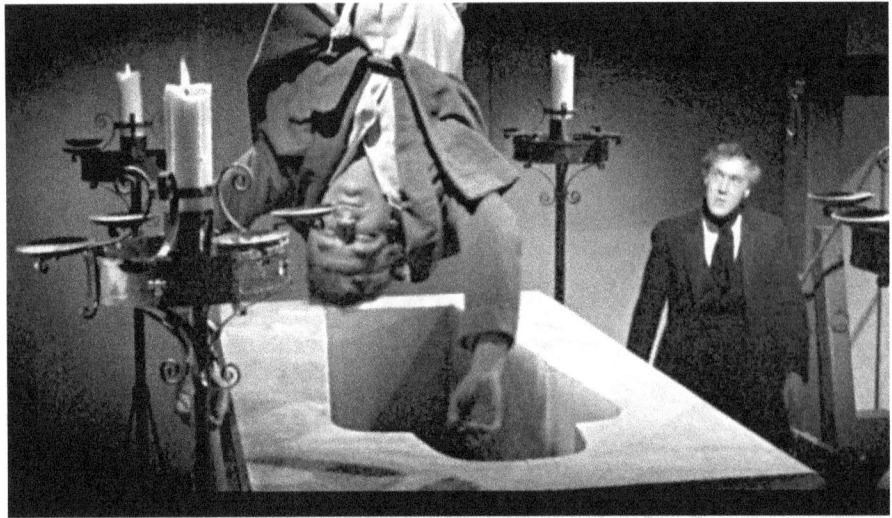

After Klove stabs Alan in the back, he uses a pulley to hoist his body above Dracula's tomb and drains his blood.

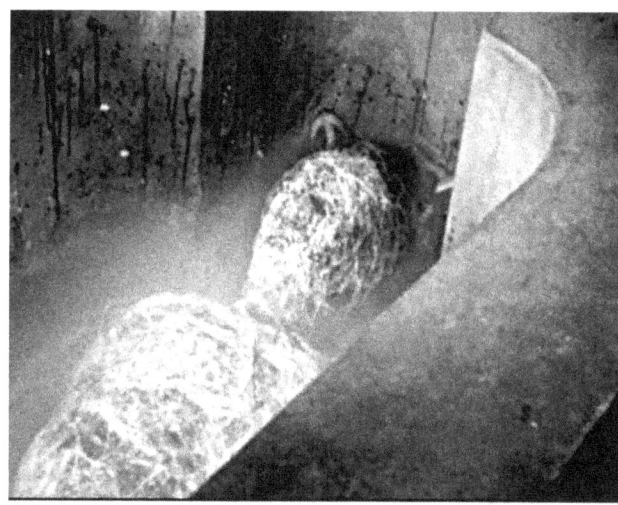

Left: The body of Dracula takes shape inside the sarcophagus; Right: When the blood ritual is finished, a newly animated hand emerges from the sarcophagus (with ring).

At 52:41, Charles returns to the castle to look for Alan and Helen, and he passes by a wall where two swords are mounted. Wandering further, he encounters the tapestry/curtain that encompasses the evil chamber of the resurrected Dracula. Like in *Horror* and *Brides*, it's an area sectioned off from the rest of the castle and represented as the unholy resting place of the vampire king. Of course, Charles ventures behind the curtain. He enters the room with the huge sarcophagus of Dracula, the vampire resting at the bottom unseen by Charles. What captures Charles' attention is a human arm extending outside a large trunk, which is revealed to be dead Alan. As stained-glass windows reveal the setting of the sun, sleeping Dracula's eyes bolt open, like the similar scene in *Horror of Dracula*, but inferior by its similarity, photography, and lighting. Charles, still unaware of the vampire's presence, rushes up the stairs nauseous, as Dracula's eyes dart around his coffin. Trying to duplicate the similar crypt sequence from *Horror of Dracula*, the sequence here pales in comparison. Terence Fisher apparently was running out of fresh ideas.

At 55:29, Klove's carriage with Diana arrives at Castle Dracula, Klove saying that her husband sent for her (which isn't true!). Leading Diana inside a very dark castle, Klove quickly exits, slamming and locking the door. Dramatic music sounds as Helen appears in a light blue nightgown, showing ample cleavage, "We been waiting for you, Diana. *He's* been waiting for you." She extends her arms and says, "Come, sister," walking toward Diana. Diana asks where Charles is and why is he not here? Helen slightly smiles, flashes a hint of vampire fangs, and says, "You don't need Charles." Helen rapidly charges for Diana, but she stops suddenly and looks terrified when Dracula appears on the balcony, stretching like an animal and hissing, acting feral. The scene is an inferior copy of the similar library scene from *Horror of Dracula*, where Dracula attacks his vampire mate, after she attacks Jonathan Harker. Here, several close-ups appear of Christopher Lee, mouth open, fangs barred, and snarling like an out-

When vampire Helen attempts to bite Diana, Dracula appears in feral mode atop the balcony, an inferior imitation of the library scene from *Horror of Dracula*.

When Charles intervenes to save his wife Diana, diseased Helen goes for her brother-in-law's neck.

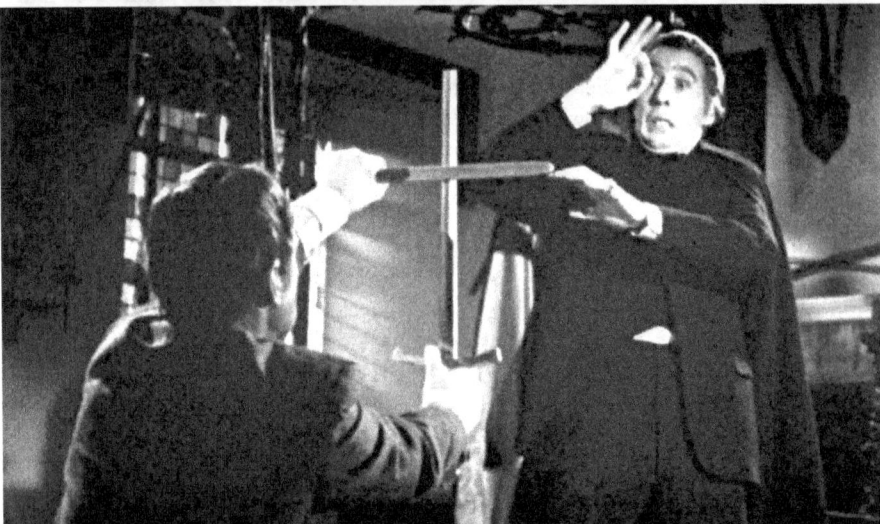

Top: Dracula is about to break Charles' sword in half; Middle: Charles uses the two broken pieces of the sword to form a crucifix; Bottom: Dracula strangles Charles.

raged animal. Dracula pounces down the staircase, grabbing Diana, dragging her by the arm. Suddenly Charles appears as Helen, arms still extended, rushes toward him. Helen goes to embrace Charles, hugging and telling him, "Let me kiss you." As her mouth opens wide and her fangs go for the throat, Charles pushes her back. Diana rushes to Charles again, as Dracula advances and starts choking Charles, as the vampire predator pushes him further back. And then Dracula, with all his supernatural strength, pushes him down very hard in front of the fireplace. The *Dracula* theme plays as Charles, profusely sweating before the raging fire, tries to loosen his collar. Dracula, fangs blazing, loses his triumphant mood once Charles rushes and grabs one of the swords off the wall. Charles cautiously approaches Dracula, who at first waits and then comes at him. Dracula grabs the sword with little effort and breaks it in half, throttling Charles around the neck. The vampire king gains momentum and slinks nearer to his prey, again opening his fangs wide for the kill. Meanwhile when Diana rushes to her husband, a small crucifix brushes against Helen's arm and burns its impression. She wisely holds up the necklace to Helen, who backs off in fear, and then she turns the necklace toward Dracula, who stands still, transfixed, but quick-thinking Charles forms the broken pieces of the sword into a crucifix, Dracula turning in fear and backing away. With their crucifixes, one aimed on Helen, one on Dracula, they back toward the door, not knowing that Klove has entered, drawing his knife. As Dracula and Helen cower in fear, the couple see Klove at the last second and Charles bashes him in the face with one end of the broken sword. They flee outdoors and rush into their waiting carriage. Helen cuddles up to the stoic Dracula, who angrily pushes her aside. His cape spread in the night breeze, strides majestically outside his castle, repeating a similar short scene from *Horror of Dracula*.

At 1:13:47, Diana is sleeping alone in a monastery cell, when she hears tapping on her window. She awakens to find Helen banging outside. "Diana, please let me in. It's cold out here, so cold. Everything is all right now. I got away from him. Oh, please Diana, let me in. I'm freezing." Diana tentatively opens the window and Helen lurches for her arm, quickly biting it. As she tries to free herself, Diana sees Helen pulled back and Dracula takes her place, with intense burning eyes. Diana is screaming when Charles and Sander rush in. When Sandor sees the vampire's bite on her hand, he orders her husband to sit her down so he can hold the burning lamp under her arm, Diana screams in pain. Fisher repeats a similar scene, less dramatically, from the last movie. Sandor sends Brother Mark for salve and bandages. He is then told of the tinker staying the night outside the monastery, and he seems angry he wasn't told. He rushes outside and places two crucifixes in each of the two wooden coffins inside the wagon, so the vampires can't return to them by morning.

Finally, this transformation of Helen from the formal all-so-proper Elizabethan woman to the sexually liberated free spirit is illustrated at 1:16:51, when a brother announces to Father Sandor, "We have caught the woman. She was hiding in the stables." Charles and Sandor venture inside to find two brothers alongside Helen, each holding an arm. Helen twists and writhes with manic strength, continuing to hiss and squirm as she is laid upon a large wooden table. One of the priests/brothers hands Sandor a mallet and wooden stake. As she is held down by four men, still struggling and squirming, Father Sandor places the stake upon her chest and slams the mallet down, producing oozing blood. This animalistic vampire represents little of the old Helen. In all these sequences with Helen, the distinction between vampire predator and human being has never been so clearly shown.

New to Fisher's mythology is the resurrection of a Dracula sequence, to become a staple in future Hammer vampire projects, but this is the first Hammer vampire film to feature one. At 38:14, Alan is awakened by the still-human Helen, having a bad dream. The couple hears rustling in the corridor and Alan decides to investigate. He sees Klove dragging a trunk down the hallway, as ominous oboe music flourishes. Against Helen's wishes, Alan decides to go outside the room and investigate. He creeps around the castle in utter darkness, going behind the large tapestry, when he comes to a room with a giant stone sarcophagus. On the side of the coffin is the engraved name "Dracula." A red-lined cape rests against the candle-lit wall behind him. Thunder crackles outside. Alan passes into a curtained side room and sees an urn sitting on a small table. Suddenly Klove appears in silhouette outside the curtain, and he quickly stabs Alan in the back. A rapid cut shows Helen in her bedroom, looking frightened and very concerned. Klove drags Alan's corpse to the stone tomb as he slides the tapestry off the top, revealing a very high sarcophagus. Klove uses a pulley to hoist Alan's corpse above the sarcophagus and carefully empties the

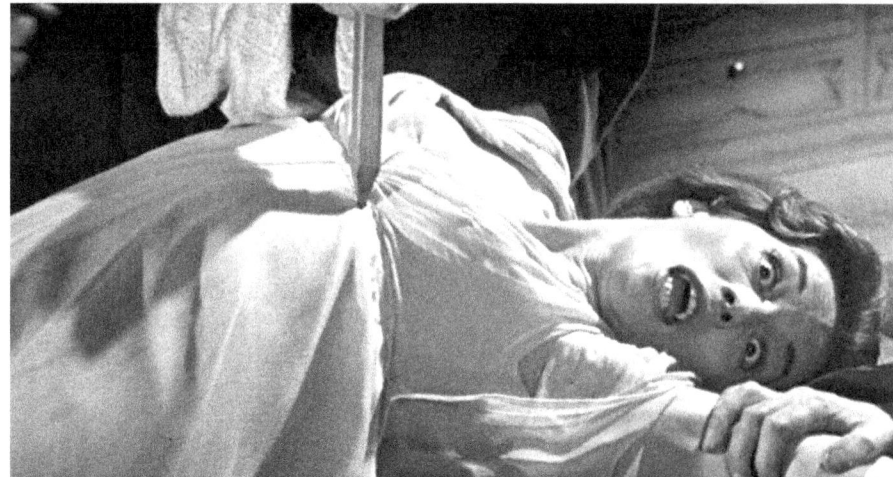
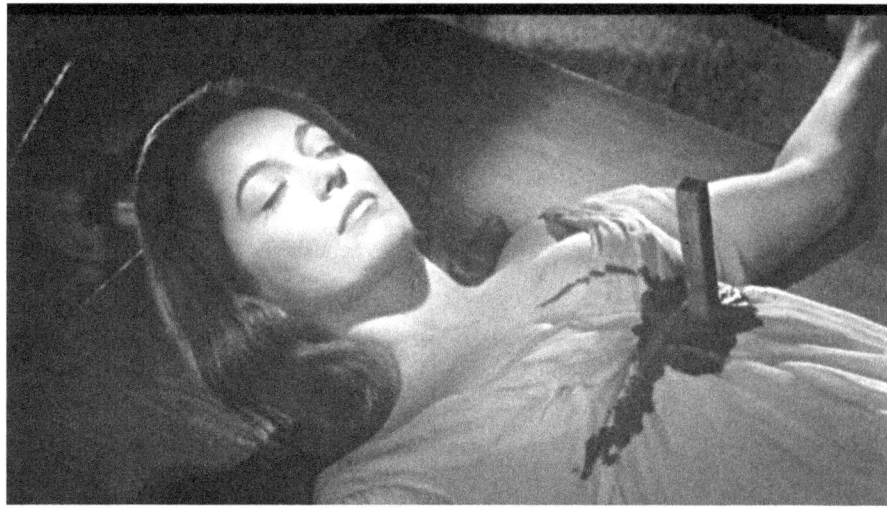

The staking of Helen

contents of the urn the full length of the coffin. Then the manservant carefully slits Alan's throat and directs the blood flow there. Klove takes a few steps backward as the fresh blood cojoins with the ash of Count Dracula's remains from the urn. Smoke rises as a body takes shape. As Klove watches, a ringed hand emerges from the top of the coffin, grasping for the edge. Intense orchestra music builds as the hand crawls around and an arm emerges as we cut back to concerned Helen's bedroom, a thunderstorm rages. Helen tries to exit her room when she confronts Klove, saying something about her "husband" and tells her to follow me. She has a horrified face and rushes out the door. No matter how Dracula was destroyed in the previous film, there is always a specific resurrection ritual to be followed to return the vampire king to a quasi-undead state.

But central to *Dracula—Prince of Darkness* is the person who is the human slave and protector of Count Dracula. First

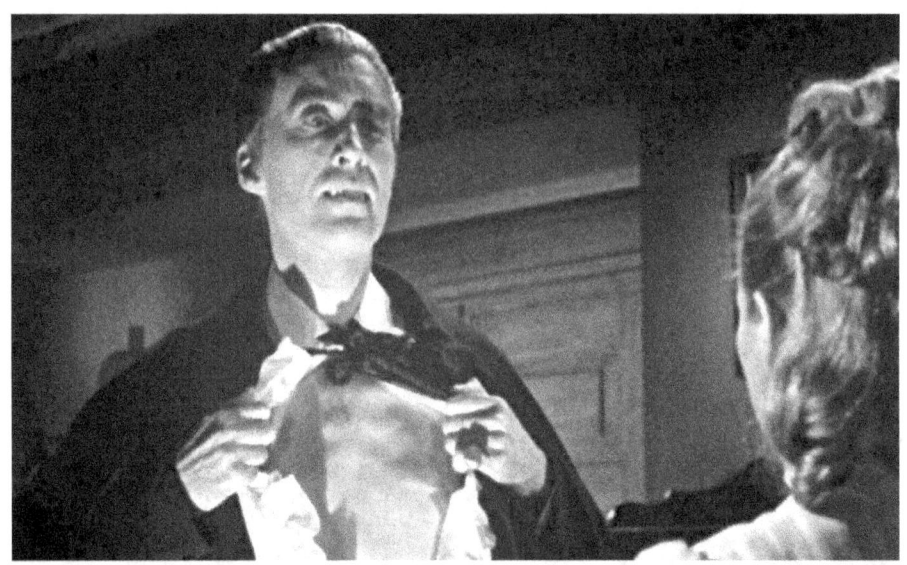
Dracula opens his shirt, exposing his chest to allow Diana to drink his blood.

Ludwig (Thorey Walters) is about to eat a fly.

introduced in *The Brides of Dracula* in the character of Gerda (Freda Jackson), who was the old nurse for Count Meinster (well before the time Meinster was vampirized). At 102:59, when Sandor first takes Charles and Diana to the monastery, he gives them a lesson on vampires and related subjects (another of those talky sequences where specifics of vampire lore are simply told for the audience's sake.) The fountainhead of this obscene cult was Dracula himself." Then Sandor says, "I thought we'd seen the last of him." Sandor relates how through the blood sacrifice of his brother Alan, Count Dracula is now resurrected. Then Charles demands, "I must kill him." And Sandor corrects him, "Not kill, for he is already dead. He can be destroyed but not killed." We hear Sandor describe the old standbys used to kill Dracula, but new to the mythology is, "Running water will drown him." Sandor says, "He is not invulnerable." "You see, there are people who help him. Apparently normal human beings who are not vampires themselves but who, for reasons we don't understand, are in his power. This Klove is such a man, spending his life at the castle, waiting for such an opportunity as you presented him with last night, a chance to resurrect his master."

Here we have two such characters, slaves to Dracula, Klove and Ludwig (Thorley Walters). We see just how instrumental Klove was in snaring the victims needed for the resurrection scene. Klove is introduced at 26:47 when the driverless carriage takes the four travelers to castle Dracula. While inside observing the blazing fireplace, four place settings at the dinner table, and their luggage neatly deposited in their bedroom, a shadow approaches the already nervous Helen from the hall, whose eyes widen in terror as Diana shows grave concern. A lanky male appears in the shadows, ominous and silent, at first misleading the viewers into believing it is the figure of Dracula, greeting his visitors to his castle, until he walks out of the darkness to reveal a man with thin features and gray hair. "I'm sorry if I startled the lady, sir. It was unintentional … I trust the rooms are satisfactory … my master's hospitality is renowned. If you are ready, I will serve dinner now." The group is very happy to have a meal and accommodations for the night, but Helen is still dreading remaining in the castle and wants to leave immediately. Even though not yet introduced by name until he serves a meal, this is Dracula's manservant Klove (Philip Latham), a rather mysterious but polite servant. He says his master Count Dracula, now dead, left orders that the castle remain open to receive all visitors.

Later that evening, at 32:50 Klove checks in on Helen and Alan, in their bedroom. Looking like a character out of *The Rocky Horror Picture Show*, asking them, "Is there anything further you or madame require, sir?" All their needs have been

Ludwig goes outside the monastery to invite Dracula inside.

Alan's arm extends out of the trunk.

Dracula's coffin slides down the incline.

As the sun goes down Dracula explodes out of his casket and grabs Charles.

met. "He's a strange one," Alan declares after Klove wishes them a good night and leaves. Helen responds, "Strange and frightening … I can't get through to you that everything about this place is evil … This whole situation is like a bad dream … The worst part of it is that I'm the only one that can see it. Oh, Alan. Let's go, please!"

And lastly, Klove is the tinker who drives the carriage with Dracula's and Helen's coffin to the monastery at 1:05:57 to ask for shelter for the evening. When he is denied, he is told by a brother that he and his carriage can remain outside the monastery for the night, allowing the two vampires admittance to the monastery with a little help from another servant of Dracula, the strange Ludwig. Besides being Dracula's slave, Ludwig represents evil on the inside, contrasted to evil on the outside, represented by Dracula and Helen.

At 1:05:37 Ludwig, who lives at the monastery, requests to see Sandor. Sandor reveals, "He was a traveler, like yourself. I found him one night near Castle Dracula. Something he had seen or heard unhinged his mind. He lost his memory completely. We brought him here. And here he has remained these past 12 years." Working alone creating a cover for a new ornate folio, Ludwig (Thorley Walters) sings to himself while catching a fly, which he secretly eats. "Flies, Ludwig?" Sandor asks. Ludwig answers, "A small aperitif, Father Sandor. It will soon be dinner. I finished the cover of the third folio. I wanted your opinion of it. Is it exquisite or merely magnificent?" Father Sandor smiles, "Exquisite." Charles notices Ludwig is kept locked in his small room. Father Sandor responds, "He has been known to erupt." Ludwig is suddenly overtaken by the urge to look for something outside, something he hasn't felt in 12 years, the urge to help Dracula. He might be called Ludwig here, but essentially, he is a recrafted Renfield, a fly eater, and defender of vampires. Thorley Walters, like Michael Ripper, was another hidden treasure within Hammer, playing semi-comical character roles, very eccentric, and a standout in every Hammer film in which he appeared. Thought to be mostly an unhinged but devoted artisan, he is not closely watched when he helps Dracula and Helen. Once again in Fisher's vampire mythos, evil from outside can be defeated if there is the concerted effort to defeat it. But evil from the inside is much harder to identify and defeat.

At 1:09:10 it is agreed by Sandor and Charles that once she is well, Diana will be sent home to England. Sandor says, "You and I will do what must be done. We will pull that castle down stone by stone if necessary … Last night Dracula was robbed of his prey, your wife. He has seen her and touched her. He considers that she belongs to him already. He will want her badly." Charles is concerned about Dracula coming to the monastery. Sandor says, "It is unlikely, and even if he does, he will not get in. What the inhabitants of these parts don't realize is that a vampire cannot cross a threshold unless he is invited by someone already inside. And if he is, all the garlic flowers in the world won't keep him out." We immediately cut to Ludwig opening a small window as he says out to the darkness, "Yes, master, yes," as he hammers at the window bars, bending them so he can get out. Dracula finds Ludwig waiting outside, so he can invite Dracula inside through the monastery door. Again, we have the re-invented plot angle reprised from *Horror of Dracula* where Dracula desires and must possess the wife of the man who comes to Castle Dracula.

To view the real power of Ludwig, at 1:20:08, Ludwig invites Diana to meet

Dracula has to balance himself on a piece of ice, looking like a novice surfer.

A new aspect in Terence Fisher's mythology could be executed a little more realistically and far less silly.

Sandor in his study. The brother watching Diana protests, but Ludwig says everything is under control. Ludwig leads Diana to the room, a chamber shrouded in darkness, and he leaves, closing the door. Next, a hand is shown locking the door, as Dracula appears, his eyes blazing. The pair lock eyes as Dracula raises his hand and approaches Diana. He points to the crucifix necklace, which she then removes. Dracula pushes his cape to the side and opens his shirt, exposing his chest. He takes the fingernail of his little finger and opens a small wound on his chest. Then he reaches for and holds Diana by the shoulders and slowly pulls her to his torso and makes her drink. But before she reaches the bloodsucking demon, we hear Charles call her name as Dracula attempts to carry her away in his arms. Ludwig, transfixed, follows the vampire king and Diana, until Sandor calls for the brothers to take Ludwig to his cell. Ludwig, out-witting the priests and brothers, slyly has managed to sneak Dracula inside, without having been noticed. This treacherous evil festering inside is frustrating. Because when you suspect evil lurking outside, it is a shocking surprise to find evil already inside.

At 1:23:45, Dracula, driven by Klove, rapidly heads for home with Diana. "He will head for his castle. Once there he will be safe, and your wife will be lost forever. We must stop them before he gets there." Klove drives the carriage with two coffins inside at full speed, as he flies down the road. Sandor and Charles mount their horses, Charles wielding Sandor's rifle, Sandor tells him there are certain things he is not willing to do, including killing Klove. To head off the wagon the two horseback riders ride cross country and fortunately cut him off, Klove stops his carriage and attempts to strike one of the two men by throwing his knife. But Charles shoots him in mid-throw.

The driverless carriage continues toward Dracula's Castle on its own. The horses halt by a hill at the castle, leaning to the side, ice and snow covering the ground, Dracula's coffin slides down the incline and winds up in the middle of an ice-covered lake outside the castle. The men find Diana alive in the second coffin. "God be praised," Sandor declares. Sandor takes out the mallet and wooden stakes, but Charles grabs them and tells Sandor to look after Diana. Charles carefully maneuvers across the ice to reach Dracula's coffin. Reaching the coffin, Charles releases both metal shafts, which attach the coffin's lid, as Sandor notices the darkening night sky and yells, "It's too late Kent. Get away from there!" Suddenly Dracula's coffin lid flies open (like Gina's similar resurrection in the last film), and Dracula rises in his coffin to grab Charles' hand. Dracula exits his coffin struggling with Charles. Diana grabs the rifle and shoots a hole in the ice, water bubbling near Dracula's foot. Sandor utters, "Running water" (a vampire cannot cross running water), and grabs the rifle, shooting holes in the ice, preventing Dracula from crossing the frozen lake, as Charles runs to safety. The ice breaks to form a circle around Dracula, and in a ridiculous scene, Dracula must teeter

In an eerie sequence, Helen pleads with Diana to be admitted into the monastery.

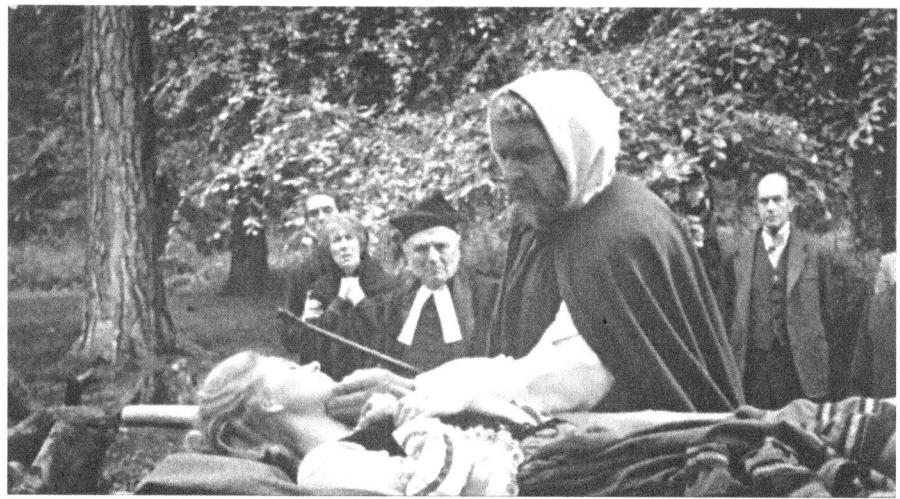

When we first meet Father Sandor, he is seeing that a poor village girl gets proper burial in the churchyard.

back and forth on a floating piece of ice, looking like a novice surfer trying to keep his balance, gradually sinking down with the ice. Dracula screams in agony as he further slips beneath the water. We see Dracula underwater, lifeless, as the credits come up. At least this is a new concept.

Finally, Fisher's mythology introduces the new vampire slayer, for the first time *not* Peter Cushing portraying Dr. Van Helsing, which really tied together both *Horror of Dracula* and *The Brides of Dracula*. Instead of having a thin, college-decorated cerebral man of culture, Hammer recreated the vampire slayer as a member of the clergy, who is a very strong rotund man, who is not averse to carrying a rifle or pointing out that people are superstitious fools or stuck in their old ways, loud and rude when Peter Cushing was sensitive and quiet. At 7:00 we see Father Sandor arriving deep in the woods to stop the staking and burning of a young girl, falsely believed to have been killed by a vampire. Sandor orders that she be buried in the churchyard, and when the local priest refuses such a request, Sandor says he'll perform the burial rites himself. The padre looks quite impressive riding on a horse, manning a rifle, and exerting his will against a small group of locals.

Fortunately at 10:25 Father Sandor enters the very tavern where our four travelers are resting, before continuing to Carlsbad the next morning. Father Sandor enters the tavern to warm himself by the fireplace and accidentally bumps into our four travelers. He disapprovingly sees hanging garlic and criticizes the people in the tavern, "There is no Boogey man anymore, and if there was, this wouldn't keep him out. Can't you get it into your thick skulls, it's over? It's been finished these past 10 years!" As he warms himself by the fire, he starts talking to the four travelers—who are planning to do some climbing, some sightseeing—and explains that tomorrow they are due in Carlsbad, and Sandor gets very serious about them not going there, especially near the castle. But it seems there is no castle on their map.

In each of the first two vampire movies, Terence Fisher introduces and expands upon his detailed vampire mythos, something Universal only half-heartedly did in the 1930s. His world vision is unique to vampire cinema and heavily populates all two scripts, sometimes becoming just as important as the narratives. In fact, one could make the claim that the script grows from this intricate mythology, and this mythology becomes the backbone of the first two stories. Unfortunately, Terence Fisher started repeating story threads in *Dracula—Prince of Darkness*, and when he added something new, the results were underwhelming and sometimes silly. It was time for Fisher to stop making Hammer vampire films. Besides, who could better *Horror of Dracula*?

We explore the solitary nature of the vampire with perhaps the addition of his sole/soul mate in *Horror of Dracula*, while the concept of Dracula's disciples and the cult of the undead is explored in *The Brides of Dracula*. *Horror* features a distinguished and older vampire predator, while *Brides* features a younger vampire (both in age and the time since the Baron became transformed into one of the undead). *Dracula—Prince of Darkness*, for the very first time, explores retread formulas, repeating large chunks of story threads from the first two entries and trying to revise them in new wrappings. However, *Dracula—Prince of Darkness* does introduce the resurrection sequence and the aspect of a victim feeding upon Dracula's own blood, plus the concept of the human slave to Dracula is expanded.

It is this collaboration between screenwriter Jimmy Sangster (working solo or working with others) and director Terence Fisher that created period vampire costume dramas on a budget, interjecting sex and blood in color to the formula. But at the heart of these three movies lies its reliance on the world mythology of vampire customs and rules which make these three Hammer films memorable. When we see Hammer vampires on screen, Terence Fisher makes the characters truly frightening, fierce, and monstrous. His vampires are preternatural and otherworldly and become much more than smoke and mirrors. We truly believe them to be creatures of another world.

Looking like he walked out of *The Rocky Horror Show*, Klove checks on Helen and Alan in their room.

THE SADIST
Limping, Giggling, and a Bottle of Pop
by Christopher Gullo

The entire cast and crew of *The Sadist* during the original film production

Midnight Marquee reaches an amazing accomplishment with this issue—sixty years of publication covering our favorite genre films and some we did not even know. For my article I wanted to cover a film that premiered the same year as this publication—1963. Some films from that year have already been written about numerous times like Hitchcock's *The Birds* or Robert Wise's *The Haunting*. I opted to go a different route and cover a low budget but groundbreaking film, James Landis' harrowing and unrelenting tale of Midwest horror, *The Sadist*. The film was groundbreaking as it was the first to portray the exploits of real-life spree killer, Charles Starkweather, who along with his 14-year-old girlfriend, Caril Ann Fugate, terrorized Nebraska and Wyoming, in the late 1950s, taking 11 lives before finally being captured by police on January 29, 1958. Starkweather, who dropped out of high school and idolized James Dean and his rebellious image, callously killed his girlfriend's parents and then strangers they met along their way as they traveled through Nebraska. The crime spree and following court case made national headlines—Starkweather admitting to his murders but also he testified against his girlfriend, stating she too should also receive the death penalty. The jury found the pair guilty and Starkweather was sentenced to death and executed in the electric chair on June 25, 1959, while Fugate, who was the youngest female in U.S. history to be tried for first degree murder, received a life sentence in prison and was paroled in 1976, after serving 17 ½ years. The case was continuously studied by experts trying to understand Starkweather's motives and prevent a copycat killer. It also was adapted into all forms of media for the public—film, television, novels, and song. There have been at least five films heavily inspired by the Starkweather killings—*Badlands* (1973), *Kalifornia* (1993), *Natural Born Killers* (1994), *Starkweather* (2004), and of course the very first one—*The Sadist* aka *Sweet Baby Charlie* aka *Profile of Terror*.

"There are lots of good seats here for you fans who enjoy the Dodgers and the Redlegs. If you're close by, why don't you come on down? You'll enjoy it down at Dodgers stadium—it's a gorgeous day, short sleeve crowd, everyone having a wonderful time." Three schoolteachers—Carl Oliver (Don Russell), Ed Stiles (Richard Alden), and Doris Page (Helen Hovey) plan on doing just that, as they drive through the desert on their way to Los Angeles to attend the Dodgers game. But a faulty fuel pump along the way forces them to stop at a garage off the highway. There they find a graveyard of automobiles and parts—but no owner. Ed decides to repair the car, while Carl searches for

After killing the two motorcycle cops, Charlie (Arch Hall, Jr.) and Judy (Marilyn Manning) hide the motorcycles as not to attract attention.

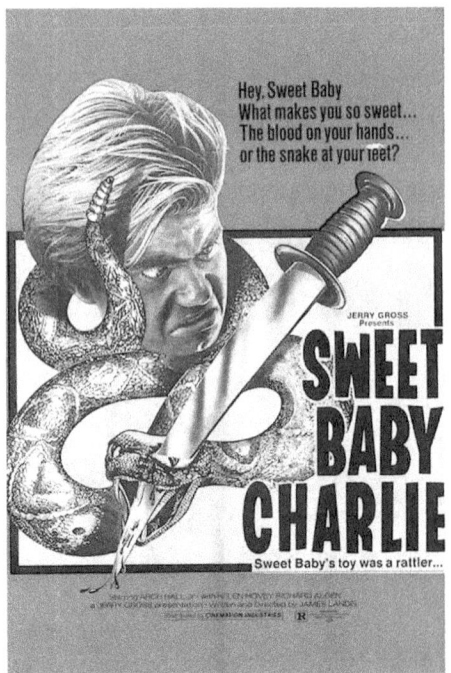

Sweet Baby Charlie was an alternate title used for *The Sadist*

any employees. Upon finding half eaten warm food in the owner's house, Carl quickly returns to alert Ed and Doris that something is wrong, but it is too late—a murderous pair of killers—Charlie Tibbs (Arch Hall, Jr.) and his teenage girlfriend Judy Bradshaw (Marilyn Manning) surprise the teachers and hold them at gunpoint. Tibbs has been on a killing spree in Arizona and is also currently stranded at the garage after being on the run. He quickly demands at gunpoint that Ed finish fixing their car so he can escape with Judy. While Ed desperately tries to stall for time and come up with a plan, Charlie proceeds to torment the teachers mentally and physically, for his enjoyment. He pistol-whips Carl, shoves Doris' face into the dirt, shoots near the frightened teachers—and when that isn't enough—Charlie finally shoots Carl in the face and tells Ed and Doris they are next. Ed tries to figure out how many shots Charlie has left in his gun, but he misses his opportunity before the killer reloads. Two motorcycle cops arrive on patrol at the garage, but Charlie locks Ed in a car trunk and has Judy hold Doris at knifepoint. When Doris struggles and screams for help, Charlie shoots the two police officers dead and tells Ed they have 15 minutes left before he shoots them as well. Ed devises a quick plan, which he executes, to overtake Charlie by temporarily blinding him with gasoline. With blurred vision, Charlie shoots randomly, killing Judy by mistake. In a fit of rage, Charlie pursues both Ed and Doris as Ed tries to fight back but is shot and killed while Doris makes a run through the desert to escape. Charlie pursues her with the car and on foot after it breaks down again. Just as Charlie is about to catch up with Doris fleeing in terror, he falls through the opening of an abandoned pit filled with venomous rattlesnakes and is bit repeatedly leading to his death. Doris makes it back to the broken-down car where she hears Dodgers batter … Ron Fairly hit a grand slam in the first inning, upon which she wanders back alone through the desert.

The Sadist was produced by Arch Hall, Sr., a former stuntman, and actor, who decided to get into production to stay involved in the business. After forming Fairway International Pictures and producing a low budget nudie pic entitled *Magic Spectacles* (1961), Arch Hall, Sr. enlisted his son Arch Hall, Jr. to star in his next project, made the same year, the juvenile delinquent film *The Choppers*. The father/son duo went on to make five additional films: *Eegah* (1962), *Wild Guitar* (1962), *The Sadist* (1963), *The Nasty Rabbit* (1964), and *Deadwood '76* (1965). Arch Hall, Jr. had starring roles in some films, supporting roles in others, and even his dad played supporting roles, a true family business. For *The Sadist*, Arch Hall, Sr. not only produced the film but also provided the opening narration for the television version. James Landis, a writer who had experience dating back to 1950s television productions, wrote the script based on the real events of the Starkweather killings. Landis would serve double duty also directing the film, and it would be the third feature film under his belt. A benefit to adapting his own script meant that Landis had a full understanding of what he wanted to achieve in this tight-paced thriller.

A foreign poster for *The Sadist*

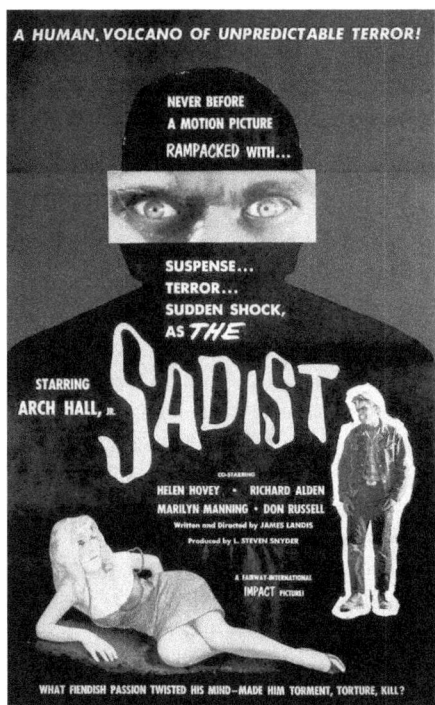

The US 1 sheet for *The Sadist*

Judy holds an ice pick at the throat of Doris (Helen Hovey)

Another huge help for the film was future Academy Award director of photography winner Vilmos Zsigmond, who then was credited as William Zsigmond in *The Sadist*, which was the first film he worked on. Zsigmond, a Hungarian who filmed the battle of the Soviet invasion of his homeland before escaping to the United States, started his career working on low budget films in the 1960s, including some more for Fairway International Pictures. He would elevate to big budget productions like *McCabe and Mrs. Miller* (1971), *Deliverance* (1972), and *The Deer Hunter* (1978); he worked with well-known directors including Steven Spielberg, Brian de Palma, and Woody Allen. Zsigmond's biggest success was his Academy Award win for his work on Spielberg's *Close Encounters of the Third Kind* (1977). What made Zsigmond's photography stand out was his attention to natural light and use of color to create the mood of the film. *The Sadist*, while filmed in black and white, benefitted from Zsigmond's use of the bright sun which seemed to add additional punishment to the hot, sweating teachers as they waited out their fate from their captors. Another unique touch courtesy of Zsigmond was the point of view shot from Charlie during his introduction, slowly raising his gun and pointing it directly at the teachers. This put the audience in the eyes of the killer and worked well and sets up Charlie's dangerous nature before the viewers even see him. The killer point of view became more common after John Carpenter's *Halloween* (1978) and seemed to be a staple of most 1980s slasher films.

The Sadist features a small five-person cast, not including two real police officers, who appear as the would-be saviors to the teachers. Helen Hovey, who played teacher Doris Page, was a cousin of Arch Hall, Jr. Marilyn Manning, who played Charlie's girlfriend Judy, was an office secretary, while Don Russell doubled as not only the production manager but also teacher, Carl Oliver. Canadian actor Richard Alden was a professional, but he had only a few roles completed by 1963. Each player brought something unique to the story. Hovey's character started as an uptight teacher unaccustomed to the real world, until she is forced to accept it by gunpoint. She plays a very important role as her character serves as the moral center of the film, versus the contrasting immorality of Arch Hall, Jr.'s Charlie Tibbs. Manning brings a sense of immaturity and jealousy to Charlie's girlfriend—the viewer never really hears her speak, but every time she whispers into Charlie's ears, you just know something bad is going to happen. Russell's respectability as the elder teacher sort of makes him the leader of the group—his explanation of the rules of baseball to Doris is particularly amusing as she cannot get the point of running the bases after a homerun. It is shocking when Carl is targeted and eliminated by Charlie first. After Carl's murder, it is up to Ed to become the hero, which he tries to be as Doris is depending on him. Although a former soldier in the army and muscular, Ed is still held powerless by the gun-toting Charlie, who seems cleverer than his appearance lets on. Ed's desperate stalling for time while fixing the

ARCH HALL, JR.
•
PERSONAL MANAGEMENT
SHEILS & BRUNO
HO-2-3383

Doris watches as Ed (Richard Alden) works on the car to stall for time so they can get the jump on Charlie.

car to come up with a workable plan is made believable by Alden's steadfast portrayal.

Arch Hall, Jr., putting in a career highlight as thrill killer Charlie Tibbs, was enacting his fourth role for his father's production company. Jr. was a good pick to portray the fictional Starkweather, albeit with a different last name—both men featured a baby face and sported a pompadour hairstyle. Arch Hall, Jr., under the direction of Landis, added to his performance a slightly hunched walk to mimic Starkweather's birth defect that caused his legs to be bow-legged, and he adapted a maniacal and unnerving giggle for which the real killer was teased in school. What makes his character so terrifying is his unpredictability—the audience knows he is a killer and will most likely kill again, but when … and will the teachers escape his wrath? At the beginning of the film, Charlie's voice is heard as a close-up of his wild eyes look on, "I have been hurt by others, and I will hurt them. I will make them suffer as I have suffered." To that end he certainly does make everyone suffer, particularly Carl—whom he immediately has a great hatred for after learning he is a teacher, apparently Charlie wasn't a model student. After forcing Carl to hand over his wallet, Charlie gleefully removes and rips up the tickets to the Dodgers game. The look on Carl's face tells the viewer that he knows his fate is now sealed. Props can certainly aid a performance, and Arch Hall, Jr. makes use of a seemingly innocent one: a bottle of soda pop. As Charlie begins to chug down his bottle of soda in the hot sun, he tells Carl he will shoot him as soon as he finishes—which true to his word he does in brutal fashion. This bottle routine is also repeated later in the film to highlight the climax. Arch Hall, Jr.'s acting career was not long lived, as it wasn't his true love; he also had a band, Arch Hall, Jr. and The Archers, following his film appearances, and he went on to become a pilot for Flying Tiger Airlines.

For a villain as evil as Charlie Tibbs, it makes sense that mother nature has to take care of what man cannot. Carl's reasoning, Doris' pleading, Ed's planning, and even the arrival of two police officers does nothing to stop the unrelenting terror and violence of Charlie Tibbs. It makes sense then that the only thing that could put an end to Charlie's reign of terror is a pit full of poisonous rattlesnakes, which he falls into during his chase after Doris through the desert. There is some foreshadowing of this serpentine revenge in the beginning of the film when Doris first bumps into some snakeskin and screams, thinking it is a real snake, and then again when she sees a water hose Ed removes from the car he is working on. Trapped

Charlie Tibbs aims his gun at teacher Carl Oliver (Don Russell), forcasting a bad end for the veteran educator.

HELEN HOVEY, a small town schoolteacher faces ARCH HALL JR. portraying the infamous killer in THE SADIST opening at................ theather.

"THE SADIST"

The Cast

Charley Tibbs	Arch Hall Jr.	Judy	Marilyn Manning
Doris Page	Helen Hovey	Carl Oliver	Don Russell
Ed Stiles	Richard Alden	Police Officers Etc.	

The Crew

Producer	L. Steven Snyder	Sound Mixer	Alan O'Day
Writer/Director	James Landis	Art Director	Mark Von Berblinger
Dir. of Photography	William Zsigmond	Property Master	Doug Kersting
Editor	Anthony M. Lanza	Makeup	Linda Noonkester
Production Manager	D.D. Russell	Wardrobe	Addalyn Fay
Musical Director	Rod Moss	Executive in Charge of	
Script Supervisor	Joan Howard	Production	Nicholas Merriwether

Running Time 90 min.

SYNOPSIS
(NOT FOR PUBLICATION)

Three small town high-school teachers enroute to Dodger Stadium, to see a ball game, have car trouble and stop at a garage, on a lonely road. The place is mysteriously deserted. Ed Stiles, a physical education instructor, (Richard Alden) decides to repair the car himself. Carl Oliver, (Don Russell) a history teacher, prowls the place, while Doris Page (Helen Hovey) observes. Suddenly terror! From behind a wrecked car steps Charles Tibbs, (Arch Hall Jr.) and his girl friend, Judy Bradshaw, (Marilyn Manning). Charley wants the teacher's car to make a get-away.

Stiles recognizes Tibbs and the girl from a newspaper story. Charley has run amuck on the nation's highways in a killing spree that already has claimed a dozen lives.

Charley, the sadist, torments them and then kills Oliver because Judy doesn't like school teachers. Then he humiliates Doris because she is "a goody, goody, good girl." Charley turns to Stiles, a Korean veteran, who makes every ingenious attempt to out-smart his sadistic captor. When two patrolmen stop in the station for a coke, Charley kills them both from a gun hidden in a grease rag.

Desperately, Stiles turns a gasoline hose on Charley's face. Temporarily blinded, Charley shoots at anything that moves . . . and he kills the only thing he loves, Judy. Discovering his error he goes insane, screaming and shooting. Stiles stalks Charley with a heavy iron bar as Doris races off into the desert. Stiles underestimates the mind of the sadist and is shot down. Charley leaps into Stiles car and chases Doris. He goes to a deserted house which Doris seeks as a refuge. The sadist's car stalls in the sand and he races after her, knife in hand, and then a miracle happens. Doris, with no possible means of escape, is saved by a quirk of fate, as Charley Tibbs accidentally runs across an old water well covering. The rotten boards give way and screaming with shock, Charley is in the middle of a den of rattlers. He fights to climb out, the earth crumbles in, the rattlers strike, and Charley slashes at them with his knife, but they come from everywhere.

Outside, Doris staggers up the road, terror stricken, unconscious of what has befallen the killer, but mindful that some miracle must have happened. Over the abandoned car radio the Cincinatti Reds and the Dodgers are in mid-game as a happy crowd screams with excitement unmindful of any tragedy in the afternoon.

ARCH HALL JR. as the contemptible sadist with girl friend MARILYN MANNING strike cold fear on the nation's highways in THE SADIST now playing at the.........................

THE SADIST IS REALLY HAPPY

Arch Hall Jr. who plays the infamous Charley Tibbs in THE SADIST, with convincing realism, is far from a "twisted" individual. Happily preparing for his sixth starring role, he is a recording artist and a band leader when not before the cameras. THE SADIST, with HELEN HOVEY, RICHARD ALDEN, and MARILYN MANNING, in the other top roles, is playing at ....

FROM THE BLUE GRASS TO STARDOM

Helen Hovey, a Berea college girl, discovered in a church play by producer Nicholas Merriwether, brings to the screen an incredible talent in her first role. As Doris Page, a small town school teacher, she enacts the leading female role in THE SADIST, with Arch Hall Jr. Miss Hovey's performance has alerted Hollywood to the fact that many colleges produce potential stars if seen by the right people. THE SADIST opens at .... theater on ....

SINGER MAKES A BIG JUMP

Arch Hall Jr. leaps from teenage singing roles into a powerful suspense story with the ease of a veteran in portraying an infamous killer in THE SADIST opening at........ ....at the ....theater.

YOUNG ACTOR BECOMES A VETERAN

Arch Hall Jr. who plays the part of the infamous Charley Tibbs in THE SADIST at nineteen years young, brings to the screen a stark realism that ordinarily is the art of the veteran screen star. His performance is being hailed as a most convincing and extraordinary piece of acting. THE SADIST opens..................... at the ....

TAKE ADVANTAGE OF THIS INFORMATION FOR YOUR CAMPAIGN!

SADIST HERE! A HUMAN VOLCANO

A hard-hitting motion picture, depicting the terror, of THE SADIST, comes to the.... ....theater............ .... It stars Arch Hall Jr., Helen Hovey, Richard Alden, and Marilyn Manning. The screen play was written and directed by James Landis.

ACTOR BEGS TO SEE BALLGAME

Begging for his life and a chance to see the Cincinatti Reds versus the Los Angeles Dodgers, Don Russell, veteran actor, plays Carl Oliver, a history teacher who runs afoul of THE SADIST, staring Arch Hall Jr. Helen Hovey, Marilyn Manning, and Richard Alden at the.................................

YOUNG STARS ADORN THE SADIST

A host of young stars, fully equipped with the histrionics for the job, make THE SADIST, one of the hardest hitting and most realistic films in a long time. Arch Hall Jr., Helen Hovey, Marilyn Manning, and Richard Alden, lend the impact that generally accompanies only big name stars to fine filmfare. THE SADIST opens...........at the.............

TERROR IN THE AFTERNOON

When three school teachers on their way to a ball game, come face to face with THE SADIST, things happen that none dreamed possible. With documentary realism Arch Hall Jr. enacts the role of the contemptible sadist in one of the most shock packed films in a long time, THE SADIST opens ....

CANADIAN ACTOR SCORES IN THE SADIST

Richard Alden, of Toronto, appearing opposite Helen Hovey, in THE SADIST, left security in Canada for the insecurity of Hollywood. Director James Landis, after months of search, put him in THE SADIST . . . and was rewarded by a fine performance. Other young stars are Arch Hall Jr. and Marilyn Manning. THE SADIST opens a limited first run at the....................

PRETTY MISS PLAYS PRETTY BAD GIRL

Marilyn Manning, considered one of Hollywoods prettiest young female stars enacts the role of Judy Bradshaw, a fragile, imbecilic side-kick of Charles Tibbs in THE SADIST, opposite Arch Hall Jr. She dies seeking to embrace her fiendish lover who then goes beserk. THE SADIST opens .... at the .... theater.

MARILYN MANNING and HELEN HOVEY star in the terrifying film THE SADIST opening .... at the ....

RICHARD ALDEN, HELEN HOVEY and DON RUSSELL in the suspense drama THE SADIST now playing at the .... theater.

Ed is on the run, evading killer Charlie Tibbs by attempting to hide in a barn.

in the pit and armed with only his knife, a wild-eyed but for once frightened Charlie slashes at the snakes in vain as they strike him at lightning speed. He desperately tries to crawl out of the pit, but a coiled-up rattlesnake strikes repeatedly and finally does the killer in. A fitting end to a venomous villain.

What makes *The Sadist* stand out is its brutality and realism—especially for a film released in 1963. In 2023 we are unfortunately bombarded with news of shootings, but this was something new to the public viewing *The Sadist*. Compared to the fictional monsters in most exploitation films of the period, Charlie Tibbs is even more frightening, as he was real and just as evil as any other supernatural demon. In addition, I really felt sorry for the teachers involved in the story, being a high school history and writing teacher myself. I have fond memories of group trips I took part in with my fellow colleagues to sporting games and a particular one to the Gettysburg battlefield. Speaking of sports, the script was well researched in this area as well—it is noted on the radio that the Dodgers are playing the Cincinnati Redlegs—a name change from their usual Reds from the 1956 through 1960 period, thanks to the Red Scare created by senator Joseph McCarthy. Lastly, even though two of the three actors playing teachers in the film were not professionals, everyone involved still gave a believable performance, which kept me vested in their hopes of survival. The entire cast and crew working together lifted what could have been a forgotten film into a cult classic.

Interview with Arch Hall, Jr. 2022

CG: Your father started Fairway International Pictures. How did this come about?

HJ: My dad decided in sort of a midlife crisis that he loved the movie business. I loved my dad, and I don't mean to be critical at all, but my dad was just a man and was a bit shy on the business end of the operation. It's the movie business, and my dad was always on the creative end as a writer, actor, and stuntman. He thrived on being around younger people who shared his passion for being creative. That doesn't have a whole lot to do with the business part. Let me be clear, he never failed at anything, but business was not his strong point. My dad was in different businesses prior to producing. My dad was in radio and would have made a natural transition to television as his longtime friend and army buddy Clete Roberts did. Roberts became a foreign war correspondent and eventually a television news anchor in Los Angeles after a distinguished career in radio, KNXT, a CBS affiliate. KTLA channel 5, owned by Gene Autry, hired Clete after his run with CBS, and he finished his career there. My dad's health is what I believe held back his transition to television. You see my dad was a heavy smoker—at the height of his radio career he was smoking five packs a day. Kent cigarettes was his choice of cigarettes in the 1950s. I remember TV ads with a doctor in his white lab coat explain why Kent with their proprietary "Micronite" filter were so much safer than the other brands of filter cigarettes. My dad used to roll his own cigarettes, with

Two dead cops

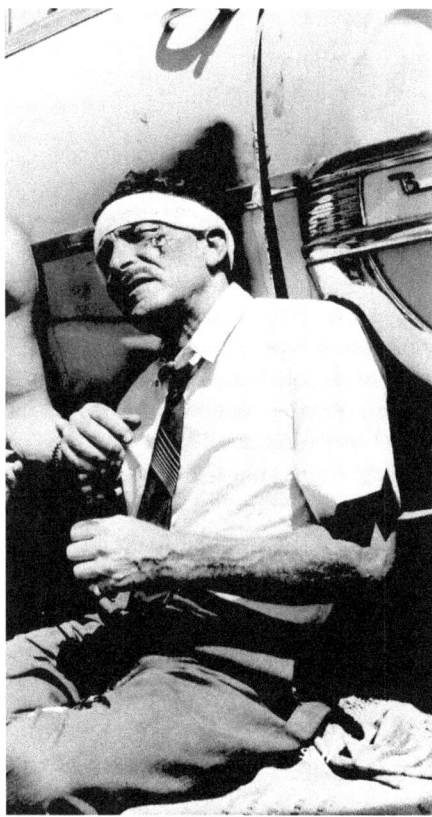

Carl is pistol-whipped by Charlie before being killed by him.

In this lobby card from *The Sadist*, Doris on foot attemps to flee from the grasp of Charlie.

one hand, as a cowboy on the ranch. It wasn't until years later that we found out about Kent's "Micronite" filter: It turns out that "Micronite" was mostly a derivative of asbestos. My dad started having to use the microphone cough switch on the air a lot. I think he was diagnosed with chronic bronchitis or emphysema back in the day. Today it's called COPD. This was a career ender for a live radio announcer. So instead of transitioning to television, he moved on to other endeavors. He had a company called Cozy Homes in southern California. He specialized in four different home models that he would offer people who owned property. He didn't have a contractor's license, so he hired a Brazilian lady and a sub-contractor who already had licenses. She was a sales manager, while my dad oversaw the day-to-day operations. They built a lot of houses, but there may have been some "funny" business going on with money being perhaps misappropriated. I related it to my dad's cowboy honesty and trusting people too much. He was an old school cowboy who spoke the native language of the Lakota Sioux and operated his whole life on the honor system of a handshake. If someone gave him their word, it was good enough for my dad. From that business, my dad went into trucking after being talked into buying a large aging fleet of 10-wheel drive dump trucks, whose core business was hauling gravel and hot asphalt. He named that business Hall and Company, as a spin-off of our surname.

While my dad still had the trucking company, he decided to branch out as an independent film producer, and his first production was *The Choppers* in 1959. He had formed a company by the name of Rushmore productions. The name stemmed from Mount Rushmore in South Dakota, where my dad first worked in the film industry. *The Choppers* unfortunately languished in the can for over two years because my dad couldn't put together a deal for distribution. That was the reason for the birth of the film *Eegah*, because now we had a double-bill and would be off and running. During production of *Eegah*, my dad decided on changing the name of the company to Fairway Films and later to Fairway International, when he sold the film distribution to overseas markets. The name stayed until the company's demise in the late 1970s.

CG: Did you research Charles Starkweather before taking on the role in *The Sadist*?

AHJ: I didn't do any research into Starkweather before taking on the role. Starkweather was more of an inspiration for the writer and director, James Landis, who could be a very obsessive and forceful individual. Jim, as he was called, came by the Fairway compound one morning during post-production. My dad was away, and Jim offered to treat me to lunch at the Tallyrand, which was a little restaurant on Olive Avenue in Burbank. We dubbed it the Fairway International Films "unofficial commissary" because we were there all the time. So, we're sitting at the restaurant deciding what to order and Jim pulls out a photo and passes it to me under the menu I was reading, and it was an image of Starkweather and his girlfriend Caril Ann Fugate. I was aware of the killings at the time, but I had not seen any images of Starkweather, so it was kind of a strange thing seeing the photo because I thought he looked like me. Jim said, "What do you think of that?" I didn't even know how to respond and asked who this guy was. Jim proceeded to tell me this guy was Starkweather, the notorious serial killer. He then explained Starkweather was the inspiration for his writing the script. The film wasn't supposed to be chronicling Starkweather's spree, but it had elements of that, of course.

CG: What was it like working for director James Landis?

AHJ: I was always fighting for Jim's approval. I think it was his deepest fear that my portrayal of Tibbs could at any

Marilyn Manning might play her role of Judy Bradshaw as a child-like innocent, but she knows how to handle a gun and kill if she has to.

time unintentionally become my "Bud Eagle" character from *Wild Guitar*. Landis initially was flatly against me even being considered for the role of Tibbs. But then he got interested in that portrayal, he could totally control me, mold me to his liking as being a novice and not really an experienced actor. I was sort of like putty in his hands, as I didn't have any real ego and he could just give me direction and I would take it to heart. Monkey see, monkey do. An example of this was how Jim directed me to use a hunched walk and giggle to copy Starkweather's mannerisms. I soaked up every nuance of Jim's direction, and he said that would be the condition of me playing this character. Because if I should fall off the mark, the whole thing would be lost, and it would be all for naught. He said, "You've got to promise to stay tuned to me and can't drift away. If you start drifting away, we'll have to stop. If you can't pick it up with the same believability, pace, and panache after any interruptions … the film will be a failure as we cannot start from scratch again. On a low budget film like *The Sadist*, time is money."

Landis was both writer and director and pretty much said he'd all but kill me if I fucked up, and you didn't want to cross him as he was a Korean combat veteran with an explosive temper. I knew that a lot of people were depending on me. Zsigmond was hoping to make a showcase of his cinematography, which he certainly did, and of course Jim was showcasing the same thing for his writing and directing. And of course, my dad was financing the whole thing, so I'd be letting everybody down. This was something that weighed heavily on my shoulders, that I mustn't screw this up. After Jim showed me the photo of Starkweather in the Tallyrand during post-production, he told me, "You know, junior, you did okay … ahh … you did a good job," as he kind of smiled while lighting a cigarette.

CG: Shooting a low budget film can sometimes force the production team to think creatively on the fly. Did you experience any of this while working on *The Sadist*?

AHJ: We had some unbelievable problems during filming to deal with, and a lot of the solutions were very high risk: firing live ammunition, poisonous snakes, etc. For Don Russell's death scene, we initially started out with a failed attempt with some property department that guaranteed they could provide an air rifle that fired a wax projectile of black wax. This projectile was supposed to simulate a real bullet hole in window glass behind Don's head. Well, after three attempts, Zsigmond just threw his hands up and said this was stupid and not working. So out went the air rifle and everybody on the set tried to brainstorm a solution. As there was no CGI at the time, my dad, who was a real cowboy and knew how to handle guns, asked if Don would be okay with him firing a real bullet over his head. Don was a real pro and said let's go for it. As it turned out, the owner of the property had a 300 Weatherby Magnum. The Weatherby Magnum is a very powerful hunting rifle, capable of taking down large animals at hundreds of yards. However, since the shot for this scene would be only a few feet away from the actor's head, my dad had to remove the scope and bolt to precisely calculate the bullet's point of impact, compensating for parallax error. So, my dad used calculated science, but it was still high risk. This also

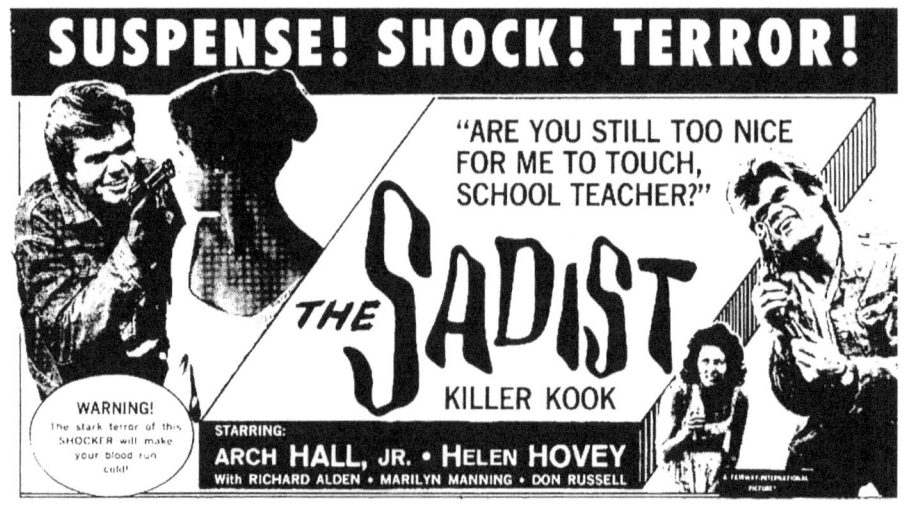

The point of view of the killer as he aims his pistol at the three teachers; this shot became very popular in *Halloween* and films that followed in its wake.

had to be a one take event as once the glass was blown out, we had no replacement auto glass for the derelict Kaiser. We rehearsed the scene several times for timing cues until everybody was good to go. My dad asked Don one last time if he was still okay with this, and he gave a thumbs up. Don had complete trust in my dad. So as Vilmos began filming and slated "MOS" [without sound], the countdown cadence was called out, my dad fired the rifle, and a hole replaced a tiny grease pencil "X" in the glass about 12 inches above Don's head. The blast concussion was so horrendous that it didn't require much acting on Don's part; he was truly terrified as evidenced by his facial expression.

Another thing we did for Don's death scene was a bit over the top, pardon the pun, and which got the ire of the censors. This was a flash insert from another angle from the same scene where my dad fires the rifle. We had this prosthetic scalp with a wig filled with bloody lambs' brains that would come flying out in a couple different directions when clear monofilament lines were pulled. This had to be synchronized, and because it was an MOS scene (without sound), the boom operator, Dave Sullivan, who was also the drummer in the "Archers," shouted out a countdown marching cadence from five to zero. It was a difficult scene to do because, even though it was synchronized, there were two monofilament lines—one pulling the brains and one pulling the scalp, as Don threw his head back. Anyway, the final product was a pain in the ass to do, but it turned out to look pretty good. Jim was happy with it as he wanted Don's death scene to be graphic, but the censors had a conniption and demanded that the entire scene be cut out. Don's death scene that you see in the film is a shot from behind him with me firing a blank in my Colt 1911A1.

I did use live ammunition in the running scenes near the end of the film. That was also very complex. No one would consider doing that today—the insurance companies and lawyers would go nuts. I put a three-foot wooden dowel in the bore of the .45 1911A1 pistol. We walked slowly through the choreographed scene where I'm chasing Richard Alden, who is running away through this old barn with rotted wood. I maintained the bore axis of the pistol always at a safe 20-degree deviation angle away from actor Richard Alden. From the camera POV it looked like I was pointing the gun right at him. We practiced that scene several times. I would say "bang, bang" for each round I was supposed to be shooting. Jim was on one side of me, my dad on the other, and Zsigmond was behind the camera. Jim would track the bore axis as I aimed the pistol to make sure it was kept safely out of Richard's stance. An additional spotter was also there at another angle. This all being said, it was still a risky thing because we were firing through rotten wood and, of course, the wood was exploding from the bullet's impact and there is always a chance of a knot or a nail deflecting the bullet and causing a ricochet. After running the scene a few times, we went ahead and filmed it, another one-taker. Everything went fine. Richard Alden was good with it. He said, "Let's go for it—and please don't shoot me!" So, there were elements of risk using the real firearms with live ammunition on a movie set. We mitigated risk exposure down to what we felt was an acceptable level through careful analysis, planning, and cheating camera angles. This was 1963 and post-production effects were rarely used.

My dad, who was concerned about using firearms on the set, put me in charge of all the firearms to assist with everyone's safety. When we first started filming, we didn't know we would have to use live ammo, so I had various types of blanks. Theatrical blanks are loaded from

Doris Page becomes the moral center of the film, innocence being contrasted to the totally evil Charlie Tibbs.

Charlie and Judy, killers that started ultra violence in the movies

very low charge settings, some are five times powder load because there is no real projectile to operate like a semiautomatic recoil-operated pistol. In lieu of that, they put in heaving wadding and a huge charge of powder. Even though I had blanks they still could be dangerous as far as the wadding was involved, especially at close range. Anything within 20 feet could still hurt somebody with the wadding from a blank, especially the eyes without protection. I discussed the safety aspects with Zsigmond and he said he didn't need any firearm pointed at someone's face because they could make it appear that way with the angle of the camera. Zsigmond was not aware of the dangers involved, even in using blanks, so it was important that I explained it to him. Don Russell wore a face shield for the scene in which I had a gun pointed near his direction, and he also wore eyeglasses for his character.

Modern accidents involving guns have certainly occurred on movies sets—one infamous example was Brandon Lee's death on the set of *The Crow* (1993) and most recently the death of the cinematographer from a gun actor Alec Baldwin was handling on the set of *Rust* (2021). That was a low budget film, and they were cutting a lot of corners and getting a lot of breaks from the union. There was a lot of descension and problems on the set. On our set of *The Sadist* using firearms which I was overseeing, only myself and the two California highway patrol officers had actual guns on the set—and we were all well versed in how to use them safely. The officers would do film work on their days off. They were good guys and I met with them on set when they arrived, and I showed them my .45 and explained we would be shooting blanks and would be careful with the wadding and some live ammunition, which I kept separated from the blanks for safety. They brought their Cadillac versions at the time. One guy had a Colt Python and the other a Smith & Wesson Model 27. Both were premium .357 Magnum revolvers commonly used back in the day, long before the move law enforcement regarding semiautomatics. They didn't use those during the filming as they were too nice looking. They stowed their guns away and I gave them two four-inch Smith and Wesson revolvers, which were used in the scene with the motorcycle cops. We put blanks in those guns, but they never shot them during the scene as my character ambushed them. They ad-libbed their scenes like the spilling of the coffee, and I think they did a great job and Jim was very happy with it.

CG: Your character's death scene in *The Sadist* featured real rattlesnakes, which must have been nerve-wracking to film. Can you explain how the scene was filmed?

AHJ: My death in the snake pit was highly orchestrated, but there were also some problems there. There was a guy we hired who was a snake wrangler. Anybody by that definition is kind of a weird person, and this guy kind of fit the bill. He was an expert who raised snakes and was used to handling them. He had this utility truck with all these trays in the back of it which housed the various snakes that he brought to the set. The pit that my character fell into was a real pit, and we dug a cutaway version for the pit's interior on the side of a gully so it could be shot from a side angle. So, the wrangler would put the snakes into the pit and then the snakes had to be stirred up to act aggressively, before they got angry and began striking. Jim inquired if the wrangler could have the

Charlie for the first time registers real terror, as he finds himself in the snake pit.

Charlie falls into the deadly snake pit and his hair style changes.

snakes bite, which the wrangler insisted they would. The wrangler then proceeded to explain that he had what he called "cold" snakes—which were snakes that had their mouths sewn shut with monofilament. He apparently did this like a fisherman with a hook knot so they could be safely removed. The result was that these snakes couldn't open their mouths to deploy their fangs. But the snakes would still strike you, and when they hit me in the leg, it felt like somebody punching you. It was still unnerving to prepare yourself to be struck by these dangerous snakes and stay in character.

We rehearsed my death scene, and we were losing light so we had to curtail everything and pick it up in the morning at around 8 a.m. This was to be a similar matching light to that which Zsigmond had originally shot the scene. Zsigmond said the light was down too much and wouldn't intercut. So, we wrapped that night and came back the next morning, and our film shoot was taking place close to the wintertime, so it was naturally cold. Everybody was on set ahead of time to do make-up and wardrobe and sound. But the snake wrangler never showed. His wife had drove him back to a motel the night before in her own car, so his utility truck was still on set. Time is starting to burn up and now it's close to a quarter to eight and he still wasn't there yet. Jim was starting to get nervous and Zsigmond is going, "What's the deal?" This was before cell phones, so we had no way of contacting the wrangler and didn't even know which motel he was staying in. By 8:30 still no sign of the wrangler or telephone calls from him. Zsigmond at that point inquired if we knew which snakes the wrangler used so we can set the scene up and shoot a bit until the wrangler arrived. Jim asked me if I was okay with this, and I answered yes, at this point we thought all the snakes were "cold" and it would be safe. A couple of grips found the rattlers in the utility truck. They said they were like sleeping in the trays, so they took a couple out and laid them in the dugout cutaway of the pit. The snakes were now on the ground and doing nothing. But it was about 34 degrees, still very cold as we were up north of the San Fernando Valley. So, I got into the pit with the snakes as the camera was being set up to film the scene. A car then arrived on set and the snake wrangler gets out, sees some of the compartments are open on this truck, and he runs over shouting, "What the hell are you doing?" Jim explained he didn't show up on time and they needed to shoot, but the wrangler said you can't do that, some of these snakes are "hot," and then proceeded to explain the difference. He said these snakes don't have any lines closing their mouths—they are dangerous, especially the Eastern Diamondbacks, which were huge and vicious but not indigenous to Southern California. The wrangler immediately fished out the snakes with a snake hook. He said you put your actor in there and all the snakes put in with him are hot—Diamond rattlers, Timber, and Eastern Diamondbacks. He said the only thing that saved me was that the temperature was so low, and the snakes were lethargic. When the wrangler gave us the correct cold snakes Zsigmond had to put high intensity lights on the snakes to warm them up, so they would become active and then they started to strike my leg. I could laugh about it afterwards, but the snake wrangler went berserk saying we were out of our minds, these are poisonous snakes. He said didn't you know that? Zsigmond retorted, "Yeah, that's what we paid for!"

We were lucky to avert a tragedy. It was triggered by the snake wrangler not showing up on time and Zsigmond being worried about the lighting. He wanted morning light, which would match evening light, and he was getting irritated. Jim had probably been up since 4 a.m. and was on his 20th cup of coffee and had a short fuse, so he wanted to get things moving with the film. It was ignorance on our part as we were way out of our area of expertise, and we learned our lesson in that you don't mess with people's stuff.

CG: What do you think of *The Sadist* still being remembered today, and what do you think the rest of the crew would think?

AHJ: Looking back in the rear view mirror some six decades now, knowing that with a bit more budget to work with and a couple of name actors, it may have had a major impact. Yet the original did not go unnoticed by Hollywood insiders. So much so that a few key elements obviously influenced later films. It has even been studied in film schools.

I believe all those who participated in the making of this little film must be smiling down, pleased that it hasn't been forgotten. *The Sadist* lives on, streaming on many Internet platforms.

Angels and Ministers of Grace Defend Us! More Dark Alleys of Classic Horror Cinema by Gregory William Mank; McFarlandbooks.com; Order 800-253-2187; 448 pages (7x10); softcover $49.95

In his fascinating *Introduction*, Greg Mank first set out to write this latest book as what would become emotionally "a vacation," but conflicts immediately came into play. After writing two recent books about anguished celebrities (Colin Clive and Laird Cregar), Mank thought it would be easier to approach various movies instead of tormented personalities. But now he realizes there are "tormented movies," movies that are "frequently emerging *not* what it ideally was set on becoming, but what it ultimately *became*." A film starts off with its "goals, ambitions, and dreams," but ends up "scarred, broken, and compromised."

Mank states in this book, he relied as "much as possible" on primary source material. The "discovery of new information" caused the author to "re-examine" several films that he had already written extensively about in previous books over the years. Mank thought "he wrung every drop of blood out of *Bride of Frankenstein*," but such new information revealed "Universal's in-house civil war, the hang-ups of the scenarists, and the many censorship travails." Which caused him to re-examine the films in a brand new light.

Mank finally offers "a word of friendly warning: This books scorns contemporary conventional wisdom and progressive re-evaluations, including film history … As such, this book defies all present and future sledgehammer attacks on *Dr. Jekyll and Mr. Hyde* for its abuse of women, *Island of Lost Souls* for its abuse of animals, *Murders in the Rue Morgue* for demonizing an oversexed gorilla, etc."

By the end of this *Introduction*, Mank has succinctly and clearly set the parameters of this latest book. He tells us 9 of

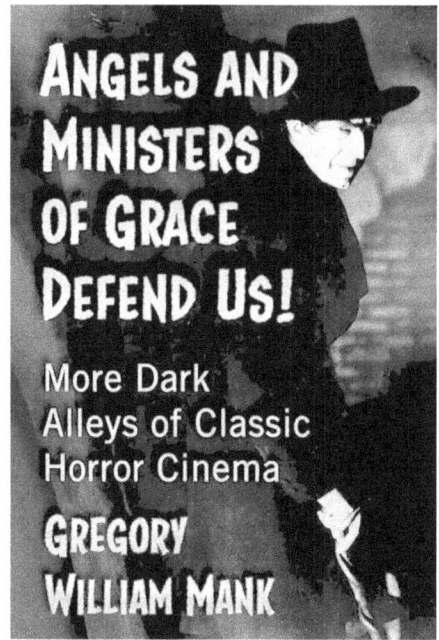

the 13 chapters included are about specific films including *Murders in the Rue Morgue*, *Rasputin and the Empress*, *Island of Lost Souls*, *Bride of Frankenstein*, *WereWolf of*

Valerie Hobson and Boris Karloff from *Bride of Frankenstein*

London, Tower of London, Dr. Jekyll and Mr. Hyde (1941), House of Frankenstein, and Mad Love. Plus, four chapters deal with specific topics concerning horror films.

For the sake of review, let us examine *Werewolf* (Mank uses the "WereWolf" spelling) *of London*: "*It's the Devil … Creeping out of Hell*, chapter five. Mank divides the chapter into three parts, starting with *Pre-production*, recapping the Universal civil war, which was occurring at Universal at the time. President Carl Laemmle, Sr. started a "coup" when his son, Carl Laemmle, Jr., was off traveling abroad to promote Universal Pictures. While gone, Father Carl, who hated the horror and "sex" films that his son favored, replaced "Junior" with his son-in-law, Stanley Bergerman, who was awarded Junior's executive producer's post, Carl, Sr. hoping for more family-oriented entertainment in the future. Junior, crushed by the betrayal, vowed to return to Universal and regain his power. In fact, he did, returning to oversee the production of *Bride of Frankenstein*, while Bergerman regrouped and established his own horror film to produce, *Werewolf of London*, which would film concurrently with *Bride*. But Bergerman soon turned the production duties over to Robert Harris.

Mank includes lengthy copy on screenwriter John Colton, who was acknowledged for writing for Broadway, and was homosexual. Many fans account for his queerness as the reason Dr. Yogami caresses Dr. Wilfred Glendon on the arm a little too long in one scene. Colton ultimately was one of three screenwriters credited on the project.

Next Mank includes a lengthy biography on star Henry Hull, detailing both his Broadway and movie work. Originally, Bela Lugosi was supposed to portray Dr. Yogami as foil to Hull's Glendon, but to Mank's disappointment, Warren Oland ultimately won the role when Lugosi accepted the starring role in MGM's *Mark of the Vampire*. Now both Junior and Bergerman mounted prestige horror productions, Bergerman "dreaming it would upstage and out-perform Junior's long-awaited *Frankenstein* sequel."

Next, Mank brings The Production Code to the forefront, as it affected *Werewolf of London* (*Bride of Frankenstein* being covered in its own chapter, with all the blood and gore). Joseph Breen approved the film except for two incidences in the script: a prostitute must be changed to a beggar and no scenes of the man-to-wolf transformation can be shown. But as the author offers, "which was the whole point of *Werewolf of London*!"

Next is the news of a new director, Stuart Walker, being signed to the production, as Kurt Neumann is assigned to another project. And Mank provides a biography of Walker, saying Bergerman was happy with the new director's talent. Then when Mank compares the production costs of *Werewolf* to *Bride*, it becomes apparent *Bride of Frankenstein* is the favored production, having 15 more days for filming and a budget roughly twice as much as *Werewolf of London*.

The second part of the chapter, *The Shoot*, details sometimes an hour-by-hour description of the filming. And it is well researched and interesting for sure. But Mank asks who is the "muscle" of the production, who wields the most power? He claims for *Bride of Frankenstein*, it was James Whale, who won all disputes, especially against Boris Karloff, who did not want the Monster to speak. But in *Werewolf of London*, it was not director Stuart Walker or star Henry Hull. It was make-up artist Jack Pierce, who was "at his peak" in 1935. According to Elsa Lanchester, as she told Mank, Pierce on the set of *Bride* "thought he was a god, who made these people." And according to Mank, the *New York Times* gave the bulk of its coverage on *Werewolf of London* to Pierce.

Mank continues with *Pretty Lisa* (Valerie Hobson) and *The Giant Madagascar Carnalia*. But when he approaches *Dr. Yokohamma and Lycanthropes in Love*, he skirts dangerously close to allowing revisionist criticism in his book, something in his *Introduction* he claimed this book scorns. But he mentions screenwriter John Colton being gay and including in his script a tender moment between Yogami and Glen-

Henry Hull as the *Werewolf of London*, half werewolf, half devil

don, Oland touching Hull's wound on the arm which reflects his concern over hurting Hull as a werewolf earlier in the picture. But Mank refers to modern revisionist criticism that envisions Yogami falling in love (or lust) earlier in Tibet where his attack "was a virtual rape," a metaphor concocted by screenwriter Colton as "love in bloom." Mank mentions the dog in the film was named Sappho (an ancient poetess from the isle of Lesbos), another gay reference.

Next the author covers the transformation or "transvection" sequences. Unlike Lon Chaney, Jr. in 1941's *The Wolf Man*, Hull's werewolf self is a melding of "wolf and devil" that is decidedly un-hairy when compared to Chaney, Jr., which is perplexing when considering Jack Pierce concocted both make-ups. But in the next section, *Hull vs. Pierce*, Mank addresses the reason why. Even though the author stated earlier that Jack Pierce was the "muscle" of the production, Henry Hull did not want Pierce making him up as a "teddy bear," where people could not recognize him. So, Hull took several production stills of himself, and using pen and ink, created the concept make-up of the werewolf and told Jack Pierce to bring his concept to life. Jack Pierce was reduced to technician and "hit the roof," as such an act of defiance was "blasphemy" at Universal. Pierce created a make-up for Hull, like the 1941 version Chaney, Jr. used, but "Hull had refused to wear it," forcing Hull to write a letter to Junior Laemmle, angering Stanley Bergerman, since he was producer of the picture, not Laemmle. But Carl Laemmle, Jr. was the vice president of the studio, and that trumped Bergerman's position as executive producer. Laemmle agreed with Hull, and Pierce was forced, bitterly, to render the Hull make-up.

Fifteen pages remain in the *Werewolf of London* chapter, but I don't want to reveal everything. But as the chapter thus far has shown, Mank is a magnificent film historian and storyteller. Instead of being a strictly factual writer, Mank adds a dramatic flair to the cold facts and attempts to bring film history to life, where it bleeds and breathes. For well over 40 years, Gregory William Mank has been perhaps our finest film historian, or at least the most interesting. For as long as he has written about *Bride of Frankenstein*, he even finds new things to say about it in 2022. That is simply amazing. And this book comes with the highest of recommendations.

Apocalypse Then: American and Japanese Atomic Cinema, 1951-1967 by Mike Bogue; McFarlandbooks.com; Order 800-253-2187; 305 pages (7x10); softcover $30

In his *Foreword* to the book, chemist and dinosaur expert Allen A. Debus tells us he discovered author Mike Bogue two decades ago, in print, in the pages of *Scary Monsters* and *G-Fan*. Then in 2014 both fans eventually met at a sci-fi convention held in Chicago, *G-Fest*, where Bogue wanted Debus to be on his panel, *Atomic Age Connections*. The two hit it off chatting about sci-fi cinema late into the night.

Debus describes Bogue as an affable gentleman and says the roots of this book were laid down at this convention, but he had been a fan of *Atomic Cinema* since a child, growing up during the 1950s, living in the shadow of the hydrogen bomb, fall-out shelters, Soviet intercontinental missiles, the Cuban Missile Crisis, JFK's

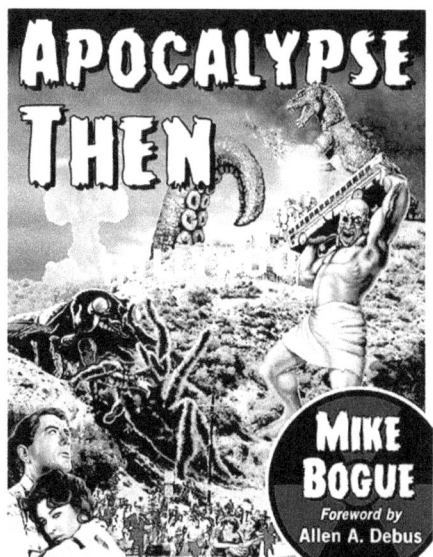

American and Japanese Atomic Cinema, 1951–1967

assassination, and the mushroom cloud. "How odd to be so nostalgic about living with the threat of being nuked!"

In his *Preface* to his book, Mike Bogue opens by telling how he was scared to death snoozing on the couch when he was rudely awakened by an ICBM that just struck Fort Smith, Arkansas, a mere 37 miles away. Bogue thought this was the end of the world. He cleverly compares the American atomic cinema to the Japanese by saying in American cinema the genie appears to be able to be put back in the bottle, but Japanese cinema felt once the genie was fed, there was no returning to the bottle. The term "nuclear threat" took on real meaning in the 1950s and 1960s, creating a worldwide fear that electrical threats of the 1940s could not muster. Allen A. Debus rolls out the concept that all giant monster films occurred in the wake of hydrogen bomb testing and such subconscious fears led to metaphoric personification of nuclear threats in such movies. Bogue goes on to clearly explain terminology and concepts of his book, and states the book is divided into three sections: *MUTANTS* (humanoid), *MONSTERS* (non-humanoid), and the *MUSHROOM CLOUD* (serious treatment of nuclear war) and describes the problems he faced in categorizing each film. Finally, in his *Introduction* Bogue gives swift discussion to American and Japanese "atomic cinema" and paints some interesting facts concerning films he covers in the book.

For the sake of review, let us cover one film from the MUTANT section and

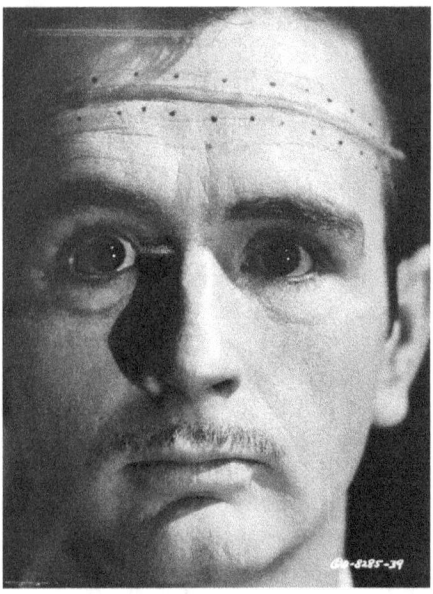

One of the atomic zombies from *Creature with the Atom Brain*

one film from the MONSTERS section and see what kind of insight he brings to such films. So, randomly, let's pick *Creature with the Atom Brain* and *Tarantula*.

The first section, MUTANTS, is broken down into four sections: *All-American Aberrations* (where *Creature with the Atom Brain* is found), *Mutations American Style*, *Rising Sun Terrors*, and *Marty vs. the H-Man*. *Creature with the Atom Brain* opens with a description quote from *Castle of Frankenstein* magazine that uses harsh opinion to sum up the movie (with added wit), Bogue saying the "decently made B-grade programmer" will appeal to baby boomers and probably no one else. Then a lengthy synopsis occurs in this 3-page critique, which Mike Bogue comments, "It's probably unfair to probe the script too much," commenting the B-feature was just there to be the second half of a 1950s "thrill-bill" double feature. But retelling the plot makes Bogue think of a few "plot oddities" which he raises and tries to explain.

Bogue supposes if the film were made during the 1940s, electrical energy would have been enough to bring such creatures back to life, but being made in 1955, the film uses attributes of the nuclear age to modernize the old-hat formula, thus adding: "Geiger counters clicking, military trucks searching, fighter jets soaring." Bogue ends the discussion with a quote from Bill Warren's *Keep Watching the Skies!*

The second section MONSTERS is divided into three sections: *Red, White, and Blue Behemoths*, *Walking H-Bombs*, and *Honda vs. Harryhausen*. *Tarantula* appears in the first section. The almost four-page coverage is five pages long by virtue of the reproduction of the one-sheet, which occupies one page. So, all the film coverage is roughly three-four pages in length (but special chapters might run as long as 16 pages).

The chapter opens with detailed cast and credits list, which can be found in numerous other locations, including the IMDb. Bogue opens by stating "this may be the quintessential 1950s grade-B monster movie. Yes, it's that good—and that typical." Then Bogue breaks as usual into his detailed synopsis before he tells us why it is that good, having to accept his appraisal at face value. After the synopsis ends, he tells us that "*Tarantula* is an exciting little item," not "the quintessential monster movie," but he praises the final 20 minutes. He recommends the movie for being the kind of entertainment you watch in your den, "scarfing down popcorn and cola." And he says it encourages people to talk back at the screen. Then Bogue offers critical review punchlines from Turner Classic Movies, Rotten Tomatoes, *Castle of Frankenstein* magazine, and Leonard Maltin.

Bogue cites a sequence at night, with horses in their corral whinnying in terror, as being "the film's most powerful sequence." The tarantula climbs over a hill, slowly eying the terrified animals before the creature goes in for the kill. The author also notes that a giant prop of the tarantula was constructed for publicity

Leo G. Carroll and Mara Corday in *Tarantula*

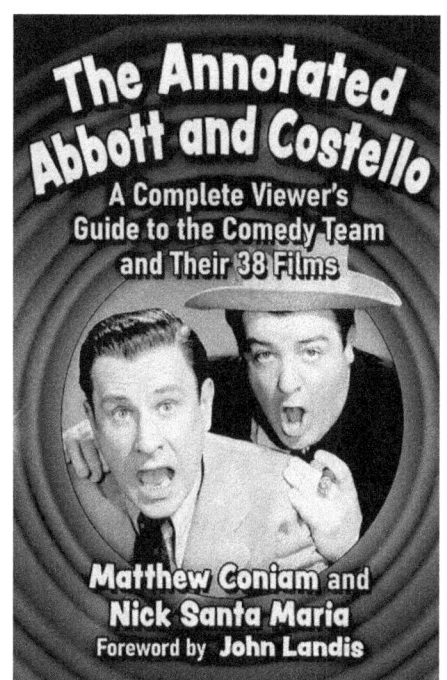

and the movie itself, being used only in a few scenes because the moviemakers generally relied on actual tarantulas. Puffs of air moved the actual creatures on set. Then Bogue praises the acting of John Agar and Leo G. Carroll and reveals the two actors' other credits.

"The spider symbolizes the bomb, in that the arachnid is deadly and keeps growing, just as in real life the nuclear threat kept growing. Also, the bigger the arachnid gets, the harder it is to kill—and the greater the nuclear arms race escalated, the harder it became to control." It is a stretch to call a mutated animal a powerful weapon. Isn't the giant tarantula a symbol of what unharnessed nuclear power produces, that it can mutate insignificant creatures into monsters that can easily kill? But I don't see the fall of the bomb being equal to the force of a giant living thing.

Bogus ends his discussion with a profound point ... *Tarantula* depicts "America awash in innocence and trust." The movie displays social, religious, and political institutions "as trustworthy," painted with more than a dab of 'Dudley Do-Rightism." The author says today, a white male in his 70s might remember "the 1950s as a golden age," while an African American in his 70s might remember the 1950s "as more than a bit tarnished." But the author leaves us with one final point, the sci-fi films of the 1950s evoke "wonderment." "Yes, too much wide-eyed-ness can distort discernment, but too much snarkiness can choke the soul." Perhaps Bogue's point was not as clearly written as it should have been, but I received his point loud and clear.

Bogue did *not* have much to say new about these films, but every so often he managed to hit the nail squarely on the head. More of these moments would have transformed a good book into a great one.

The Annotated Abbott and Costello: A Complete Viewer's Guide to the Comedy Team and Their 38 Films by Matthew Coniam and Nick Santa Maria; McFarlandbooks.com; Order 800-253-2187; 482 pages (7x10); softcover $49.95

Noted film director John Landis writes the brief *Foreword* for this book and argues that "horror and comedy are the two most difficult and unforgiving genres. The audience either laughs or it doesn't. The audience is either scared or they're not." Landis mentions Low and High comedy, referencing co-author Coniam that Abbott and Costello got little respect for all their successes. Then Landis recounts some of his favorite skits by the comedy duo and invites us to further delve into the book.

In his *Introduction One: The Case for Abbott and Costello*, director John Landis asked Matthew Coniam, "Why do you feel the need to justify a book on Abbott and Costello" when shown a rough draft of this *Introduction*. Coniam answers him, "All critical theory is ... just fashion. And fashion reflects more on the critic than the film itself." And then Coniam goes on to defend the comedy duo and says, "There is still really no secure critical consensus when it comes to these guys." Many critics still consider the team to be "comedy hicks," and like The Three Stooges, fodder for "indulgent kids." Many people say admitting to liking Abbott and Costello is akin to liking a MacDonald's hamburger. *The National Society of Movie Critics on Movie Comedy* finds whole sections on Harry Langdon, Jerry Lewis, and Blake Edwards, but "only manages to give Abbott and Costello three passing mentions," and one of them is how they surpass Laurel and Hardy in their ridicule of "all women." And one critic calls them "latently homosexual." Even though there is good stuff written about the duo, they are still considered "second raters." Their criticism remains, "That they relied

The comedy duo of Bud Abbott (left) and Lou Costello (right)

Above: Bela Lugosi as Dracula tries to place Lou Costello in a trance. Below: The boys cannot believe that under all that hay is the body of the Frankenstein Monster.

overly on a handful of routines that they used and restyled until they were ground into the dirt, and as performers they never evolved true comic personae with an existence beyond these routines." In the rest of the lengthy *Introduction One*, Coniam thoroughly manages to justify the comedy team's antics, working in biographical information and interesting facts.

In the second *Introduction* by Nick Maria, he covers *The Art of Abbott and Costello*, defiantly never apologizing for associating the word "art" with the comedy duo, who "are the most visible and valuable exponents of the art of burlesque comedy, but their level of performance far exceeds what their contemporaries had to offer." Maria confesses he has been a comedian for 45 years, and as a child of five years old, he knew what his profession would be, even though he would not start in the comedy field until his mid-teens. "I also noticed early on that he [Costello] was actually superior to adored comedians like Curly Howard (brilliantly funny, but without depth), and even Stan Laurel." Maria says to prove his point, watch Laurel play a "real" person in his post-Hal Roach productions, such as *Air Raid Wardens*. To me, whether Stan Laurel can play a "real" person in the inferior Fox films has little to do with his comedy personae. What about the Hal Roach films made with sympathetic directors and supporting casts, where he had more creative control?

Older routines from burlesque such as "Who's on First" demonstrate a commitment to their craft akin to what "Olivier was to *Hamlet*." Maria states their best-known routine "Who's on First?" to be "perfect." He acknowledges the jokes and routines are mostly older than the boys themselves. Maria admits their talent makes old jokes and routines relevant and fresh, but Laurel and Hardy create material brand new and relevant to their unique personas, not rehashed bits.

Maria continues his long chapter explaining the art of Abbott and Costello, and he does a commendable job, but does he constantly over-praise the comedy duo at the expense of denigrating other classic comedy teams? He can like what he likes without criticizing The Three Stooges (he calls them "cartoon characters") and states Oliver Hardy could have survived solo, but Stan Laurel could never have a solo career (even though he was the genius of the team and created the master-

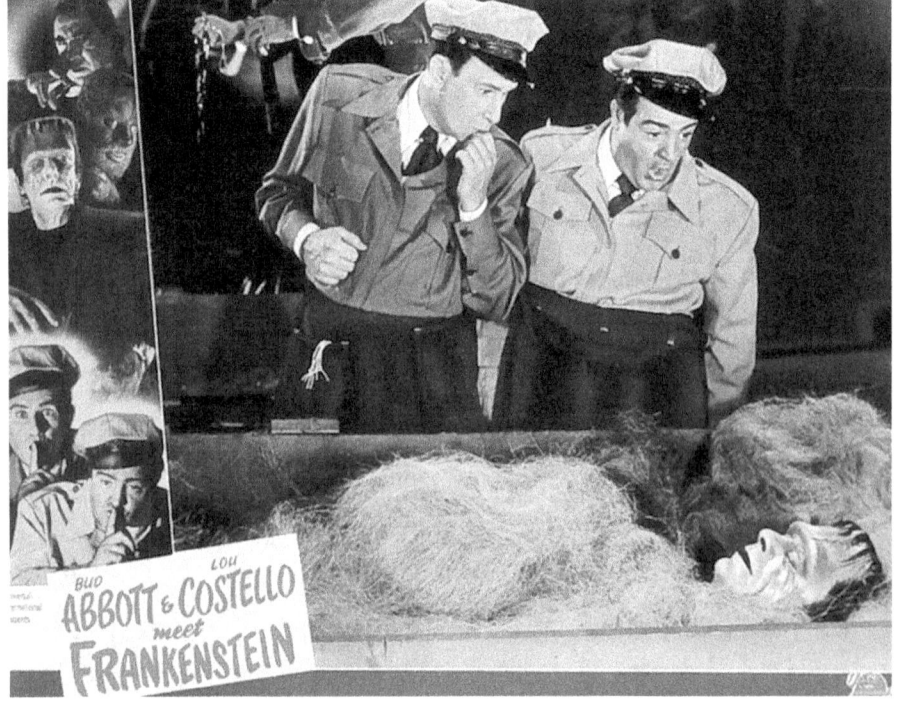

ful routines). He criticizes the great Buster Keaton whom he says "relied on recycled material" once he was near 40, but well-advertised alcoholism affected his creativity. And who should be criticizing recycled material? To my mind Maria is guilty of praising Abbott and Costello by chopping at other comedians and bringing them down, and he is guilty, as is true, of many other critics of over-stating the obvious.

Then the two writers pen insightful critical analyses of the duo's 38 films, but with the bonus of annotation. To see what that means, let us explore their coverage of *Abbott and Costello Meet Frankenstein*. The chapter, 10 pages long (longer than most), is written by Nick Santa Maria. Maria, again guilty of overstatement, calls the movie "the greatest comedy horror film ever made." Maria is correct in stating the secret of the film's greatness is that the monsters play it straight to counterbalance the comedy. But many felt "this killed off the Universal Monsters by making buffoons out of them." But Maria rightfully insists the monsters were played with absolute respect. Maria adds the boys hated the script and did the film begrudgingly because they were used to ravishing the past for routines and "did not like learning new material." Even though the duo's chief creative artists were involved in the production—director Charles Barton and screenwriters Robert Lees, Frederic Rinaldo, and John Grant—Abbott and Costello were not happy campers. Maria then spends a little time talking about Jane Randolph who was happy, in this, her final movie, and Lenore Aubert, who was not. Then Maria clears the air about who did the title credits: Water Lantz or Dave Fleisher? Lantz is generally given credit, but animation expert Jerry Beck says Walter Lantz was on the outs with Universal in 1948-1949, and Maria feels the most likely candidate that did the title credits is Dave Fleisher. Even though the duo did not like doing the feature, it may be their best and "one of the most perfect films ever made." Besides, it made a heap of money and inspired the "Meet The" monster series of the 1950s.

Then this chapter is completed with annotations. Such as (they always note the minute and second where a specific scene can be found) at 06:47, he recounts the encounter between Lon Chaney (on the telephone) and Wilbur, as MacDougal arrives looking for his exhibits. Then at 12:40 Maria recounts the scene when the boys deliver the crates to MacDougal's House of Horrors. Maria tells us there Costello gets to do his terrific fright takes and he tells us John Grant again included his "Moving Candle" routine from *Hold That Ghost*, and Costello first meets the living monsters here. And such "annotations" continue for this and the other movies. What Coniam and Maria see as "annotations" are generally the favorite sequences in the film, where as if you didn't want to watch the entire movie, these are the scenes to watch. Yes, we learn little facts such as the moving candle scene was from the earlier *Hold That Ghost* and other necessary info, but we mostly get plot and not true annotated and well researched facts.

Despite over-defensive analysis overall, and annotation which rarely is, the book is a good one, not great, but most fans of Abbott and Costello will find it more than enjoyable enough.

THE FLASH GORDON SERIALS, 1936-1940: A HEAVILY ILLUSTRATED GUIDE by Roy Kinnard,

Tony Crnkovich, and R.J. Vitone; McFarlandbooks.com; Order 800-253-2187; 204 pages (7x10); softcover $29.95

According to the Preface, *Flash Gordon* was conceived by 24-year-old artist/writer Alex Raymond and debuted in the "funny pages" on January 7, 1934, as a direct rival to the already established sci-fi comic strip, *Buck Rogers*. But according to the authors, "*Flash Gordon* quickly eclipsed *Buck* in popularity." As the authors say, "*Flash Gordon* was imbued with swashbuckling romanticism and exotic interplanetary settings that transported world-weary audiences of the time into another, more entertaining world." In these pre-war Depression years, the Sunday comics attempted to satisfy the unsatisfied with garish color and stories that made our world seem better or told of distant more fascinating worlds. While *Flash Gordon* originally tried to compete with the similar sci-fi oriented *Buck Rogers*, they were fundamentally very different. *Buck* "emphasized sci-fi gadgetry and jargon" while *Flash*, "with its towering heroes, beautiful women, and unspeakably evil villains, was more fantasy oriented." The authors go on to explain the universe controlled by evil dictator Ming the Merciless and his monster-filled planet of Mongo. And they fill in the characters that surround Flash Gordon. The authors mention how the three successful serials inspired other movies, including the *Star Wars* universe, after "the films retained their popularity

Buster Crabbe won the coveted role of Flash Gordon over Jon Hall.

in theatrical reissues, decades-long syndicated television exposure, and now on home video." Then the structure of the book is explained and how quotes from various celebrities are sprinkled throughout.

Then the second chapter shines a light on *A History of the Flash Gordon Serials*, offering such information such as "Universal Pictures purchased the rights to several newspaper comic strips published by King Features Syndicate," realizing such comics would be enormously successful. The average money paid by Universal to make a serial in the 1930s was $200,000, but wise minds realized that to bring Alex Raymond's world to life, they better budget for $350,000. But such money had to be "stretched over thirteen 20-minute episodes for a running time of over four hours." To save on money, sets from *Bride of Frankenstein* had to be redressed and used, as well as apparatus from feature films *The Invisible Ray* and *The Mummy*. The serial was filmed so hurriedly that some over-dubbing "used to cover some gaps and inconsistencies in the dialogue" resulted with "the same voice ... used over and over." And the film's musical score "is a veritable crazy quilt blend of other Universal films of the same period." The second serial was dominated by the *Bride of Frankenstein* score. Ralph Berger, the film's art director, spared no expense in recreating costumes that are faithful reproductions from the comic strips. The special effects in the *Flash Gordon* serials look very crude when compared to current standards, but for 1930s movies, they were cutting edge. And since the first serial was filmed in only six weeks, the special effects had to be rushed. Many of the first film's better qualities can be attributed to first-time director Frederick Stephani, who was co-screenwriter, always remaining faithful to the Raymond comic strip.

Much of the charm of the serials come from sympathetic ensemble cast members including Buster Crabbe (who won the role of Flash over Jon Hall), Jean Rogers, Charles Middleton, Priscilla Lawson, and Frank Shannon. Crabbe said, "They had to be in make-up at 7 a.m. and on the set by 8 a.m. ready to go ... and had to average 85 set-ups per day." Jean Rogers (the good girl) and Priscilla Lawson (the bad girl) add "a vibrant beauty" and "add a sexual element missing from most serials." *Flash Gordon* "was so successful it played evening performances at first-run theaters, one of only a handful of serials to do so." It was recut and re-scored as a 68-minute feature in 1938 as *Rocketship*, appealing to an entirely different type of audience. Then the authors go on to cover the second and third serial.

For the sake of this review, let us cover the very first chapter from the very first serial, *Flash Gordon*.

Flash Gordon Chapter One: *The Planet of Peril*. The chapter coverage opens with a summary of all feature film versions available, joined with a list of video availability. Then a two-page *Synopsis* follows in this 13-page chapter, including 13 large photos. Then following is a *Comments* section. The authors note that "Flash Gordon might have the greatest single serial chapter ever made." But the author admits short sequences are lifted from *Just Imagine* and props from *The Invisible Ray*, also, thrown-in an impressively rendered background painting of Ming's mountaintop city on Mongo. And enlarged

Flash Gordon (Buster Crabbe) and Dale (Jean Rogers)

Flash Gordon, the swashbuckling hero

Charles Middleton as Emperor Ming (the Merciless)

lizards pose as giant monsters when combined with the human cast, a technique improved four years later when used for the motion picture *One Million B.C.* Then two of the three ape-men are profiled and similar roles in earlier films are detailed. In the arena fight scene, which proved difficult to film and took one day-and-a-half to film, one of the ape men yelled "cut, cut" in the middle of the fight, causing the surprised director to act as though he was shot out of a cannon, "What the hell's the matter?" The actor said, "Mr. Stephani, I'm sorry, but I lost my fangs!" According to the authors, "It really didn't matter." Most of the chapter is devoted to Buster Crabbe auditioning and winning the starring role. Then more cast members are profiled. A few interesting stories are shared of Jean Rogers and Priscilla Lawson re-filming a few scenes for the censors when a shot of a breast was deemed too provocative for the audience, but many sequences made it past the censors and remained intact. Then Lawson had to overdub some of her dialogue in the arena fight sequence to create a more dramatic effect for her character. Carl Laemmle, Sr. ultimately remarked, "Financially, it is the biggest serial investment ever made."

For fans of a very specific series of three serials, this book comes recommended, for it does a masterful job of writing a detailed history and critique of one of the greatest serial trilogies of all time. But it will appeal to a very-dedicated but relatively small audience.

Let's face it, after multiple releases on home video, there is little reason to keep reviewing the same old movies released in different formats. The movie never changes, but its latest format does (video tape, laser disc, DVD, Blu-ray, and now 4k), and I'm not interested in reviewing the new format available. So, let me venture to various streaming channels and review the best of the classic horror films available and of interest to horror lovers who read our magazine. To make it even more of interest, all reviewed films are foreign made, showing that even other nation's films follow the American model, and that our influence extends everywhere. After being exported to the US in the 1950s and 1960s from mainly England and France and Italy, foreign horror titles begun to be licensed to domestic markets in badly cut, re-edited prints with terrible dubbing. Recently uncut prints with accurate sub-titling have begun to appear. Now, because of streaming services, international movies from often neglected countries (such as Norway) started appearing regularly on Shudder, Netflix, and Amazon Prime. So let us dig deeply into four of them.

5.0 excellent
4.0 very good
3.0 good
2.0 fair
1.0 poor

OLD PEOPLE (Germany, 2022) Netflix … 4 stars [out of 5]

A close-up of a bearded old man, wearing an oxygen mask, desperation in his eyes, opens this German film. He looks at his cell phone in a small, dingy apartment. His home care nurse arrives to find the apartment door open and ventures in, calling out his name, moving through the drab living space as she sees his empty wheelchair. The nurse spies the old man, standing but slightly slumped over, at first lethargic he approaches the woman and suddenly is overcome by an overwhelming fit of rage. He knocks the woman to the floor with his oxygen tank and he watches as she convulses on the floor, unable to defend herself. The man squats over her and brings the oxygen tank slamming downward upon her head, about five times, the sound of breaking bone proclaiming her death. The man

puts his tank down and cries in desperation, looking to his balcony and uttering an extended animal growl.

Later we see a family with two children arrive, only to find themselves speaking of their elderly father who is estranged with the visiting daughter Ella (Jolene Andersen) having fallen out of favor with her father over her divorce. The other daughter Sanna (Maxine Kazis) reveals their father is no longer living in the local village but was admitted to a nursing home and will attend the wedding festivities if he is well enough. The youngest boy, Noah (Otto Emil Koch), an asthmatic who uses an inhaler, loves his grandfather, and goes with his Aunt Sanna and his mother Ella to pick him up from the nursing home, while the oldest daughter Laura (Bianca Nawrath) goes on a high-speed boat ride with her long-distance lover. As their car travels through town, Noah eyes the old people all showing vague sad looks on their faces as the vehicle whips by. Noah is told very few people are left in the town, and the nursing home is becoming the main attraction.

As they pull up to the nursing home, they are met with a very run-down exterior, overgrown, unmanaged grass and generally a very drab place for the elderly to live. When entering they find no attendants to register or help them find their way. Food and food trays are strewn on the floor, along with scattered utensils. They venture forward looking for "grandpa," and they finally find a room with elderly people just sitting around, like kept animals. One desperate patient looks upset and pleads to the newly arriving family to, "Save me!" Another naked woman is settled in a dirty bathtub with tiles falling off. Suddenly one attendant appears to tell the lady in the tub that she is ready to be returned to bed, and Ella inquires about their "grandpop" and is told she will take them to him, "that there hasn't been a party around here in a long time," referring to the wedding. They follow along the depressive walk with Ella asking attendant Kim, "What's going on here? The old people, are they always like this?" Kim responds, "We are totally understaffed and there are more and more of them that we really can't take care of … it gets worse." They then arrive in "grandpa's" room first finding an old man in bed with a desperate, far-away look in his eyes, confined with arm straps to his bed so he can't wander off. Meanwhile, another elderly man, seeming cognizant of his surroundings, confronts Noah in the

Seemingly, the leader of the old people's revolt

hallway, a sinister half-smile on his face, motioning with his finger. Noah walks onward confronting the elderly patients with desperate looks on their faces; there's a man wearing only underwear deep in thought playing his violin. Noah continues calling out the name of "Grandpa" whom he finds sitting in a chair by the window, a look of vacant memory on his other-worldly face. Noah takes his hand and asks him about attending the wedding reception, and the old man moves his head around in utter incomprehension. "Grandpa, don't you recognize me anymore?" Noah looks around the room to see people with detached looks, once again seeing the old man he encountered in the hall, eating, who stares directly at him, spitting his food out of his mouth. Ella enters to confront her father who has a look of being miles and a lifetime away. She looks at him with dread. The old man stares at her with semi-comprehension. Ella says, "Why are they looking at me" and Kim tells her they probably haven't seen their relatives in years, "if ever." Ella kisses her father on the cheek and the elderly man sobs violently in recognition.

Laura's lover shows her a special stone statue erected far out in the woods and says, "It's a monument to the ghosts of their ancestors. The stone is almost 2,000 years old. It's supposed to protect all families, so they stay together … and honor their elders. The monument is an appropriate background as the story of the stone is told, Ella and her family are walking the shaky old man to their car and slowly placing him inside.

Soon the wedding occurs, rice throwing, and happiness abounds, however the elderly in the community stare vacantly from houses, windows, yards, and doorways. They are the forgotten. At the nursing home the patients sit in the dark, listening to the wedding songs in the distance, each alone in their thoughts remembering better days. A male attendant comes and smiles, "Why are you sitting together? You're not listening to the music; do you like it? The male attendant states sarcastically, "You want to get all dolled up in front of the mirror, put on some nice clothes, and join the others at the party? Too bad you're not invited" and he slams the window closed, thus increasing looks of sadness on the patient's faces. "Besides it's time for bed," following his job to the letter instead of allowing the old people to enjoy the sounds of the wedding for a few more moments. One older woman weakly cries, "Let us stay up a little longer and listen to the music …" The male attendant will have none of it. The woman grows agitated and forces the male attendant to strike her to the floor, blood flowing on the side of her face, something the other patients are disturbed by. The elderly man who confronted Noah throws a look of stone-cold hatred toward the male attendant, stares at him, rises from his chair, and confronts the caregiver. Another woman picks up a shard of jagged glass and stabs him. A woman attendant enters and is confronted by patients wielding weapons. In utter rage the patients surround her, now screaming hysterically. The woman attendant tries to grab the phone and make an outside call, but the seeming leader of the inmates, the patient that Noah confronted earlier, uses a solid metal rod to hit her hard on the side of her head. He drops the rod and looks at his reflection and smiles.

Then the uncontrolled army of old people party like its 1939 and venture forth into the community and begin a killing spree, forming the impetus for the remainder of the movie.

As can be easily seen, in this unique film the elderly patients are substitutes for zombies, the detached looks resemble the similar look of the undead. For the forgotten elderly among us, the utter powerlessness of old age is vanquished, in this film power is given back to those who once had it but lost it. While the true villains of the film are the people who throw their aging relatives into dank and dirty nursing homes and literally forget them. Compassion can be expressed without any cost, for example, by allowing them to listen to the wedding music, just a little longer.

An old woman sits on a swing.

This film poses a warning for all of us. If we do not care for our ever-increasing population of old people, they will rise-up and destroy the fabric of our society by striking back in ways we cannot yet fathom. Old people can no longer be swept under the carpet.

VIKING WOLF (Norway, 2022) Netflix … 3 stars [out of 5]

"So, the saga goes … in 1050 Viking chief Gudbrand the Grim set out with 20 ships to plunder Normandy. In an abbey, they discovered a secret room. The monks begged Gudbrand "not to enter." Defying the monks, Gudbrand proceeds. "The Vikings found neither gold, nor silver." Instead, they released a snarling wild dog/wolf they soon adopt. "None of them understood that they had released the hound of hell. It came along as they sailed home. Before the ship reached Norway, all the Vikings were dead. The dog leaped ashore. And thus, evil found its way deep into the Nordic woods."

This myth-creating voiceover is accompanied by short vingettes of Vikings plundering Normandy and the abbey, and blazing fires—all rendered in excellent moody detail. It really sets the atmosphere for the rest of the movie.

"Nearly 1,000 years later …" Shots of a magnificent Scandinavian pastoral community abound. Inside a house, a dog sits on the sofa watching TV as two sisters, one younger and one a teenager, sit together eating popcorn, also watching television. A bearded male hovers in the background. The oldest teen, Thale (Elli Rhiannon Müller Osbourne), gets a phone call to attend a party at the Bay and she quietly sneaks a six-pack of beer from the refrigerator. The older sister signs to her younger sister Jenny, a deaf mute, (Mia Fosshaug Laubacher) that she can't come to the party this time. Thale tells her new stepfather that she is going to visit friends. Her new parent is upset Thale won't call him "Dad" or "father." She snaps back, he's not her real father and leaves. She confronts her mother Liv (Liv Berg), appearing to be returning from jogging, who tells her to be home by 11 p.m. She yells back, "Maybe!" On her bike she travels through scenic countryside to reach her party in the woods, kids are gathered and music blares. Meeting a boy there, he asks her how she likes the town. She claims it's a little "boring" for her. A cute young blonde, Edith, lures Thales' boyfriend away, as Thale opens a beer, promising not to tell her policewoman mother about the party. Thale soon ventures further away from the crowd into the woods. She comes upon an aquaduct and looks down the hill to see her boyfriend and the blonde, Edith. Suddenly the blonde screams and is knocked down, and when Thale investigates, Edith's face and arm are bloodied. She turns to see her equally bloodied boyfriend, dazed, leaning against a rock, as something powerful rushes by her, apparently attacking her. Turning back to Edith, the screaming, terrified Edith is dragged into the woods by an unseen presence. This sequence closes on a shot of the wounded, screaming Thale, cutting to a shot of the full moon.

Later, Thale is trying to concentrate in class while the amplified sound of a pencil rubbing across paper sounds like the howling of a wolf, which she thinks she hears nearby. Suddenly another blonde female pounces at her and appears to be a werewolf, with animal fangs, startling Thale, forcing her to scream and jump out of her student desk.

During the investigation of the missing Edith (who we find out is the mayor's daughter), one wizened, elderly man with a heavy accent suddenly appears in town, admitting he's been hunting a werewolf for many years.

To review what's happened, let us look at werewolf movie tropes that have occurred during the first half of the movie: disturbed teenage girls (Thale is cut right out of *Gingersnaps*); kids partying and a few of them venture out in the woods; the teens attacked by a werewolf and one of them is wounded, yet survives, soon to become a werewolf herself; a sudden shock when one of Thale's classmates is transformed into a beast; a "Van Helsing" character suddenly appears in town. This Scandinavian horror tale tries to create its own mythos about Vikings and Monks a thousand years ago, which is fresh. But once in modern times, the rules, however well they are applied, are tried and true tropes having been done too many times. There is something too American, too re-used, never allowing the movie to reach its potential, especially after the inventive opening sequence. The film is done well, but it seems like a retread.

The werewolf and deaf mute younger sister Jenny (Mia Fosshaug Laubacher)

Werewolf-to-be Thale (Elli Rhiannon Müller Osbourne) examines herself.

Deaf-mute Jenny desperately signs to her werewolf sister Thale.

But the film's ending is original. [SPOILER ALERT] After Thale's younger sister confronts her in full wolf mode in the streets downtown (and Thale is an actual wolf, not a human hybrid), Jenny bravely approaches her signing "sister," tears in her eyes … and fear. "I will protect you," she again signs, the wolf approaching her, an animal that stands as tall as Jenny while on all fours. As the wolf monster approaches, sister Jenny continues to sign "sister" and "I'll look after you." Jenny's mother Liv finally arrives, sneaking up behind her as the wolf snarls more furiously. Another policeman approaches from the other side and fires a tranquilizer dart at the werewolf, which sticks in the wolf's side. The wounded animal still has plenty of energy and charges the three running humans as they shoot their way into an abandoned store. The frantic wolf charges the store's door until it slows its attack and simply lurks. The mysterious werewolf hunter rams the store's front door with his car, and bloodied, is vulnerable to the wolf's slow stalking and attack. Mother Liv is next, using an object to stick in the animal's mouth to keep the beast at arm's reach. To save her mother, Jenny picks up the dart and stabs the wolf in the back, rendering it unconscious in seconds. Liv and Jenny hug one another, trembling.

The scene changes to a makeshift medical lab where the wolf Thale is unconscious and connected to IVs and monitors. "I'm sorry sweetheart … mommy's here," the weeping Liv approaches the sleeping werewolf. She shushes her unconscious daughter. Then she draws her revolver and places one silver bullet in the barrel. She cocks the gun and places it against her daughter, breathing heavily. The screen goes dark, and no gunshot is heard.

The scene changes to the police station as Liv leaves to go home. She looks very sad as she's driving, finally arriving home, looking at herself in the mirror. Liv sits on her bed, a photo of Thale displayed on the bedside table. She places the silver bullet meant for Thale, but obviously never used, in front of the photo, and smiles, the camera going in on a close-up of the bullet, as the cinematographer fades to black to end the movie.

The acting is compelling, and the mood is sensitive. But this is a well-made werewolf movie that feels as though we have seen it all before. True, it is Scandinavian but that's hardly an excuse for ultimately making a werewolf film we vaguely seem to remember. The film adds a few novel touches to color the standard tropes, but it needs to be more original for 2022. Norway needs to create its own culture and mythos. It's simply too Americanized for its own good.

DARK GLASSES (Italy, 2022) Shudder Channel … 3.5 stars [out of 5]

A brunette is driving her sporty car, swerving around the city, silently watching people in apartments, alongside the highway, in parks, seated on bath towels, watching a solar eclipse with dark glasses or dark film, protecting their eyes. The brunette, Diana (Ilenia Pastorelli), parks her car and joins others alongside the road, donning dark sunglasses and watching the sun disappear.

The sky grows dark in the middle of the day.

Meanwhile a prostitute is ending her session and reminds her client she has yet to be paid, and the silver-haired gentleman smiles and says, "You make me lose my mind" and hurries and gets her payment. She quickly exits the hotel lobby as the desk clerk asks her if she needs a cab. "No thanks, Carlo." She walks to the parking lot as we cut to a shot of a shadowy man pulling open a thin cord, as the woman screams and is pulled into the dense brush. Her screams continue as the cord is tightly wrapped around her neck, bleeding, as blood spurts from her mouth. She staggers out of the bush, holding her hand to her mouth. A car with a man and woman stops to help the bleeding woman but end up holding each other, as the

Diana (Ilenia Pastorelli), now blind, gets advice how to cope from Rita (Asia Argento), an instructor for the blind.

Director Dario Argento does publicity for his latest film.

woman bleeds out, a small crowd gathering.

Soon it is revealed Diana is a call girl. Later she services a client, still wearing her sunglasses, saying the eclipse irritated her eyes, but she will have no trouble "finding his big ole pendulum just the same." The client tells her that he wore eye protection, adding, "Neither the sun nor death can be stared at."

In another scene a bearded client comes to Diana's apartment. She tells him that he stinks; he responds sheepishly that he just came from work, where he works with dogs. She orders him to take a shower or it's "no go." After a while, the man slowly comes down the stairs and looks at the waiting Diana, "I stank, huh. See you, slut," and he walks down the stairs out the door. Eventually Diana meets a third client who wants her to try "fisting," but she claims she does not do that kinky stuff. She tells him, she does not want orgasms, especially with him and peppersprays her way out of his apartment. As she walks to her car, a white van appears to be watching her. A man approaches her slow-to-start car, but it finally cranks up, and she flies away, closely followed by the hooded man in the van. During the high-speed chase, she runs through an intersection, hitting a car. Diana awakens to a dark world with a few swishing colors, and her doctor tells her she will probably never see again, but "consider it a miracle that you're alive." The police tell her she is the fourth prostitute victim they found recently. And that only a seven-year-old boy survived in the other car involved in her accident, the father killed, the mother in a coma.

Enter Rita (Asia Argento), an instructor for the blind, who was sent to help her re-adjust and make her self-sufficient. She gives Diana aids to help her, including a white cane, and shows her how to walk independently. Diana asks what Rita sees, and when she mentions a white van among other things, she panics and tells Rita it might be "the maniac from the accident." Diana asks Rita to identify the man in the white van, but she tries and cannot. Finally, Rita takes her to get her seeing-eye dog and show her how he is trained.

Mostly this film lacks the Argento visual touch, but it features a few unique scenes. For instance, when two police investigators are returning to Diana's house for a second time, they find the house dark and empty; apparently, she went out. When the male investigator goes down a near-by alley to check, he sees the white van turning and coming right at him. Foolishly, he stands in the middle of the road, holding his gun extended, ready to fire as the van speeds up, striking the policeman and knocking him backward. He lands harshly on his back, his face a pool of blood. The female investigator runs to check on him, feeling his neck for a pulse. She says "no" as she sees the white van, fires one shot, and approaches the door, which flings open, knocking her down, her face bleeding as she crawls to reach for her gun. Then Argento cuts to a scene of a huge knife coming down in her back, with a loud thud. We cut back to the female's hand which falls to the ground and stops moving. Cut to another shot of the male investigator lying still, the white van's headlights shining directly behind him. At least a little of the old Argento magic remains.

It must be mentioned the score is composed by Arnaud Rebotini, who composed the "Pagan Dance Move" in *Blair Witch* (2016). He wrote a typical Argento

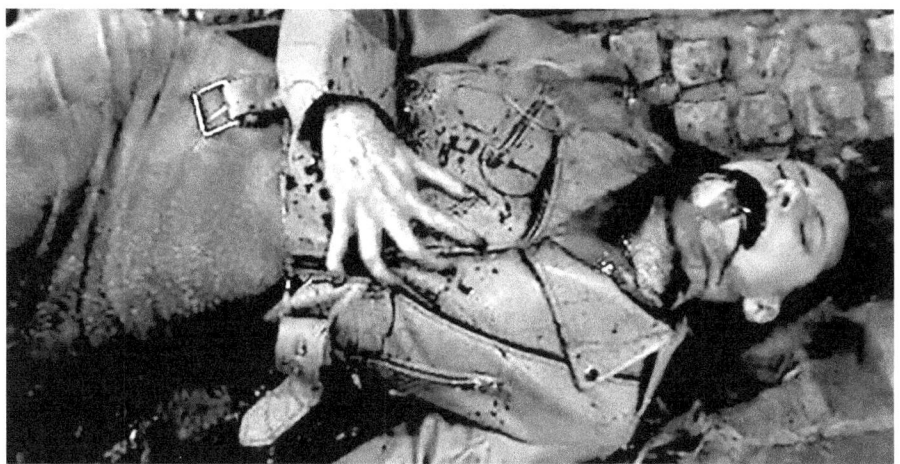

The first victim, attacked in the shrubby with a wire, lies in a hotel parking lot.

score, much like what Goblin might have done—all bombast, crescendos, loud, and in your face. The score accents all the crucial sequences and helps Argento's movie succeed.

It is curious to see an older Asia Argento in her father's films, taking on a character who does not rely on youthful sex scenes. No longer a girl in her 20s, she has now morphed into a lovely mature woman, with more normal roles, in this film becoming a best friend to the blind girl, Diana. Asia is now playing a middle-aged woman and doing it very well.

The film's final chapter is about to be revealed, surprising many of his fans by pulling off a good film, even if it pales when compared to *Suspira*, *Deep Red*, and even *Opera*. But *Dark Glasses* is much better than his recent films, such as *Argento's Dracula*. It will be interesting to see his future work.

TROLL (Norway, 2022) Netflix … 4 stars (out of 5)

In the Norwegian mountains, a blonde teenager, Nora (Ine Marie Wilmann), also called "Tiny," is mountain climbing with her father, Tobias (Gard B. Eidsvold), when she slips, falls, and is saved by her rope. They finish climbing to the top when the father announces, "The Troll Peaks." Nora recites the legend, "Once upon a time, at a big troll wedding, 13 drunk trolls lost track of time, the sun rose and turned them to stone, and now they're mountains ... Blah, blah, blah.

Tobias responds, "You do know that … there's some truth to every fairy tale."

"They're just mountain peaks," Nora responds.

"You have to believe in something to see it," her father tells her. "Can you see them, Nora? … not with your eyes, with your heart. Believe!"

Twenty years pass and we are in northwestern Norway, in a makeshift scientific camp. Nora has grown up and is leading the scientific excursion hunting for dinosaur bones and relics. After digging endlessly up and down the coast for six months, the university is threatening to cut off their funding. Nora says, "We just need more time!" And she adds, 'If there was one thing my father ever taught me, it was to never, ever … lose faith," just before her shovel hits something hard, a huge fossil buried in the sand.

Meanwhile, in the Hjerkinn Dovre Mountains, a massive construction project is being protested by those vehemently again the building of a railroad through the mountains. The noisy protestors are chanting, "Let the mountain live … let the mountain live." But the huge group of workers continue to dig, drill, and tunnel through the mountain. One worker holds an electronic detonator pointed toward the protestors, and he pushes the switch down resulting in a huge underground explosion. The underground workers are exposed to deep rumblings and hear soon an animalistic howl. "Everybody out!!!" the foreman yells. The workers run for their lives as giant rocks crumble behind them. Screams echo everywhere.

We cut to the Norwegian Armed Forces Operational Headquarters, Akershus

Fortress, Oslo, where the military is trying to understand just what happened in the Dovre Mountains. "I'm getting a message

Tobias (Gard B. Eidsvold) and Nora (Ine Marie Willmann) flee for their lives from the hand of the Troll.

about high seismic activity in Dovre," one agent reports. Soon, fighter jets are being sent there. The Prime Minister is about to be shown video of the mine explosion with seemingly gigantic footprints walking away from the underground site. The Prime Minister's aide Andreas (Kim Falck) is told to find an "ologist" who is qualified to comment, and we cut back to Nora's archaeological camp, which is now having a massive celebration about her find. A military helicopter lands at the campsite and a man tells Nora, she will be flown immediately to Olso, where she will meet Andreas in the remains of the underground explosion. "You guys know that I dig up fossils, right?" Andreas replies, "This really is top secret." Nora is led to an impromptu military headquarters in the bowels of the cave. "The incident at Dovre is geological in nature," a general reveals. Then there is a dialogue between all the great minds assembled, a mishmash of mumbo jumbo before common sense prevails when Nora interrupts with, "Everyone sees they're footprints, right?" Immediately a female operative abruptly enters with a cell phone video of the incident, taken by one of the protestors. The footage shows protestors chanting, then a guttural roar sounds, as rocks explode from the underground and seem to follow the panicking protestors, many of them crushed. Nora asks the woman to run footage backwards until we hear the roar … "That sound, like some kind of animal." The video keeps running until Nora yells "stop" again. The video pauses on a shot of a humanoid rock creature come to life, a living troll perhaps?

Every country has its favorite giant monster. Godzilla in Japan is a creature representing the power of the atomic bomb and the terrible radiation which lingers from its use. The destruction caused by its rampage is like a nuclear explosion. In America, we have King Kong, just like those innocent natives, living in peace on a far out-of-the way island, Kong represents royalty and is a god at home. King Kong loses all respect and sense of power when captured and brought to America. Just like the African slaves were overcome and forced to live as strangers in a strange land, shackled and chained, to be exploited for money. And now we have trolls in Norway, creatures turned to stone, vulnerable to sunlight which can destroy them. Trolls are happy living in Norwegian splendor, very content. When civilization expands by building a railroad network, they have little choice but to strike back.

Norway has learned much from America about creating giant monster movies. Just like the black-and-white Harryhausens, the monsters are only hinted at during the first parts of the movie, viewers watch as buildings fall, rocks explode, and haunting howls erupt. When the monster is finally shown, it does not disappoint, remaining one of the best CGI creations ever conceived. The creatures often reminding American viewers of the cartoons and breakfast commercials, that show fuzzy little creatures who live in trees. Here the troll is savage but seems more than a little pleasant with its congenial nature and warm face.

Troll is a personification of Norwegian culture, just as Kong represents American culture. The fairy-tale creatures represent Norway's ancient culture, primitive and wild, becoming rock creatures, happily embedded in its natural environment, that is until civilization attempts to invade its territory and disturb its resting place. It is rudely awakened by tunnels and explosions and is forced to invade civilization with an all-out attack to protect its way of life. And what a visual attack it is, the special effects of destruction rivaling the best America has produced. For all lovers of giant monster films, *Troll* is among the best in a long time, well worth seeing.

FINAL MUTTERINGS

BY GARY J. SVEHLA

In 1963, merely 13, I was a very shy child who loved monster movies, and none of my friends were into horror films to the degree that I was. As I once revealed, after I saw *Horror of Dracula*, I paraded around my backyard with a white sheet as a cape and lay flat on my picnic table bench, which was my coffin. In 1957-1958 I saw horror movies in the theater or drive-in with my father, but I was banned from seeing any further monster movies by my mother in late-1958 and 1959, because *Horror of Dracula* made me physically ill. It destroyed me because of a little thing like no sleep and some puking. For this reason, I had to miss films such as Hammer's *The Mummy*, even though I drooled over advertisements in the newspaper. By 1960 I began venturing to the Waverly Theatre on Greenmount Avenue by myself (now driven by my father) to see all the 1950s double-features that weren't syndicated to television until 1964. At the Waverly, I saw everything from *I Was a Teenage Werewolf* to *Forbidden Planet*, attending along with a theater of screaming kids, who further fueled my passions. My Dad dropped me off before one p.m. and picked me up sometime after four thirty, allowing me time to check out a nearby newsstand that sold paperbacks, comics, and monster magazines, always satisfying my cravings for all things gruesome. These weekend excursions to the Waverly were the best times of my life as a child, and it wasn't the same when these 1950s movies stopped running at the Waverly in 1964 and started appearing on television, usually on shows called *Twilight Movie*, *Supernatural Theatre*, or *Chiller*, late Saturday night Baltimore TV programs with horror hosts such as Sir Graves Ghastly, the Ghost Host, The Great Zucchini, and later Count Gore Devol (who still survives, running his own website for horror fans to this day. He even hosts special shows and movies at AFI's Silver Theater outside Washington, DC.)

Finally, during 1964, when the Waverly wasn't showing my type of B-movie anymore, I started taking the streetcar/bus to local neighborhood theaters along nearby Belair Road, such as the Paramount, Vilma, or the Earle to see the latest Hammer and American-International movies, competing horror movie production companies, usually starring Vincent Price, Peter Cushing, or Christopher Lee. I sometimes went alone, but I often ventured out with my friends, where my love of all things horror must have rubbed off on them, but never to the degree it affected me.

What an atmosphere to start a horror film fanzine in 1963, among Aurora model kits, baseball monster cards, comics, magazines, and horror movies in the theaters and all over television. I started reading *Famous Monsters of Filmland* in 1961, which I bought at my local drugstore (which was being published along with similar magazines such as *Castle of Frankenstein*, *Fantastic Monsters*, *Shriek*, and *Modern Monsters* a few years later, plus others), and in *Famous Monsters* I began to read about amateur

Supernatural Theatre with The Great Zuccini

versions of the mighty horror film magazines or "fanzines," some of these fanzines I soon purchased through the mail. I then discovered *Horrors of the Screen* and other magazines which dazzled me with their creative printing techniques and imaginative layout. I did not know how to start or where to start, but my friend Dave was a budding artist who wanted his work exhibited anywhere and I loved writing about the movies I always adored. At Holly Beach (owned by Dave's father) that summer, Dave and I planned out the first issue of *Gore Creatures*, and when I told my father about those plans, he jumped right in to help. Even though the first issue was copied by hand and later carbon-copied, my Dad immediately offered methods to reproduce issues using at first hectograph, then ditto, then mimeo, and then in the late 1960s, I learned of the local Arcade Press, directly behind the neighborhood Arcade Theater. And the rest is history. First boss Tony Lorenzo and later Bob Gehring showed me the way.

My mother Ann, who was a fan of the *Perry Mason* novels and other mystery series, always wanted me to grow into a novelist, someone like Erle Stanley Gardner or similar writers, but my passions ran to film criticism and analysis, and even though I tried short story writing, I felt it was never my thing and I had to disappoint her. But my father Richard supported my hobby and soon ran the financial side of things in our hobby business, assisting me along the way, doing conventions and being the number one supporter of *Gore Creatures/Midnight Marquee*. And I was so lucky when I married in 1984, that my wife Sue supported me and the magazine, even writing for the magazine and creating the concept of FANEX, our 16-year convention which she organized and ran. She even thought of a way to get Christopher Lee to FANEX, by publishing an expanded US version of his autobiography. That brings up Midnight Marquee Press, our book press, which she originated in 1995, allowing her to work from home. Yes, Sue was responsible for so much creativity.

I was always conflicted about *Midnight Marquee*, imagine a grown man writing about monster movies at the age of 73. Maybe I should have tried harder to be the new Stephen King and pleased my mother. But at conventions such as our own FANEX and many others, people would come up to me and say how important the magazine was to their lives, and so was the convention, and they couldn't precisely put into words the profound effect both had on their life. At the 1999 Monster Rally where Christopher Lee appeared to premiere the American edition of his already published British autobiography, grown men were crying after standing in line to have him sign copies of the book, while many more thousands who did not attend expressed shock when he actually attended the convention. Many relinquished the chance to ever meet their favorite living horror film icon, thinking he would eventually appear at more com-

The wonderful world of the Waverly Theatre, the oasis of horror, circa 1963

mercial conventions, and that they could meet him there, but being busy with the *Star Wars* series and *The Lord of the Rings* series, he never did major appearances again (perhaps appearing to small crowds at book show signings in England in the final years), unfortunately dying in 2015.

But people discovered ways to get personal memorabilia signed, which was a big no-no in our contract, which specially stated only copies of his autobiography could be autographed. We did not even get anything signed other than our book. But our staff, who had access to his private suite, made clandestine deals to have personal items signed for themselves and friends, behind our backs. I must admit, such actions initially hurt Sue and I very much, but Christopher Lee did not seem to mind such infractions in the least, and he was the one who set the rigid rules in writing, thus making Sue and I appear to be the bad guys! Well, almost 25 years have passed, Lee is long gone, and what was done was done.

A lot of history occurs over 60 years, much of it unsaid. Sue is now preparing a pictorial book (with captions) on 60 years of *Midnight Marquee*, which will be available within the next year, and hopefully reveal more of the story.

If this is truly to be the final issue (you never know!), I want to profoundly thank every person who helped us on the way. No effort was too small. And some efforts were mighty big. It was a pleasure to work with every one of you. And who knows, we might work together again.

—Gary J. Svehla, July 2023

We are so delighted to have Allen K.'s artwork back. It's been a rough few years (or decades) for both families but it's nice to have Allen along for the 60th Anniversary issue. Allen has been busy working on many books with his amazing art. You can find his work at allenk.com or on Amazon at https://www.amazon.com/s?k=Allen+Koszows ki&i=stripbooks&crid=1A0O248CSABIO&sprefix=allen+koszowski%2Cstripbooks%2C98&ref=nb_sb_noss_1 or Centipied Press https://www.centipedepress.com/art/allenkoszowski.